IMAGES
of America

LITTLE SILVER
VOLUME II

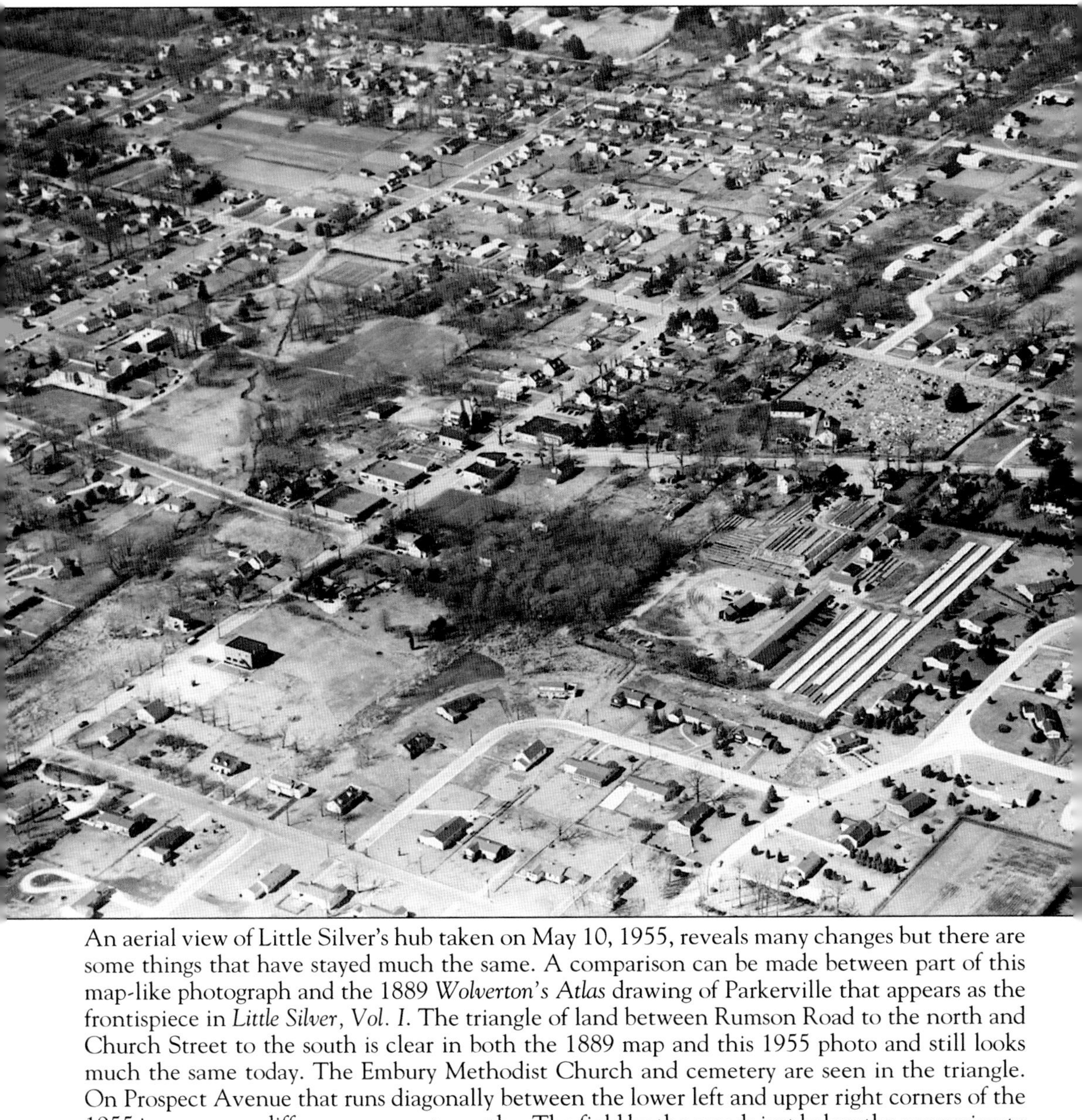

An aerial view of Little Silver's hub taken on May 10, 1955, reveals many changes but there are some things that have stayed much the same. A comparison can be made between part of this map-like photograph and the 1889 *Wolverton's Atlas* drawing of Parkerville that appears as the frontispiece in *Little Silver, Vol. I*. The triangle of land between Rumson Road to the north and Church Street to the south is clear in both the 1889 map and this 1955 photo and still looks much the same today. The Embury Methodist Church and cemetery are seen in the triangle. On Prospect Avenue that runs diagonally between the lower left and upper right corners of the 1955 image, some differences are noteworthy. The field by the woods just below the approximate center of the photo is the location of the A&P shopping center that was built within a few years after this view was photographed. The old Borough Hall that was previously the school is across from the intersection of Prospect and Church Streets. The long greenhouses of Lovett's Nurseries are in the lower right half of the picture where the Cheshire Square condominiums are now. Try taking a magnifying glass to see if you can locate the firehouse, Markham Place School, houses, stores, and streets that you know. (Dorn's.)

IMAGES
of America

LITTLE SILVER
VOLUME II

Karen L. Schnitzspahn

ARCADIA
PUBLISHING

ISBN 978-0-7385-6359-6

Published by Arcadia Publishing
Charleston, South Carolina

Printed in the United States of America

Library of Congress Catalog Card Number: 2008937063

For all general information contact Arcadia Publishing at:
Telephone 843-853-2070
Fax 843-853-0044
E-mail sales@arcadiapublishing.com
For customer service and orders:
Toll-Free 1-888-313-2665

Visit us on the Internet at www.arcadiapublishing.com

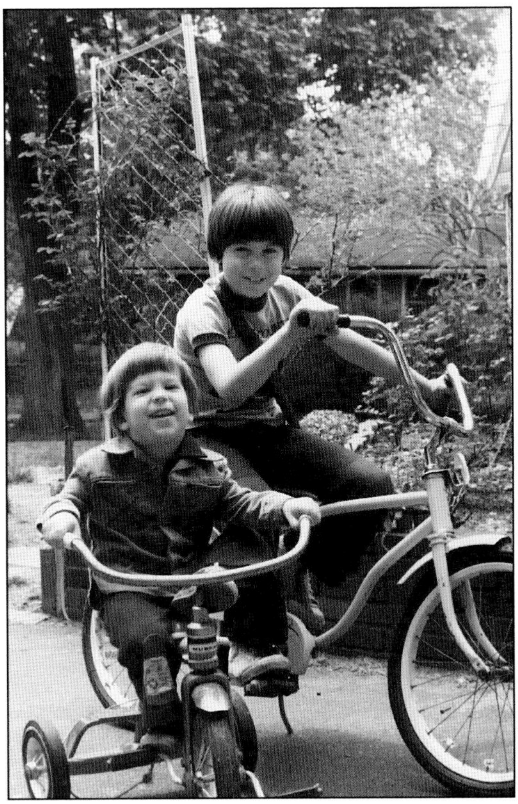

1978

This volume is dedicated to
All those who have grown up in
Little Silver,
And especially to my sons
Doug and Greg.

Contents

ACKNOWLEDGMENTS

After the publication of *Little Silver Vol. I* in 1996, many wonderful people—both past and present residents of the town—contacted me with additional photographs and information for a possible second volume. A wealth of new material surfaced. I am now proud to present *Little Silver Vol. II*, which has involved much time and dedication to compile but has been a pleasure!

I am grateful to the Borough of Little Silver, and would like to thank Little Silver Borough Administrator Michael Biehl and the staff at the Little Silver Borough Hall for their assistance. My sincere gratitude also goes once again to David E. Griffiths and The Little Silver Historical Society.

Many current residents, some who grew up in Little Silver, have helped by contributing photographs, and have helped in many ways. Special thanks go to Janet Giersch, who compiled a fine database of homes and neighborhoods in conjunction with the town's 75th anniversary that will be an enduring reference work; to Mary Christian, who is a talented writer/editor; and to Sandy Wells, writer and Little Silver columnist for the *Two River Times*. Sincere thanks (in alphabetical order) to: Ardis and Nishan Bogosian, Lois Bowie, Marion Cogan, Barbara Finch, Peggy Henneberry, David A. Kennedy, Jane Lux, Betty Jean and Karl Meyer, Mr. and Mrs. Walton Moore, Dr. and Mrs. Robert Nelson, Kathy Pearson, Barbara and Larry Pidel, Elaine and Henry Pope, Dominick Santelle, Mr. and Mrs. Richard Tetley, Anthony F. Trufolo, Keith Wells, Nancy and Obert Wood, and Cathy Wright. I'd like to thank the Little Silver Fire Co. No. 1 and especially Dan Denton, Bob Stout, Ed Burdge, Al Pound, and Don Mulligan.

My sincere thanks goes to former Little Silver residents and out-of-towners related to former residents or business owners (in alphabetical order): James V. Annarella of the Shore Point Distributing Co., Doris Shampanore Marcelli Ayers, Mr. James R. Cook Sr., Dennis Elgrim, Sara-Lee Gironda, Edwina Tucker Hazzard, Jennifer Hetzler, Mary and Barry Jerolamon, Marjorie Eastmond Johnson, George Kingston, Mr. and Mrs. William Lippincott, Jeanne Little, Dr. Susan M. Love, Betsy Parker Ruff, Tom and Pauline Satter, Mrs. Anna Scaccia, and Mr. and Mrs. Frederick P. Tompkins.

Heartfelt thanks go to author-historian June O. Kennedy (who wrote the first book about Little Silver) for all her assistance and her friendship. Special thanks to The Honorable Robert A. Schoeffling of Atlantic Highlands for sharing his local collection. Thanks once again to Randall Gabrielan, author of numerous books in this series, a good friend who has provided guidance, encouragement, and photos! Thank you, as ever, to my well-respected colleague in history and writing, Monmouth County Historian George H. Moss Jr., for his wisdom and friendship.

Thank you to everyone at Dorn's Photography Unlimited, Red Bank, and especially to Dan Dorn Jr., Kathy Dorn Severini, John Pecyna, and Jeannette Massas. Thanks also to those at O'Photo and Alphagraphics, both in Red Bank.

I would like to recognize my dear friend Nancy Giles of Little Silver who is always supportive. Thanks to Arcadia Senior Editor Jamie Carter for her expertise and her patience, to my son Doug for his editorial wisdom, and to my son Greg (aka Max). Thanks to my mother, Kari Hunt. And I thank my husband, Leon (known as "Lucky Leon" to the local fishing crowd!), who has so unselfishly given me love and strength to keep on going on.

Karen L. Schnitzspahn — June 1998

INTRODUCTION

A Walk around Little Silver

Taking a walk around Little Silver, where I have lived for almost 30 years, is a joyful experience. My interest in the history of the borough began with observations of people and places during my daily walks. After looking at hundreds of old photographs while preparing the first volume of *Little Silver*, I developed an ability to visualize the way things used to be. As more images of the past became available to me, I realized the necessity for a second volume to share such nostalgic treasures and further preserve the history of the town.

My favorite images are of the people. Pictorial histories are not merely visual documentaries of places, they reflect the lifestyles and feelings of the people during each decade depicted. It is the people who make a town. Little Silver has always been a warm and friendly place. As I walk today, most everyone says "hello" in passing. Joggers, bicyclists, dog walkers, parents with babies in strollers, students with backpacks, seniors with canes—they comprise the population of Little Silver. After looking at the old photos, it is as if I am also walking by and saying hello to families on their bicycles in the 1890s, workers at the farms and nurseries in the 1930s, and kids playing outside ranch houses in 1950s. The clothing and styles of each decade are so different, some occupations have changed, but the people themselves are much the same. We can see that in the photographs.

You can walk to a store and buy a quart of milk, as I often do, in Little Silver and feel safe here. The "village," or downtown hub of Little Silver that was once called Parkerville, is a thriving commercial area but retains the atmosphere of a small and friendly town. Many stores have changed but there are still merchants who take time to serve their customers. While walking, I can visualize, from the photos, the general store with one gas pump in front on Rumson Road in the 1940s and the family-run food market on Prospect Avenue across from the Borough Hall in the 1950s. There are more people, more businesses today, and, of course, the pace is faster. There is more traffic, more noise, and perhaps more problems as a result, but the flavor of a small American town remains.

As I walk, I find it relaxing to observe houses and how they reflect the people who built them and those who lived in them over the years. Many are historic homes that are a hundred years old or more and many were built during the housing booms of the 1920–30s and in the 1950s. The photographs reveal a variety of styles from mansions to ranch houses, all with stories to tell about their inhabitants.

On the last page of *Little Silver Vol. I*, I chose to feature images of the nature preserve on Prospect Avenue. I love to amble around there. The marshy area is a quiet respite from worries, a meditative place where the sound of traffic is replaced by the cooing of birds. This is the only large open space left in town that gives insight into what things were like when nothing else was around, in a time before the invention of photography. But if you can erase all the houses, stores, and roads in your mind (a little game I often play while walking!) you can envision Little Silver before it was settled in the 1600s. You may even see some Lenape Indians, also walking, on their way to the seashore through woods and swamps.

For this second volume of *Little Silver*, I conclude with photos of a recent event that shows the affection and respect for the past that exists here. In 1998, Little Silver celebrated its 75th anniversary (of separation from Shrewsbury Township and its incorporation in 1923). The congenial spirit and pride of the borough's people sparkled at the parade and picnic held on June 7, 1998. Most people walked to the festivities, as my husband and I did. It was a fun-filled, old-fashioned sort of day and a milestone in the history of Little Silver.

It is impossible to cover everything about a town and there are many more photographs and much more to be said. My goal with this volume was to add available images and information that were not presented previously and to add additional images that enhance certain things that appeared in the first volume. The time period depicted is again from around the 1880s through the 1970s, with a few newer photos that are relevant. In the year 2023, Little Silver will commemorate its 100th anniversary. Of course many changes will take place by then, but I feel certain that the borough will still be a pleasant place to take a walk as the friendly spirit of the people will endure.

Correspondence and comments are welcome. Please write to the author at P.O. Box 716, Red Bank, NJ 07701.

Karen L. Schnitzspahn June 1998

Author's Note: The photo on the cover of *Little Silver Vol. I* (published in 1996) features two smiling women on the front and a woman on the back cover. The entire photograph was reproduced on p. 116. The woman on the far right with the box camera was properly identified as Harriet Moore. The woman on Harriet's left has now been identified by her family as Edith Richdale. Anna Elgrim, on the far left, was correctly named, but on Anna's right is not Anna's mother but Edith's mother, Christina Richdale. Edith Richdale served as town clerk in Wilton, Connecticut, for many years. Also, on p. 116, the World War I soldier with Walton Moore who was not identified is Herbert Richdale. Many thanks to Pat Dean (Edith Richdale's daughter) and her family for making these identifications.

One

Summertime: Long, Long Ago

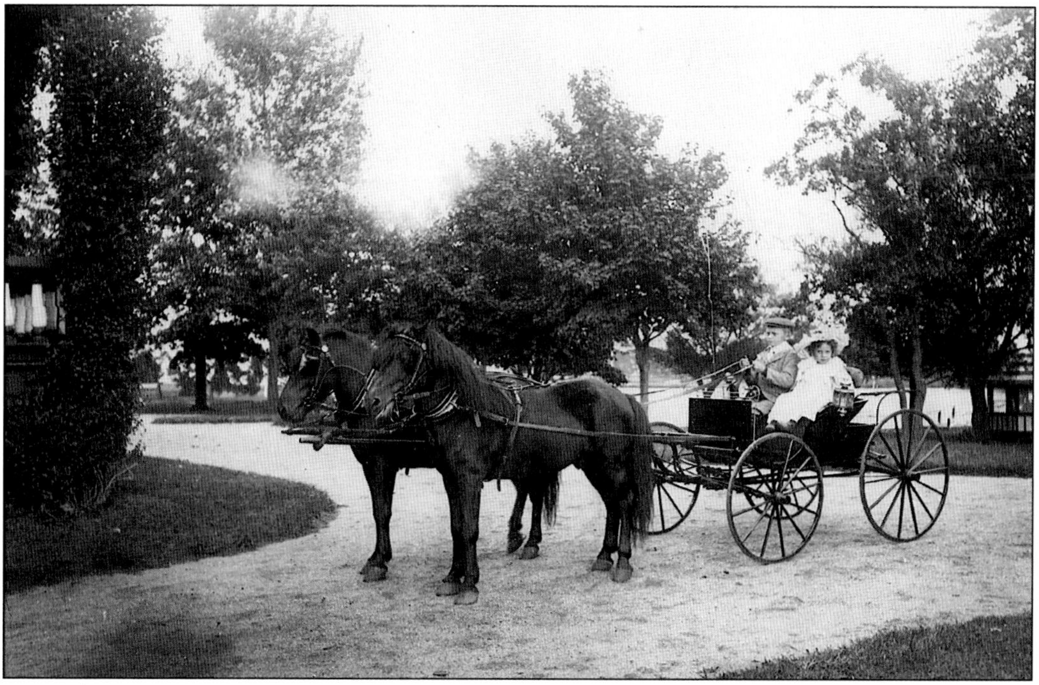

More than a century ago (1896 or 1897), two well-dressed young summer residents prepare to take a buggy ride around Little Silver. Armand Edwards concentrates on holding the reins as his cousin, Sarah Estelle Tucker, looks toward the camera. The photo was taken in front of Silver Carn, the Victorian estate that belonged to the children's grandfather, Sheppard Knapp, and was located on the northeast side of Little Silver Creek and Seven Bridge Road. (Sarah-Lee Brooks Gironda.)

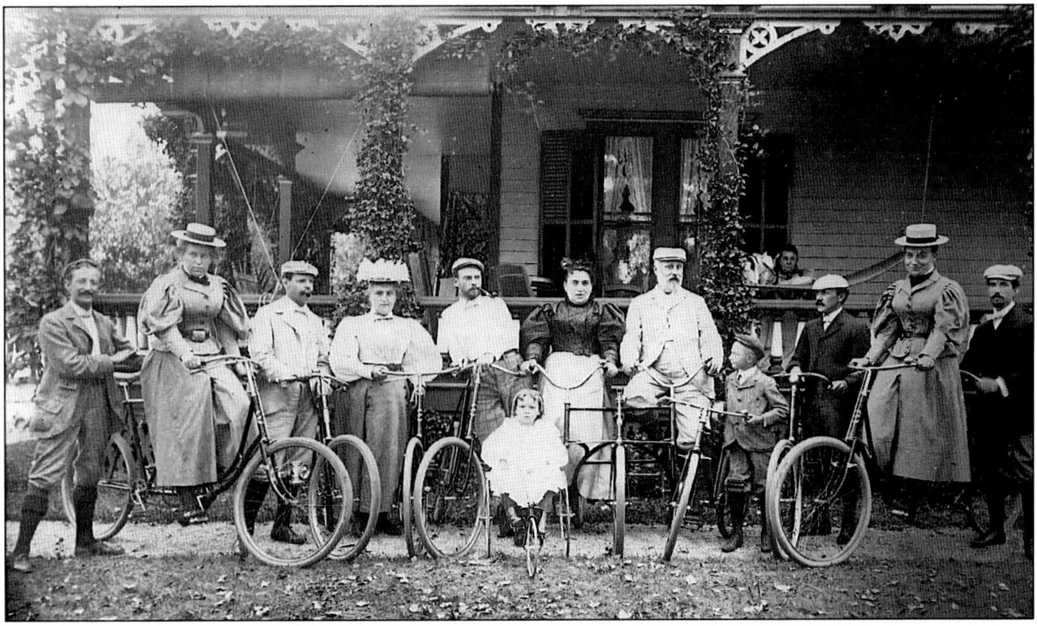

"Knapps on Wheels" is the title that Edwina Tucker Hazzard assigns to this family photo at Silver Carn c. 1897. From left to right are Walter Cramp (a family friend), Lillian Knapp, Edwin Davis Tucker and Estelle Knapp Tucker (Edwina's parents), Sheppard Knapp Jr., Sarah Estelle Tucker (Edwina's older sister on a velocipede), Sarah Miller Knapp and Sheppard Knapp (grandparents on a "side-by-side" cycle), Armand Edwards, a family friend, Henrietta Knapp Edwards, and "probably Edwards." The woman on the porch with the dog is unidentified. Edwina is not in this photo because it was taken about seven years before she was born. (Sara-Lee Brooks Gironda.)

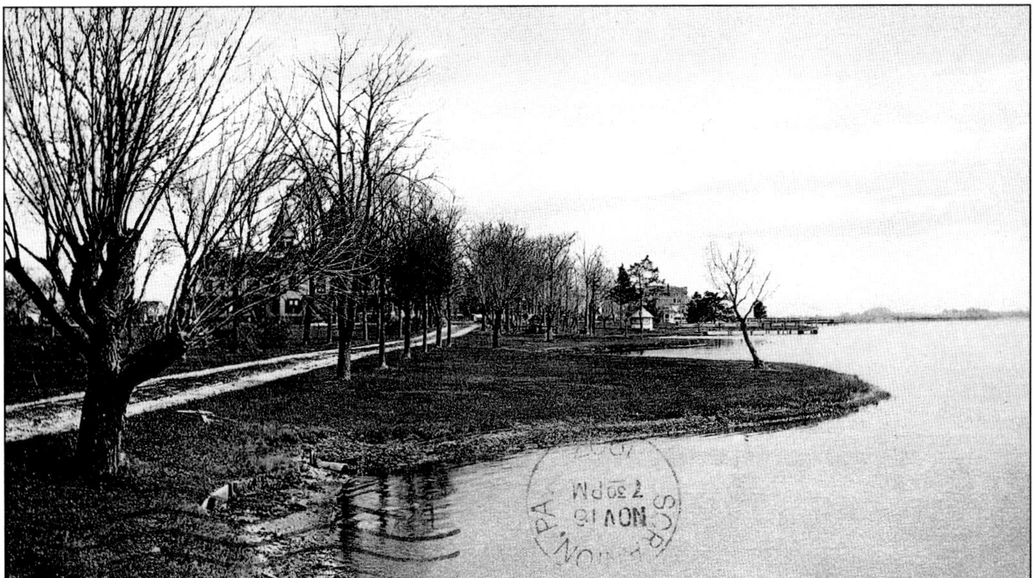

This image of Silver Carn appears in *Little Silver Vol. I*, but is repeated here in postcard form to accompany the additional photos and information that has surfaced about the estate and the Knapp family who owned it. The card is postmarked 1907.

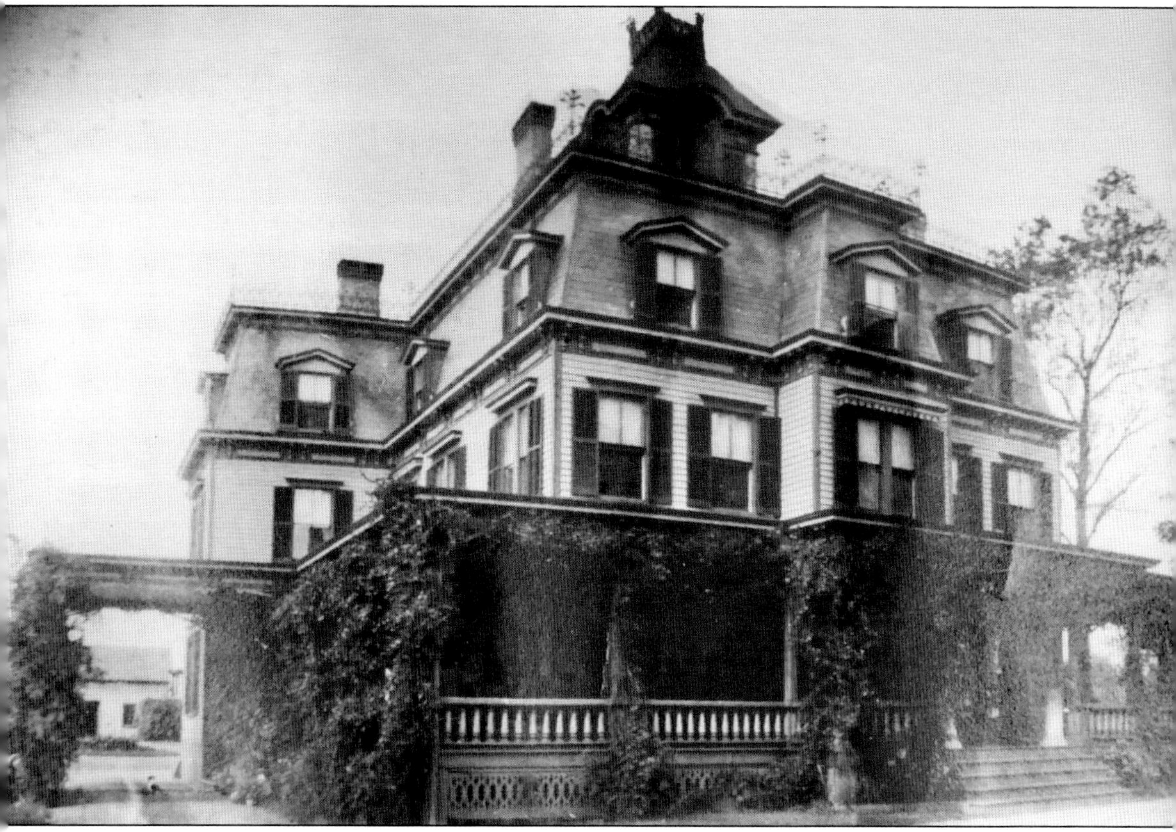

This view of Silver Carn is a seldom seen image of Sheppard Knapp's Victorian summer home that once graced the north side of Little Silver Creek on Seven Bridge Road. The house was eventually demolished and in 1929 Boxwood Manor, another fine mansion that stands today, was built on this property (see pp. 38–39 of *Little Silver Vol. 1*). Edwina Tucker Hazzard remembers Silver Carn as a child. Her family lived in New York but summered in Little Silver. She writes: ". . . I best recall the third floor (from whence I vividly remember seeing Halley's comet) where I was quartered with my parents, Edwin Davis Tucker and Estelle Knapp Tucker, my sister, Sarah, and my English Nanny, Emma . . . I am told we came into this arrangement the summer of 1906. The rooms I best recall are the huge dining room, walls painted blue-to-a chair rail and hung with fish nets into which were entwined all manner of fish/sea life; crabs, lobsters, shells, etc. Beaded curtains separated the two entrances. The kitchen lorded over by Annie, the cook, who hated children (No wonder, I locked her in the stand-up 'ice box' and then went off to play!) . . . The billiard room was a gathering-center . . . then there was the 'office' from which the farm and household affairs were run (by my mother, as my grandmother Knapp was 'frail'). The front parlor was seldom used, a stiff formal room . . . On the driveway (up from Seven Bridge Road,) stood my doll house, big enough to stand up in and 'guarded' if you will, by an almost life size cast iron deer which I and children before me, rode to faraway places . . ." (Thanks to Edwina Tucker Hazzard for sharing her memories, and to Sarah-Lee Brooks Gironda for providing the photograph.)

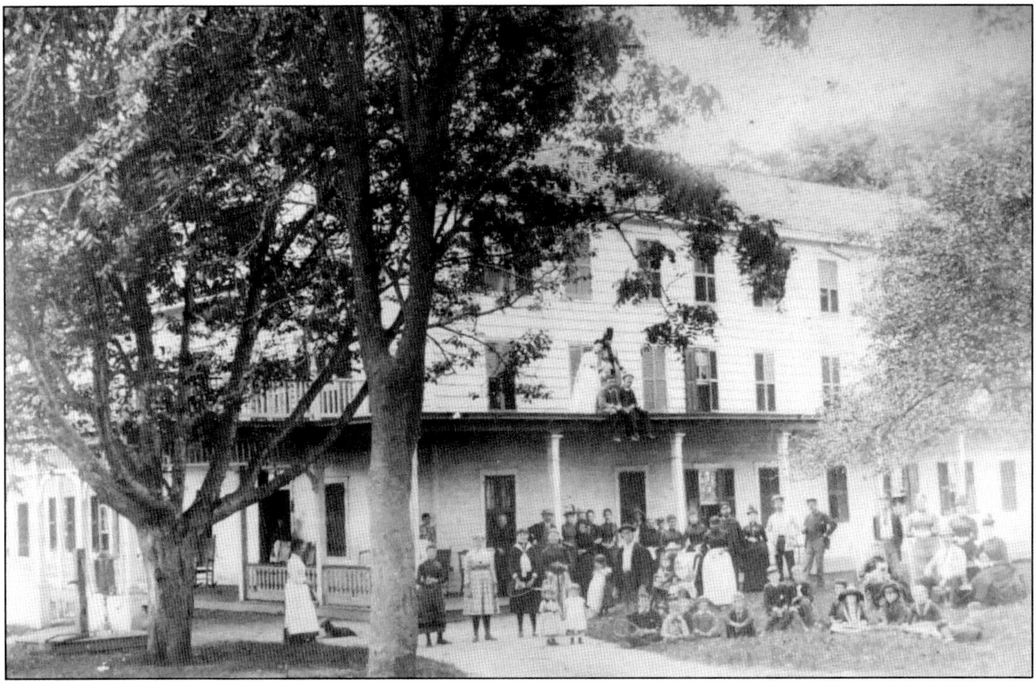

This late-19th-century image of the Silver Bay House that was on Little Silver Point provides a great look at the summer visitors who came down from New York on the Patten Line steamboats. Notice the water pump and an object on a stand that appears to be a silver water cooler on the far left by the tree. (Little Silver Historical Society.)

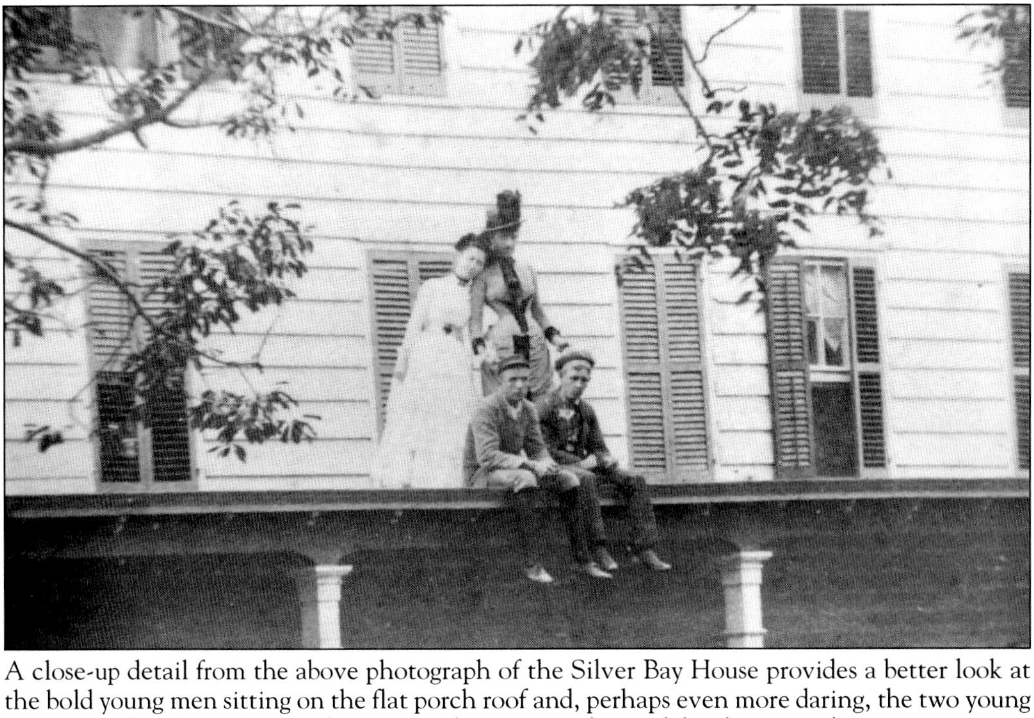

A close-up detail from the above photograph of the Silver Bay House provides a better look at the bold young men sitting on the flat porch roof and, perhaps even more daring, the two young women in their long dresses who are standing out on the roof that has no railing.

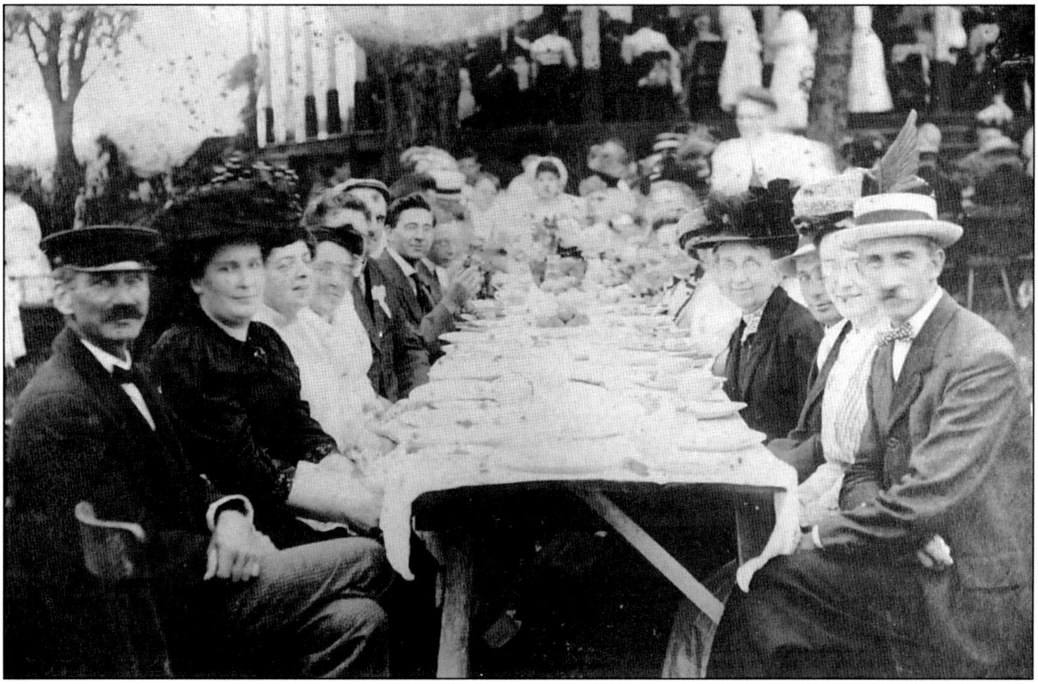

A turn-of-the-century group of picnickers takes a moment to pose for a photo on the grounds of the Silvermere Inn that was at the end of Little Silver Point Road. Identified here are Margaret and George Lippincott, the first two people on left; and on the right, Richard Bates is in front wearing a straw hat, and Ada Hoffmeir is the fourth person in. (Little Silver Historical Society.)

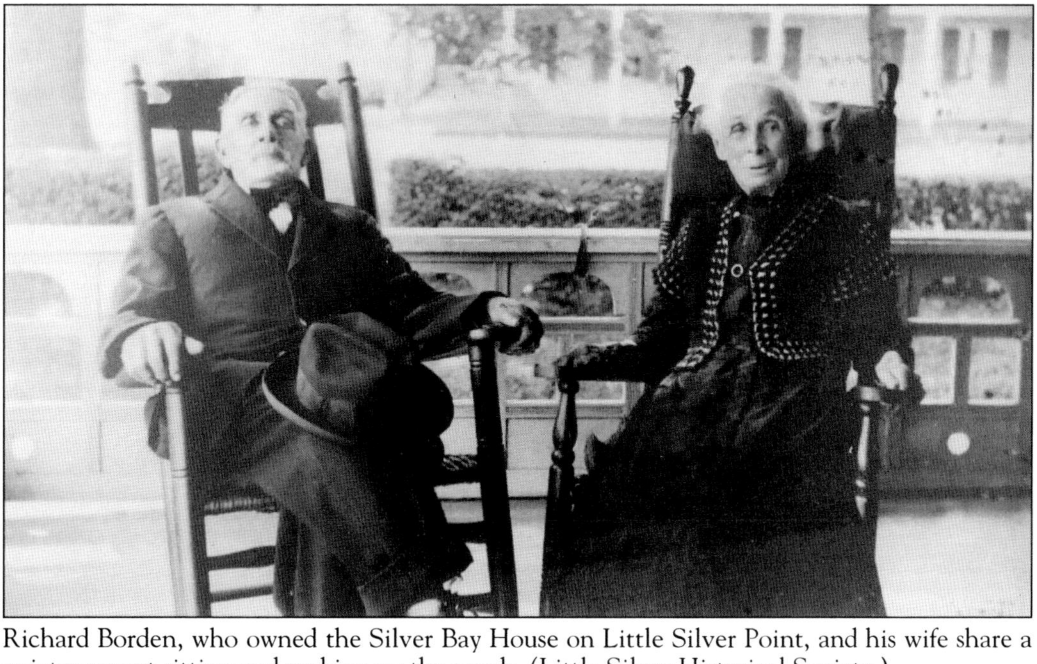

Richard Borden, who owned the Silver Bay House on Little Silver Point, and his wife share a quiet moment sitting and rocking on the porch. (Little Silver Historical Society.)

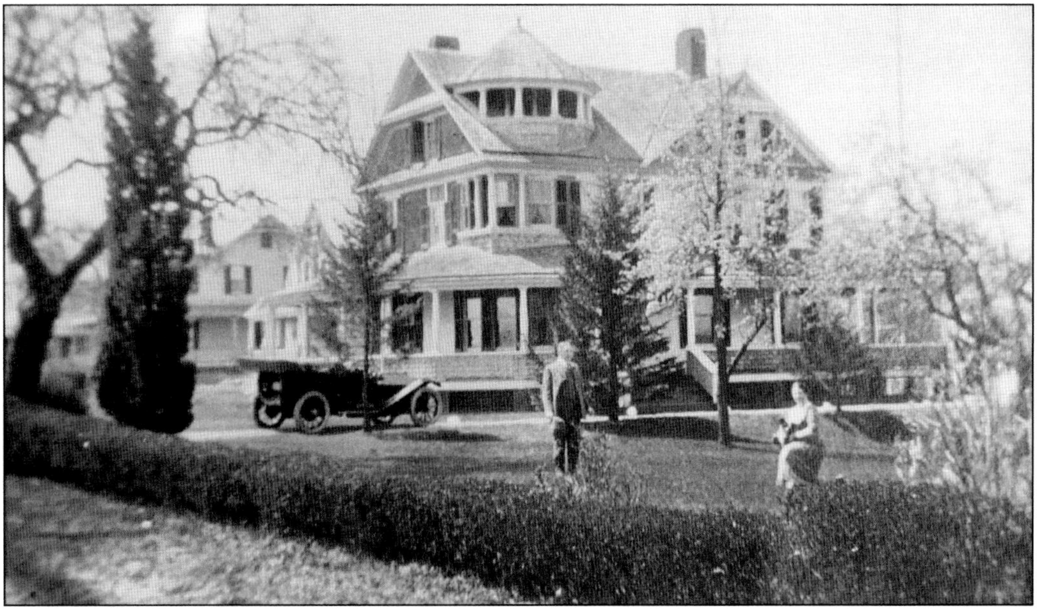

The tower with a view of the Shrewsbury River is clearly visible in this *c.* 1915 image of the Samuel Morris Borden house, 550 Little Silver Point Rd. The couple in the yard with their dog are most likely the Bordens. (A recent photo of this 1870s house that belongs to the Ostran family appears in *Little Silver Vol. I* on p. 41.) Today, the tall pine trees partially obstruct the view from the tower making the house look quite different. The smaller house next door was known as "the bird cage." (D. Elgrim.)

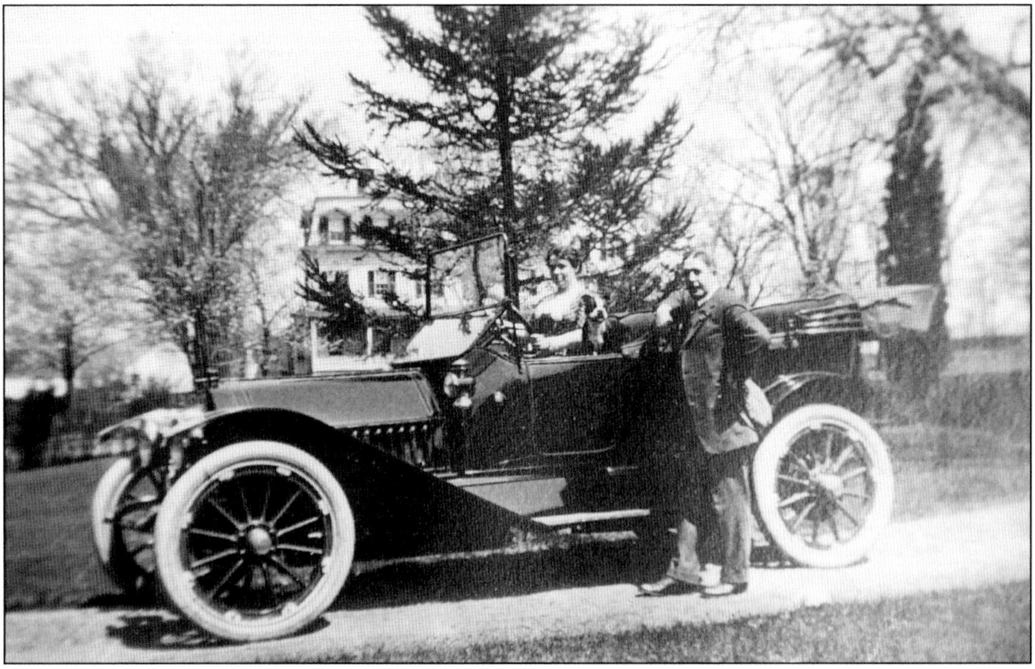

Portraits of people showing off their shiny vehicles were popular in the early years of automobiling. This is probably Samuel Morris Borden with his wife and their Boston Terrier. The image was taken on Little Silver Point Road. (D. Elgrim.)

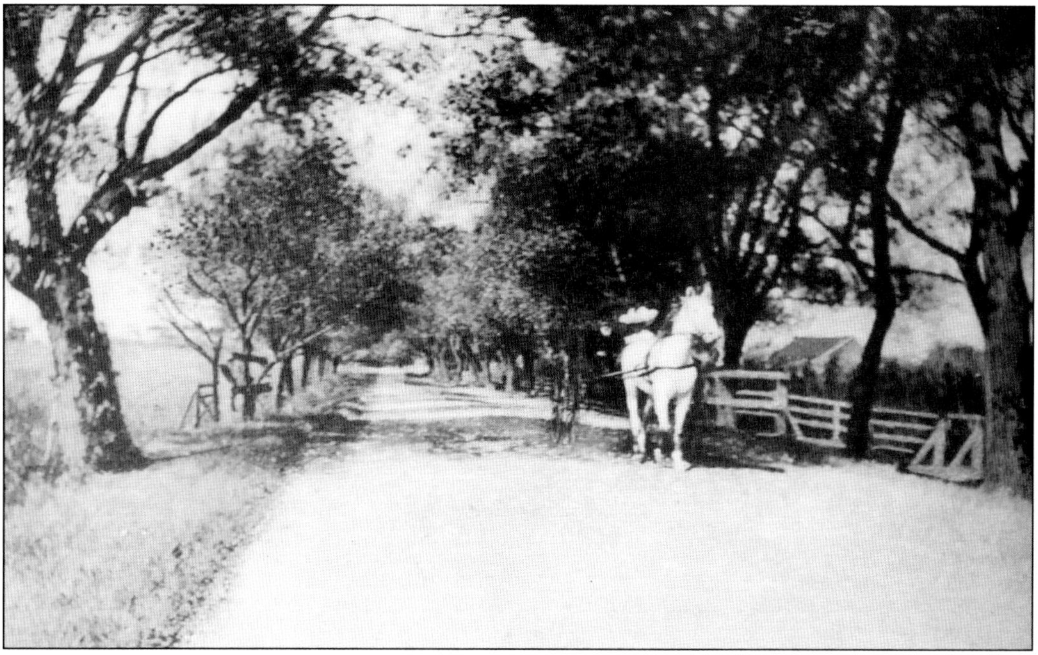

When most of Little Silver was farmland and marshes, *c.* 1905, a horse and carriage meanders down Willow Drive as depicted on this soft and lovely color-tinted postcard. (Keith Wells Collection.)

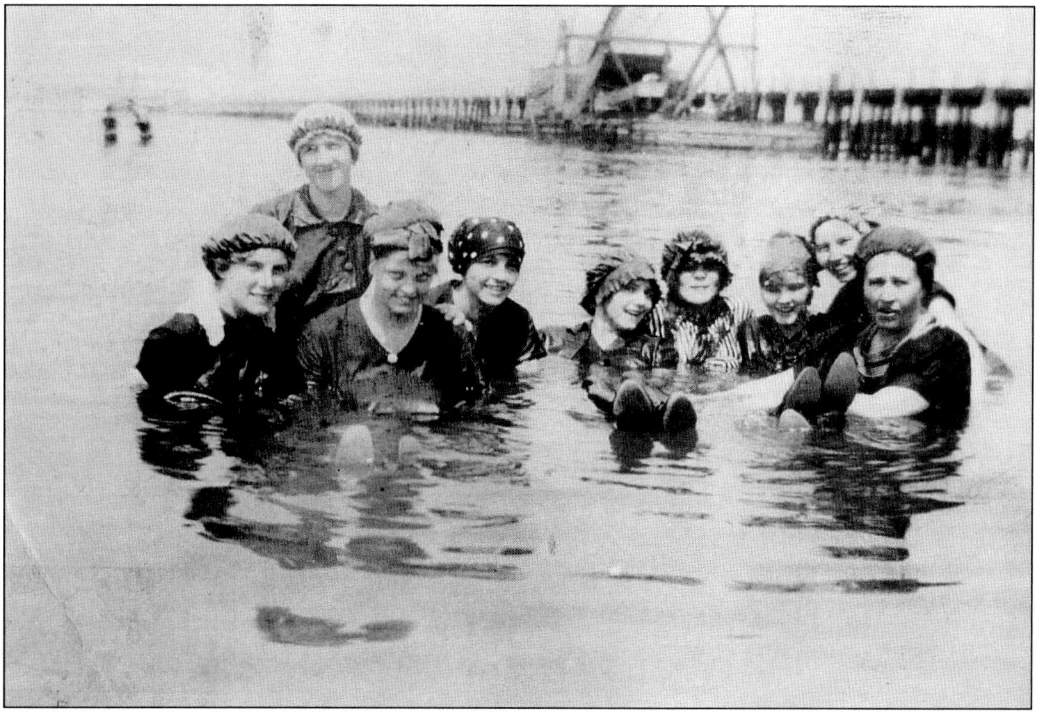

It wasn't only the summer visitors from the city who had fun at Little Silver. In this snapshot, *c.* 1918, Little Silver schoolteacher Harriet Moore (far left) and a group of local young women, all wearing bathing hats of the era, are taking a dip in the Shrewsbury River. (W. Moore.)

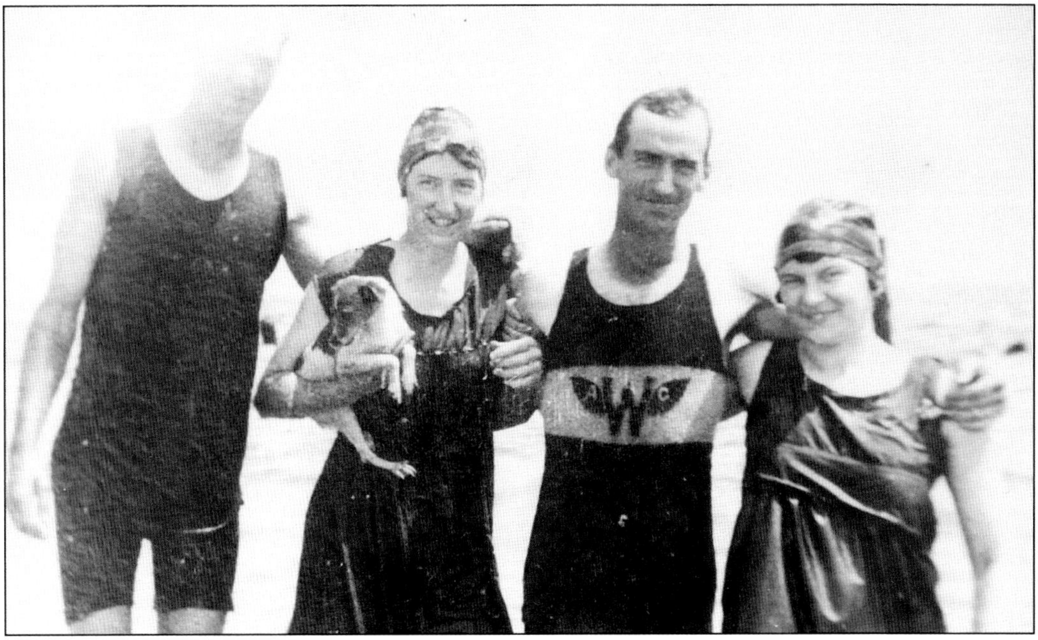

In August of 1918, Little Silver residents Julia Parker (holding the dog), two of the Parker brothers, and an unidentified girl are enjoying bathing in the surf at the Sea Bright beach. (Borough of Little Silver.)

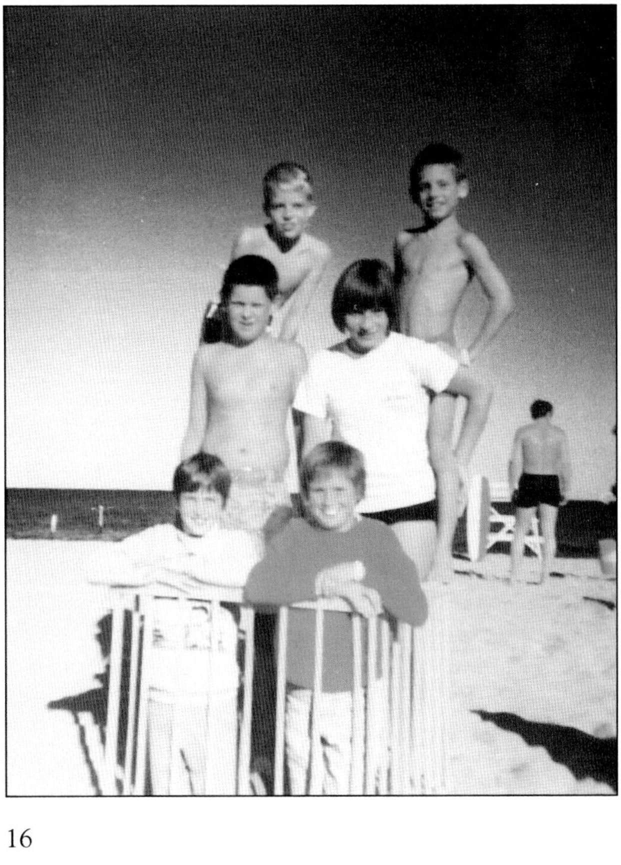

In the late 1960s, Little Silver baby boomers enjoy the beach at the Sandlass at Sea Bright. In this photo, taken by Janet Giersch, are the following, from left to right: (on the bottom) Betsy Pope (now Aras) and Susan Lloyd; (middle row) Tom Lloyd and Ginger Giersch (now Holton); (top row) John Pope and Chris Lloyd. Nearby Sea Bright remains a popular beach area for Little Silver residents who have the Shrewsbury River within the town but are inland from the sea. (J. Giersch.)

Two

THE PARKER HOMESTEAD

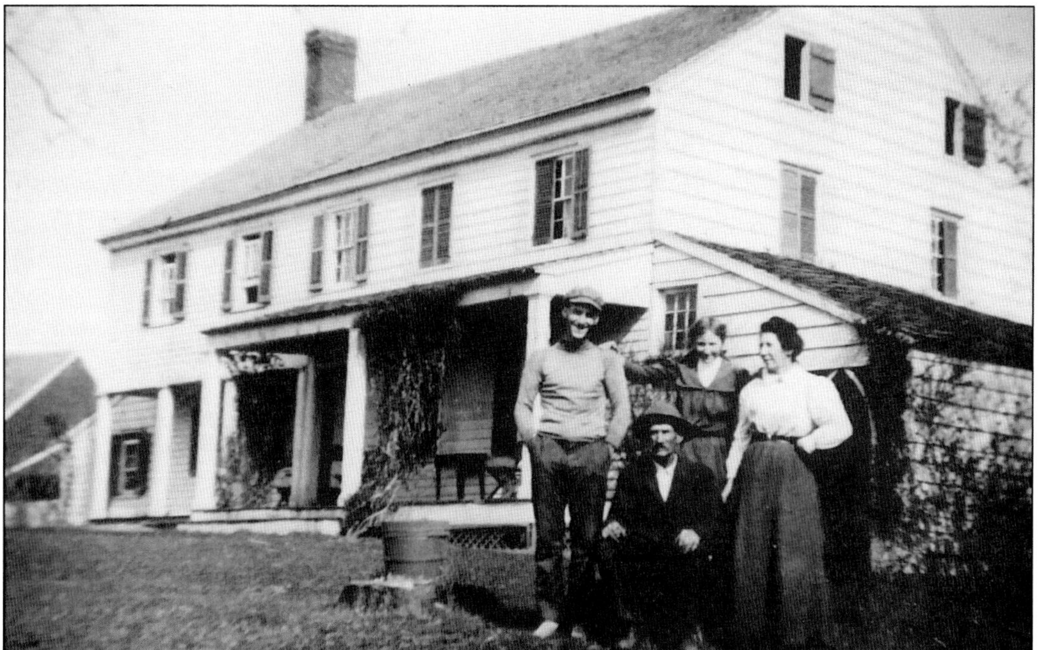

Mr. and Mrs. Michael Parker pose with daughter Julia and son Doug in front of the Rumson Road homestead in a family album photo *c.* 1917. This photo was taken shortly before the porch was expanded. The original house dates to about 1667. The Parker homestead was conveyed to the Borough to be used as a museum by "Miss Julia," the last of the Parkers to live at the property. She died in 1995.

NOTE: All photographs in this chapter are from The Julia Parker Collection that belongs to The Borough of Little Silver unless otherwise noted.

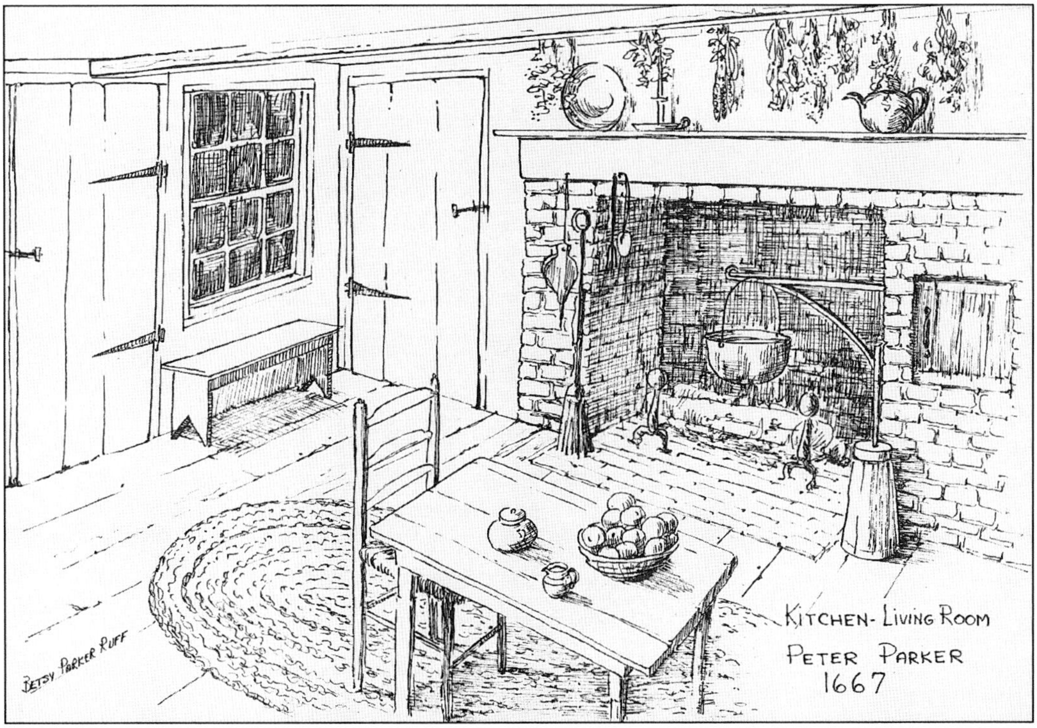

A pen-and-ink drawing by Betsy Parker Ruff, daughter of Henry Parker and a niece of Julia Parker, gives a good idea of what the simple kitchen with open hearth in the Parker homestead may have looked like in 1667 when the Parker brothers from Rhode Island settled here.

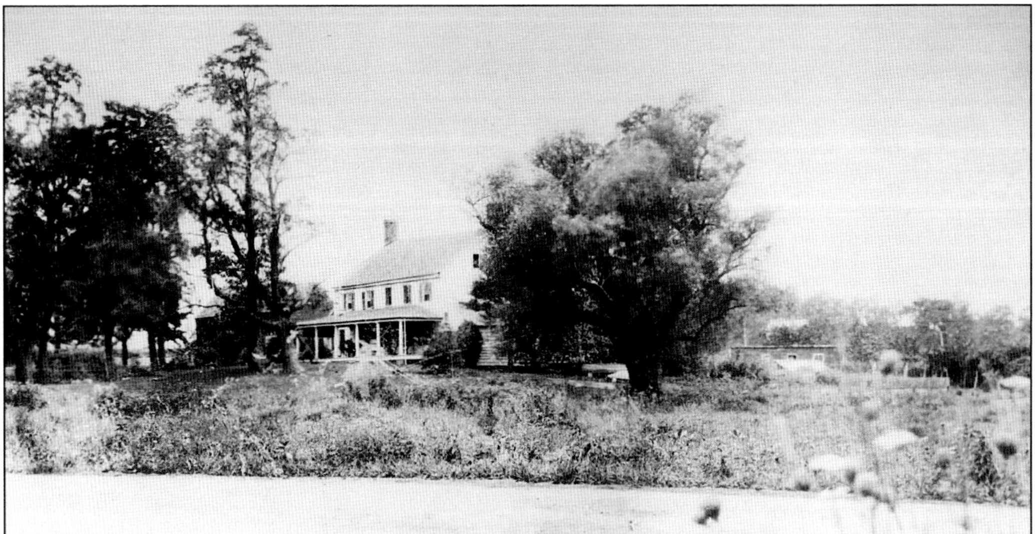

An interesting view of the Parker homestead, this image, *c.* 1917, is from the east side of the pond and gives a glimpse of the out buildings that were at the back of the house. In the summer of 1997, a team from Monmouth University led by Professor Richard Veit conducted an archeological dig at the site and many small artifacts were found. The house is currently being restored to be used as a museum and is now owned by the Borough of Little Silver.

Susan Ella Smith Parker (Julia Parker's mother) wears a fashionable lace-trimmed dress accessorized with a fancy hat, parasol, and gloves in this *c.* 1880s cabinet photo by White, a photography studio that was in Red Bank. The exact year is unknown, but this very likely was taken a few years before 1884, when she married Michael Henry Parker.

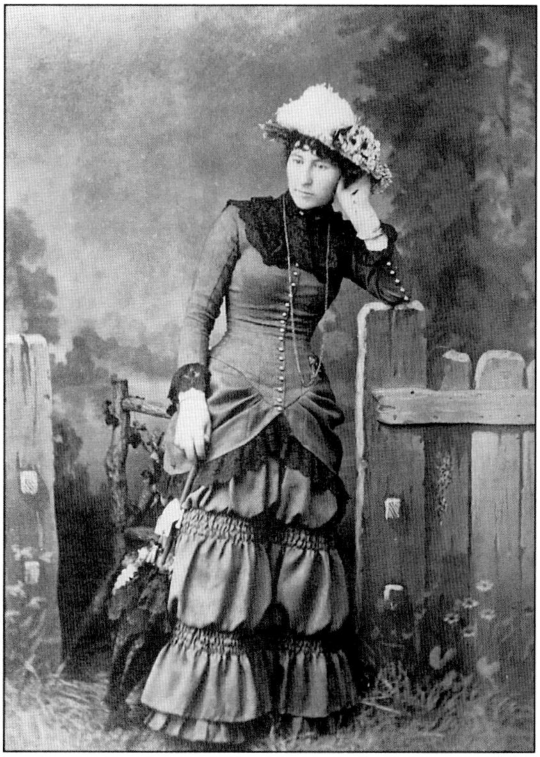

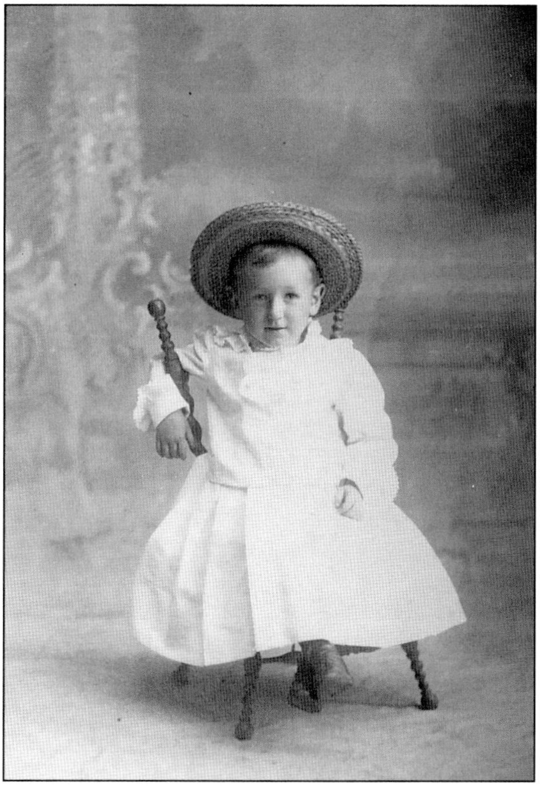

In this adorable portrait from 1898, John Stanley Parker, age two years and two months, wears a dress (as baby boys often did) and a delightful wide-brimmed straw hat.

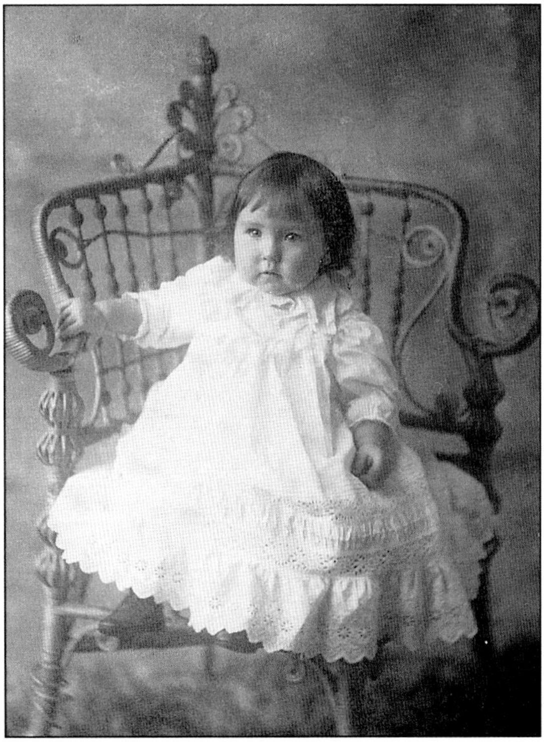

Can you recognize the face of this adorable baby who was born to proud parents Susan and Michael Parker in 1899? It is little Julia Gertrude Parker.

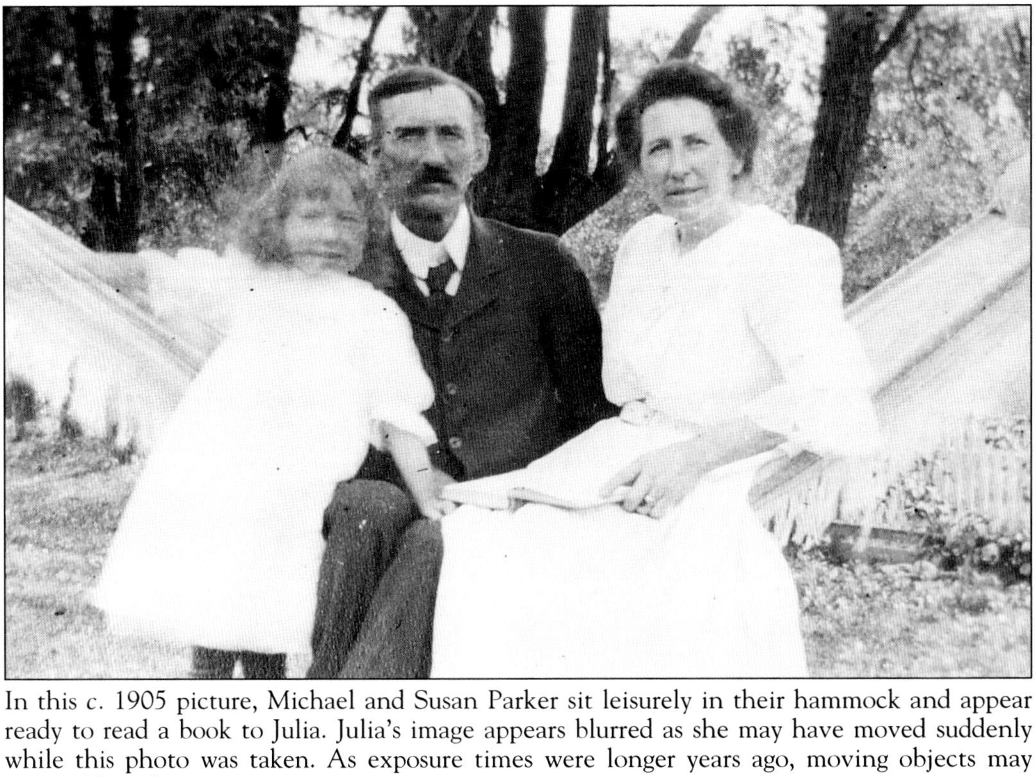

In this *c.* 1905 picture, Michael and Susan Parker sit leisurely in their hammock and appear ready to read a book to Julia. Julia's image appears blurred as she may have moved suddenly while this photo was taken. As exposure times were longer years ago, moving objects may appear blurred.

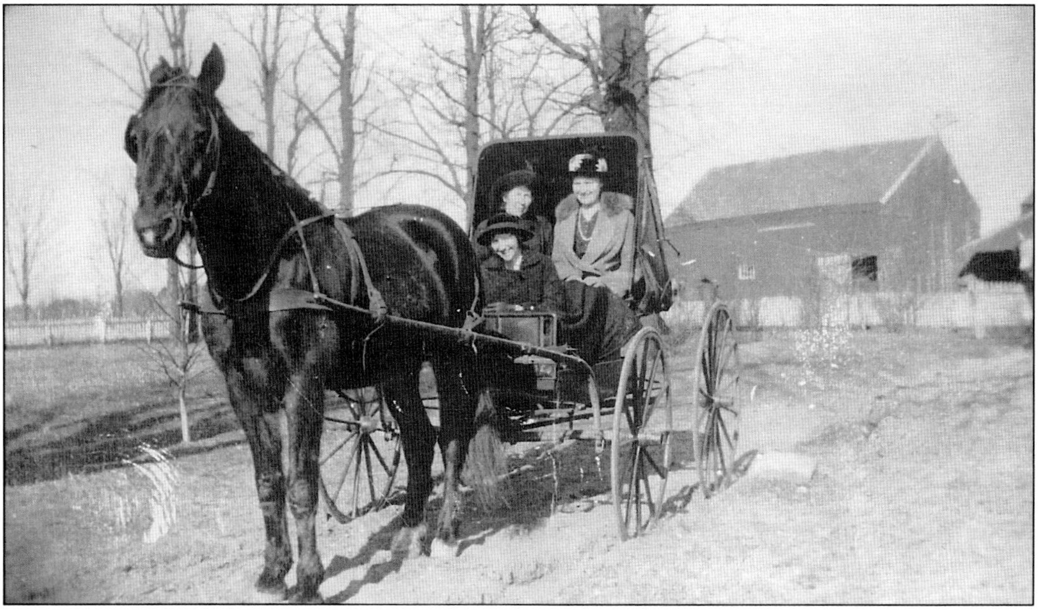

The handwritten caption on the back of this delightful horse-drawn buggy photo with Julia kneeling in the front, at the Parker farm, *c.* 1910, reads, "We are taking Linnie to the train as she starts for Eugene. After the picture was taken Julia sat on our lap . . ."

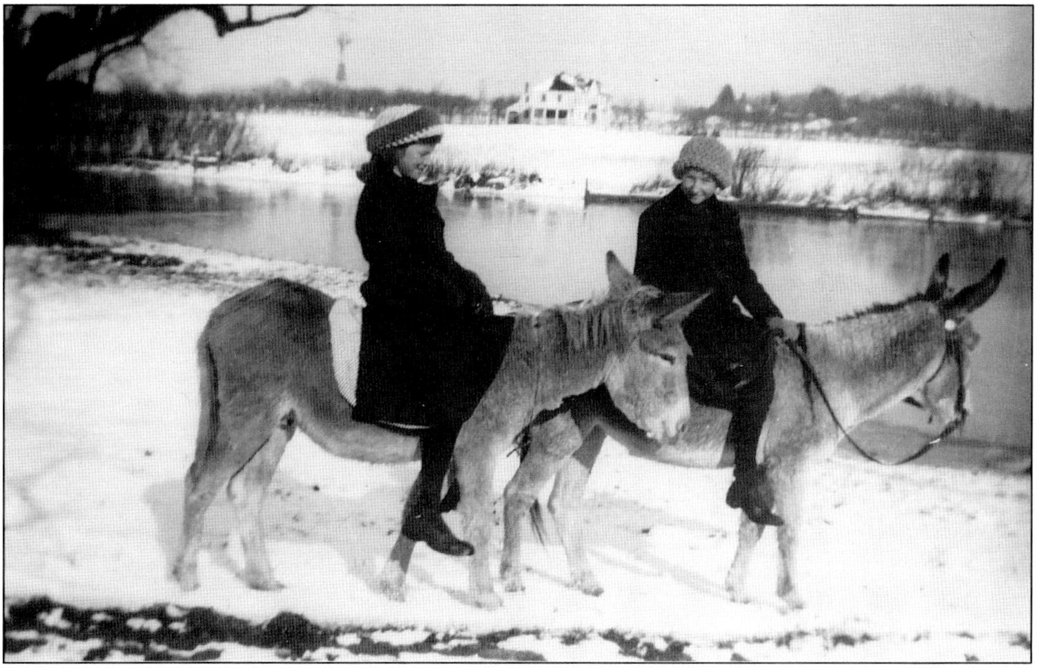

A newspaper clipping from *c.* 1908, in a Parker family album, may help to explain this photograph: "DONKEYS ON A RAMBLE—M. Henry Parker Takes Care of Them Till Their Owner Turns Up—Two donkeys which appeared to be very bewildered and worried wandered through Little Silver . . . Mr. Parker's daughter Julia and her cousin Helen Smith had great sport riding and driving the donkeys through the village." The Hasler estate on Harding Road is seen in the background.

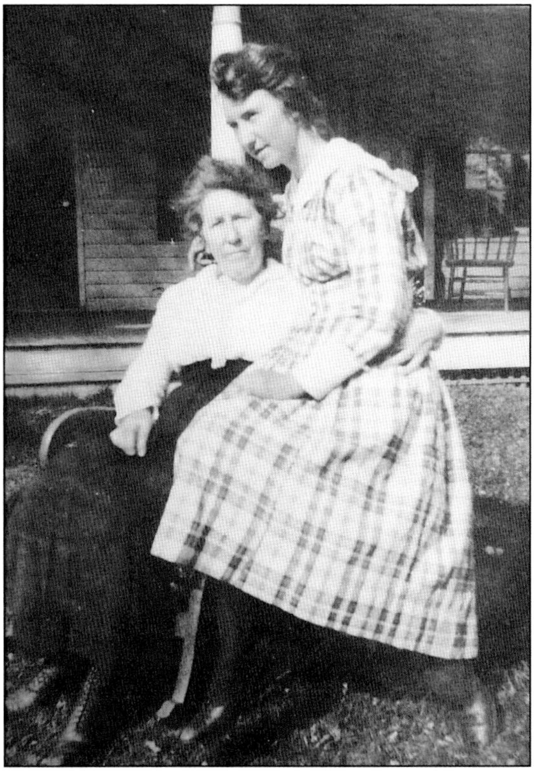

Julia Parker and her mother, Susan, obviously were very close. Wearing a pretty plaid dress, teenage Julia sits on the arm of her mother's chair in front of the Parker homestead, *c.* 1916.

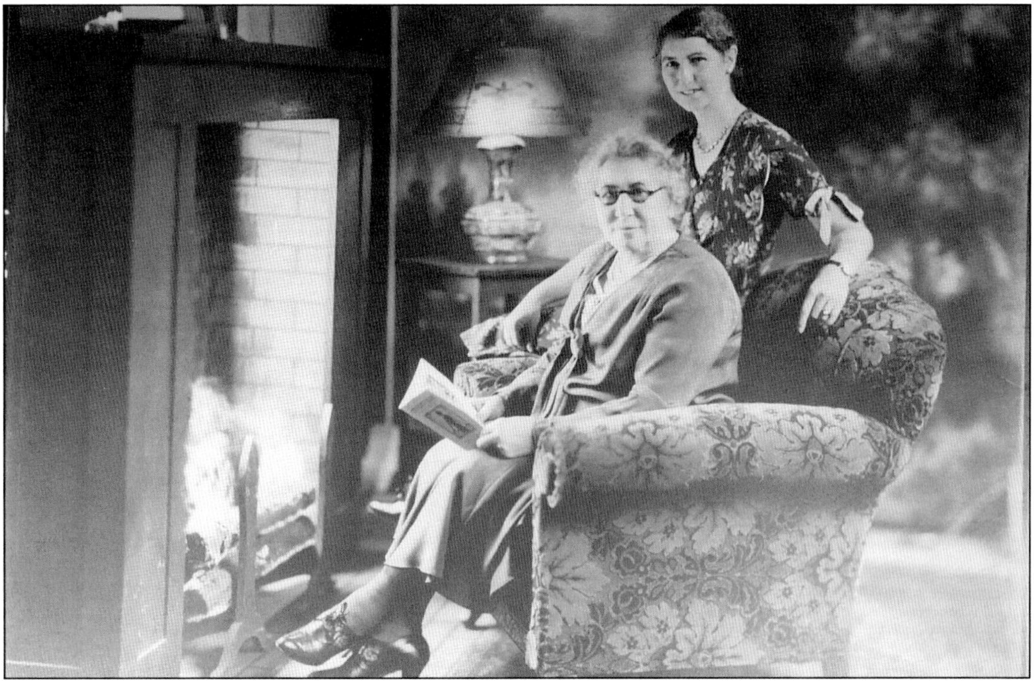

A softly lit photo of Julia and her mother, this lovely portrait probably dates from the 1920s. The fireplace and setting appear to be a set in a professional photo studio. It is not the fireplace in the homestead.

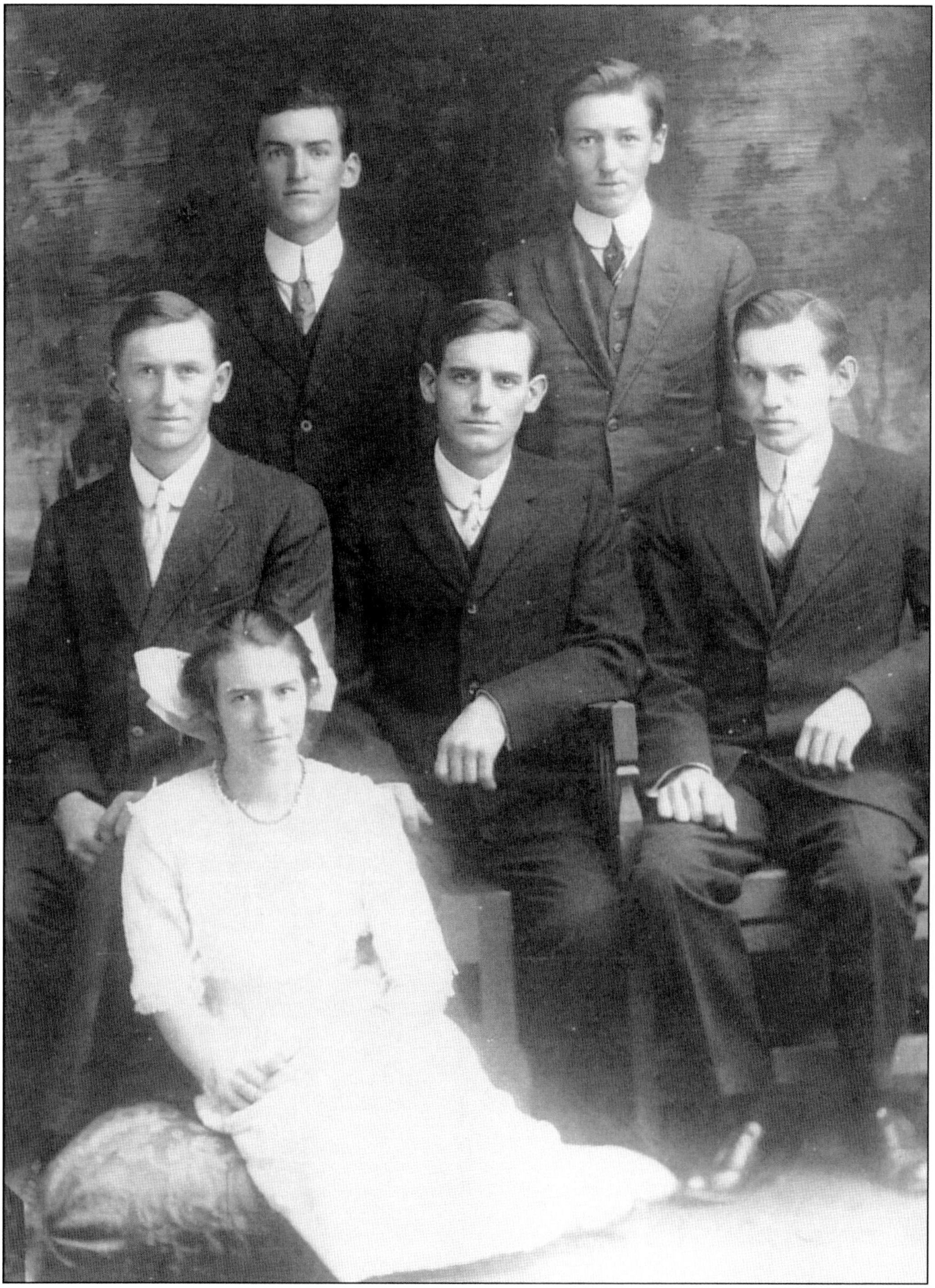

In a formal portrait of Michael and Susan Parker's six children, *c.* 1915, Julia sits in front of her brothers. Seated in the bottom row are, from left to right, Frank, Kenneth, and Henry. Standing in the back are Doug (left) and Stanley.

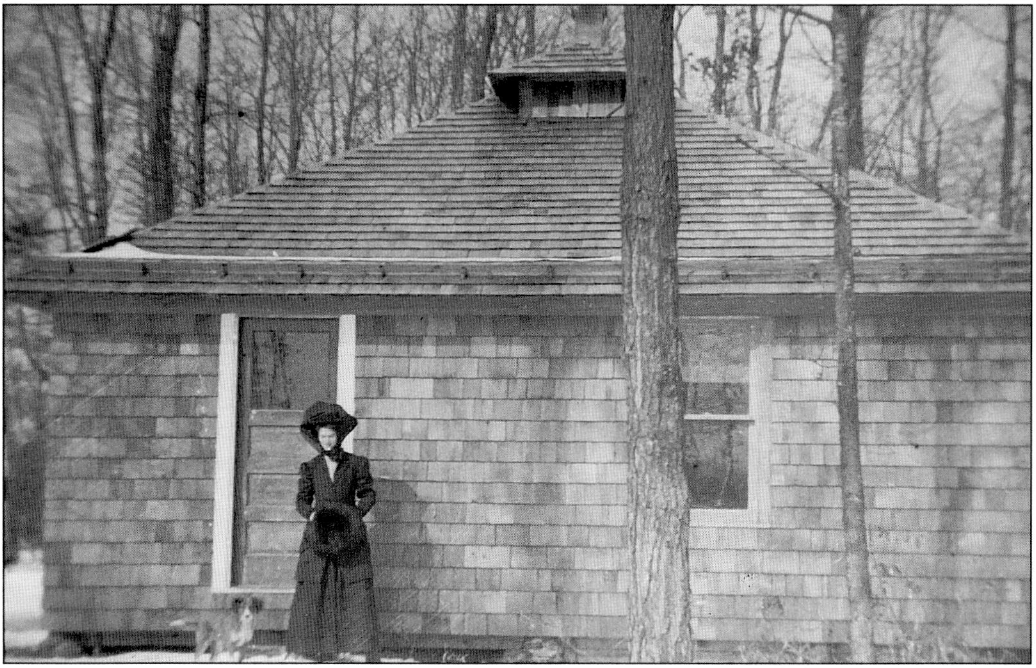

The handwritten caption on the back of this photo says: "Carrie in front of Frank and Carrie's house in the woods, Little Silver." Frank Parker, one of Julia's five brothers, and an expert carpenter, built this rustic home where he and his wife, Carrie, lived *c.* 1910. The bungalow was located "in the southwest corner of the woods" on the Parker property. In 1912, Frank and Carrie and their baby Frank Jr. moved to Arizona.

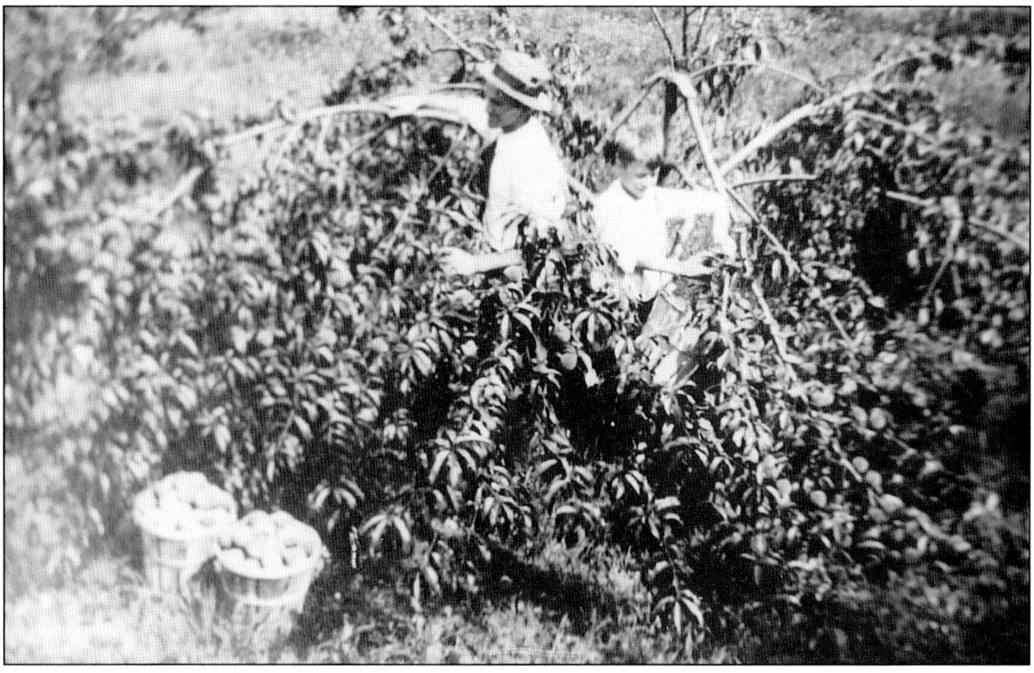

Picking fruits from the orchards on the Parker farm was a family affair as evidenced in this *c.* 1917 photo of harvesting fruit on the farm.

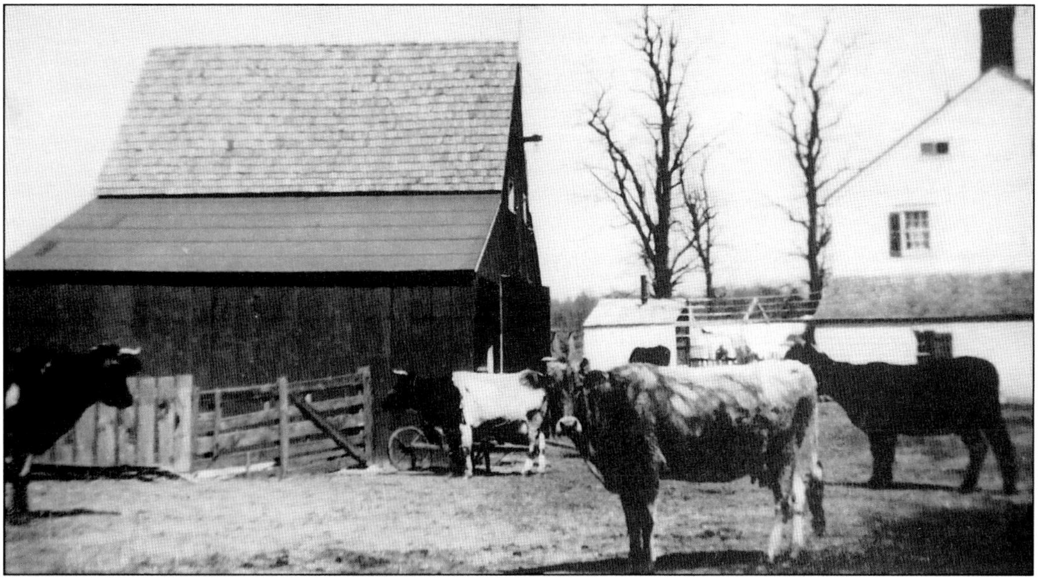

This 1917 view of the Parker barn and homestead shows that they kept cows, and also reveals a shed to the rear of the house that is no longer there.

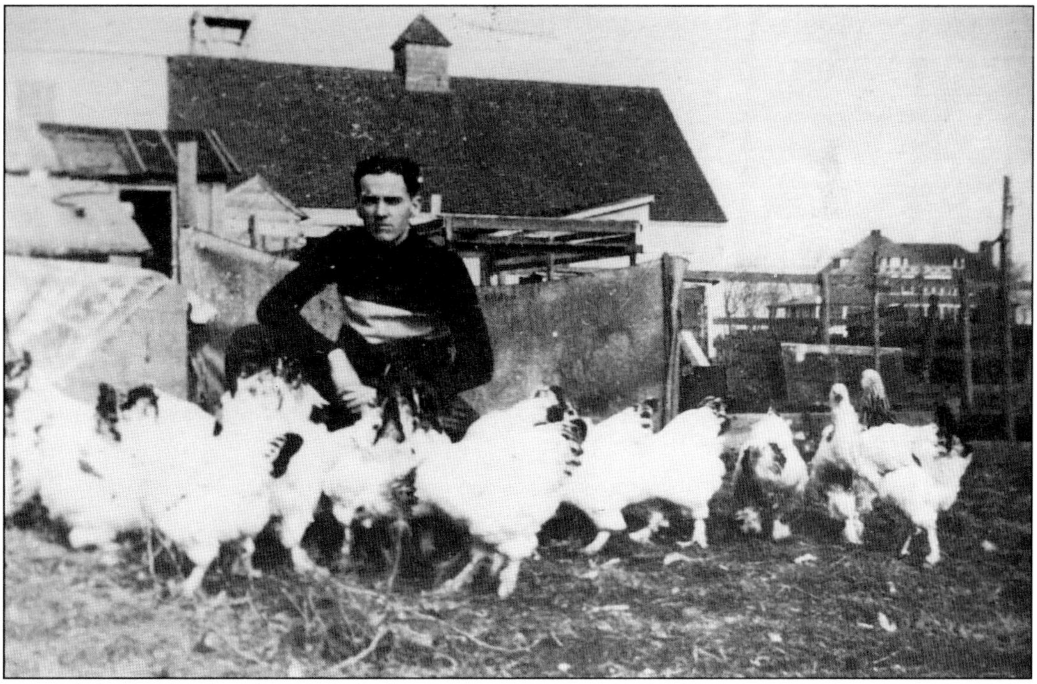

One of the Parker brothers kneels down to pose with the chickens by the coops in back of the homestead in 1917.

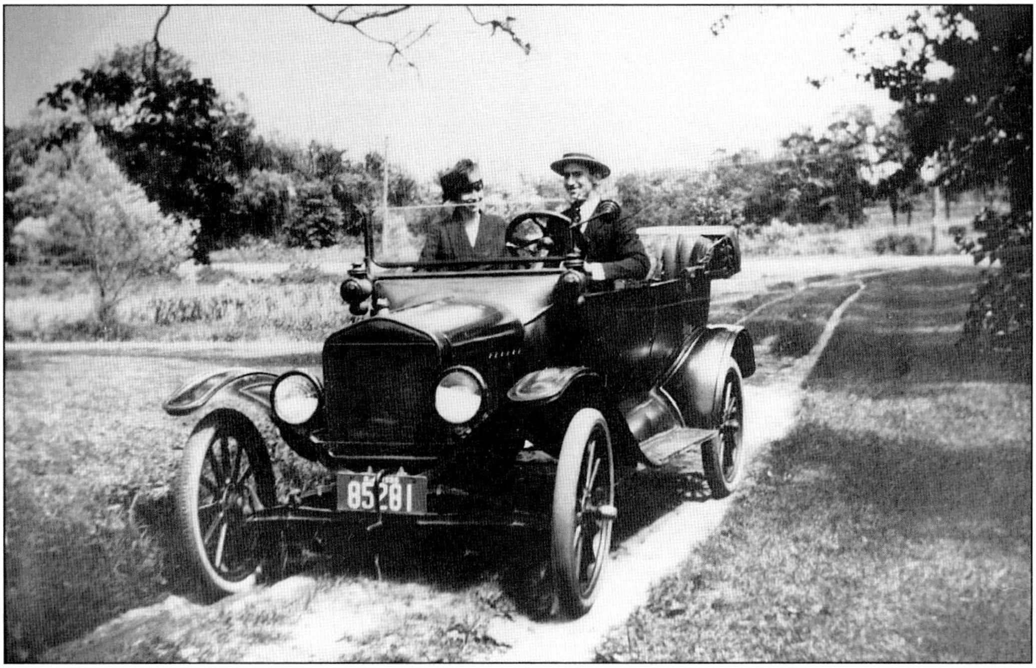

The handwritten caption on the back of this delightful photo taken at the Parker farm reads, "Doug & Roberta . . . or Julia? Our first Ford 1917."

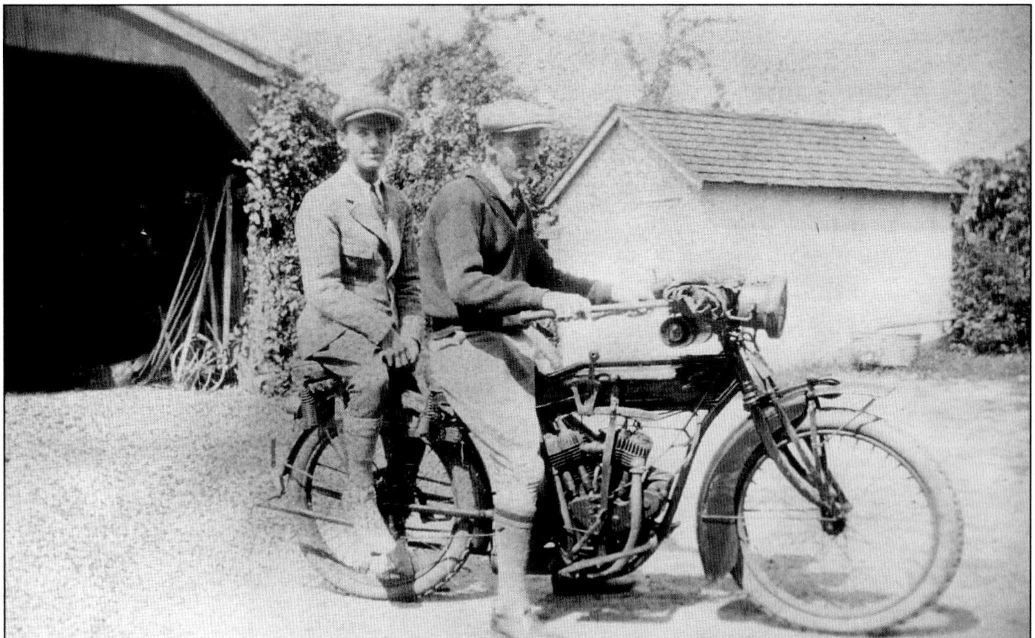

In the early 1920s, Doug and Stan Parker are ready for some fun on their Indian motorcycle.

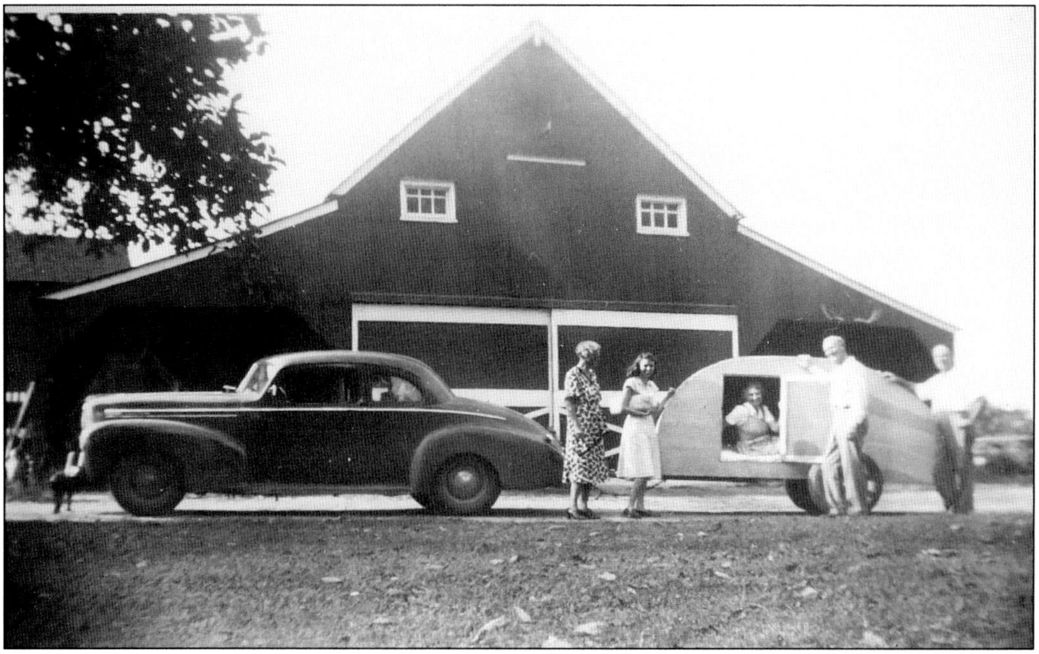

The Parker family members enjoyed traveling to western states and several of them moved west as described in Julia Parker's book about her family history. This homemade trailer apparently made a big hit with the family in around 1949. From left to right are Alice Parker, Charlotte Sickles, Julia Parker (in the trailer!), Henry Parker, and Doug Parker.

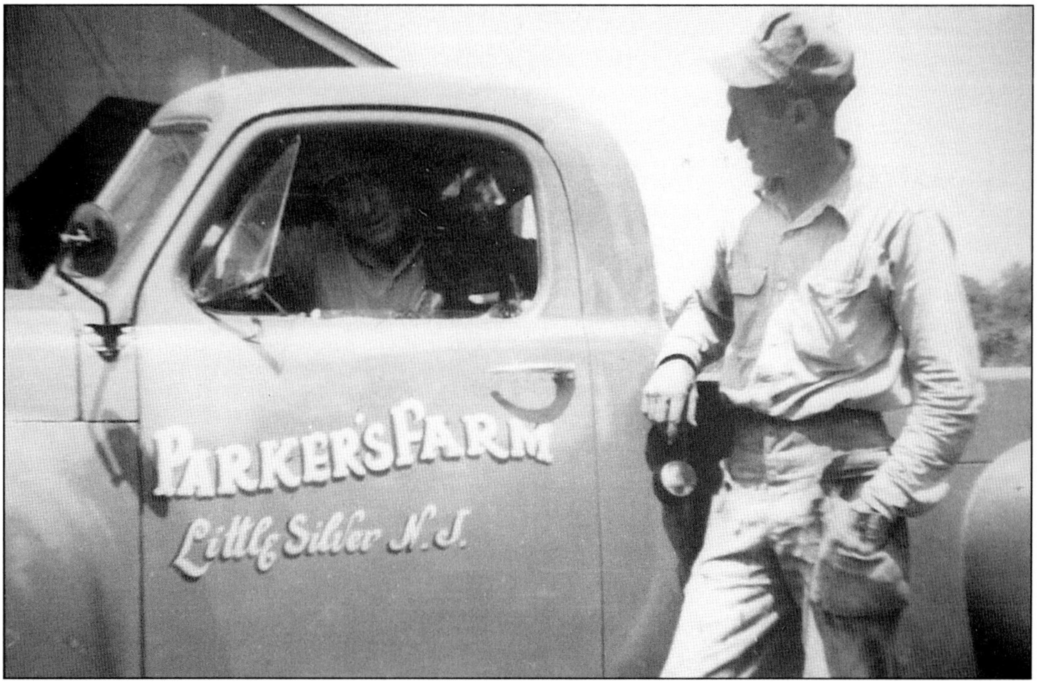

Stopping to chat for a moment in the 1940s are brothers Doug Parker (in the pickup truck) and Stan Parker. No doubt they didn't take this break for more than a few minutes, as farming is hard work with long hours.

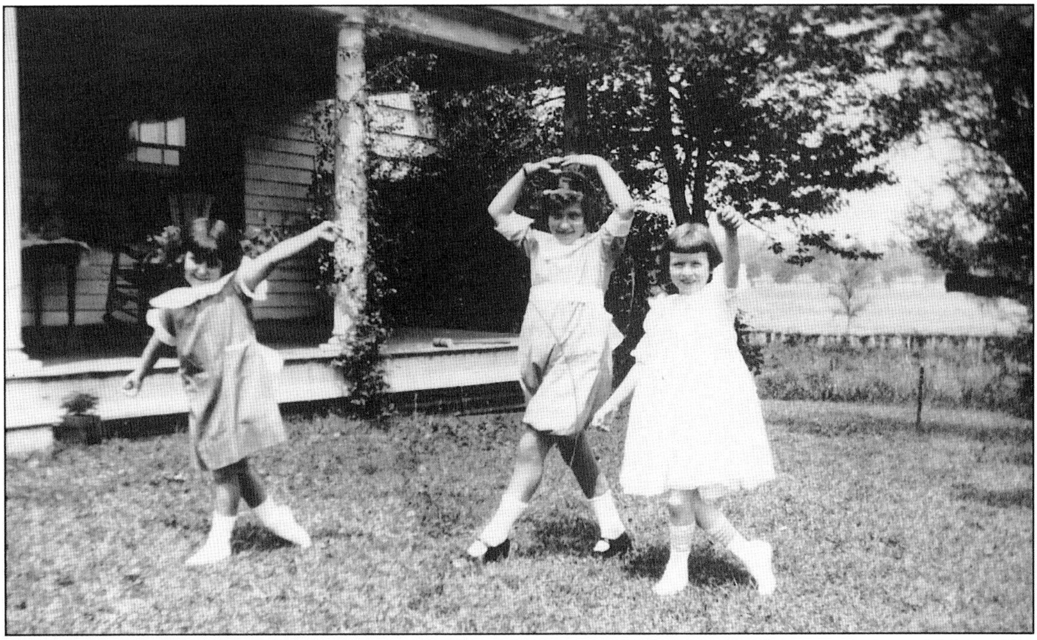

These pretty maidens are dancing on the lawn in front of the Parker homestead, *c.* 1920s. On the right is Virginia Parker, one of Henry's (Hal's) daughters. (Borough of Little Silver.)

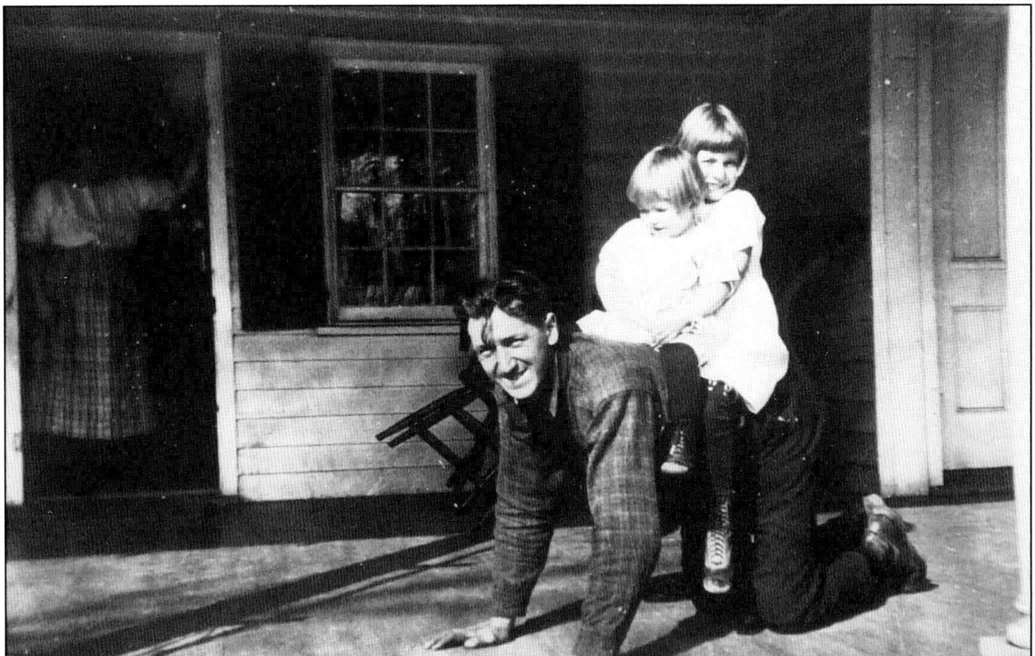

Here on the porch of the Rumson Road Parker house, *c.* 1920s, Uncle Stan (Stanley Parker) plays "horse" and gives his nieces Alice and Virginia (daughters of his brother Hal) a ride.

In the late 1920s or early 30s, cousins (from left to right) Bobby Sickles, Charlotte Sickles, Julie Parker, and Betsy Parker take a moment out from play to pose by the Parker homestead's water pump. But it is Mickey, the Fox Terrier, who upstages the children!

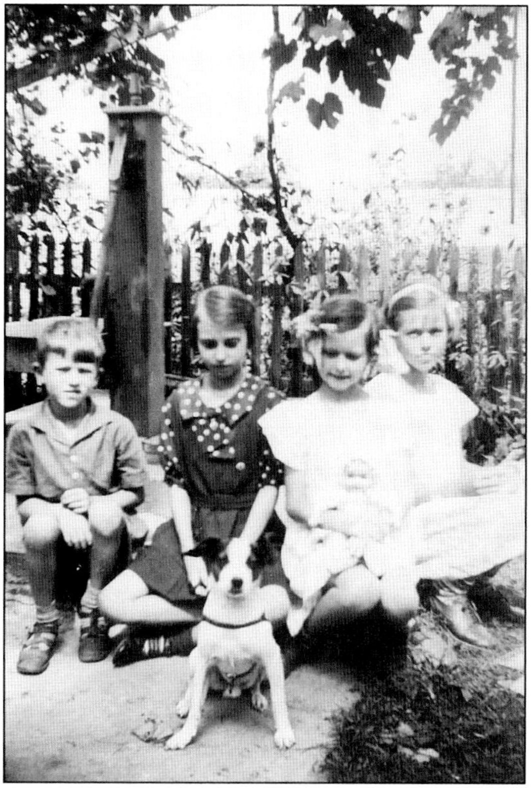

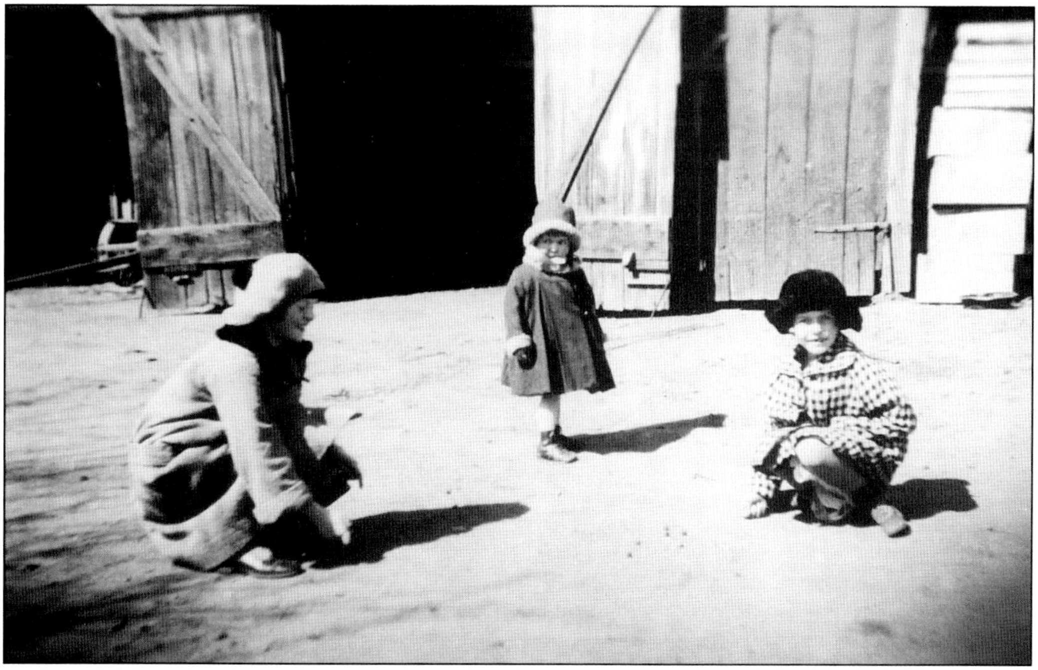

Parker children are playing marbles in front of the barn at the homestead, c. 1930s. Marbles are a popular childhood game of yesteryear that endures today. From left to right are Virginia, Betsy, and Alice Parker.

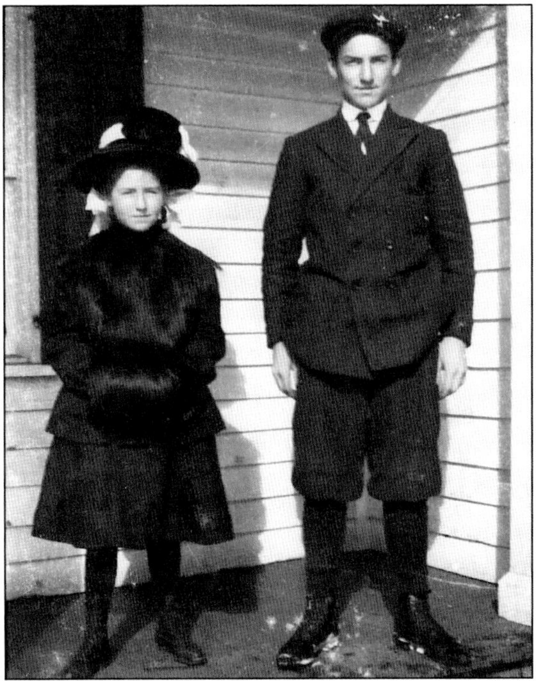

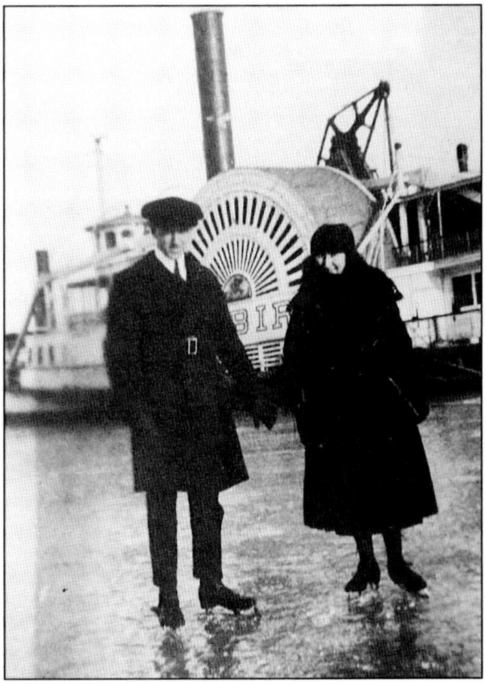

Left: In this image of Julia and Stan, *c*. 1910 on the porch of the Parker homestead, Julia is keeping her hands warm in a muff, a popular fashion accessory in those days. *Right*: Julia and Stan are enjoying ice skating on the Shrewsbury River *c*. 1917. The steamboat *Sea Bird*, which transported many passengers during the summers from New York to Little Silver, can be seen behind them, dry docked for the winter.

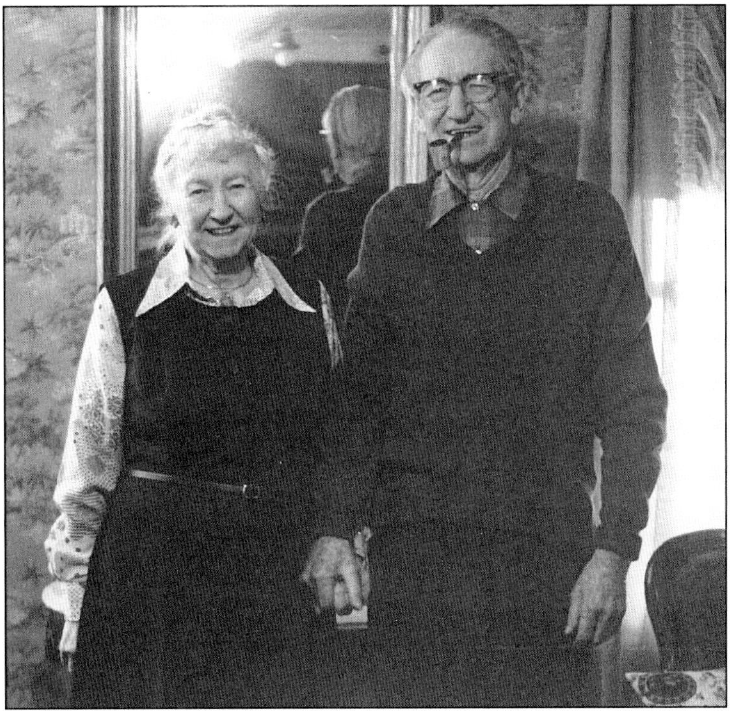

This portrait of Julia and Stan Parker from the 1980s shows that the brother and sister pair still resemble the above portrait of them from long ago, except now Stan has a pipe! The photo was taken by Leslie Sickles.

A delightfully candid image of Julia on her John Deere tractor in front of the homestead, *c.* 1980s, shows her as she was, always spunky and determined. She continued to ride the tractor well into her eighties.

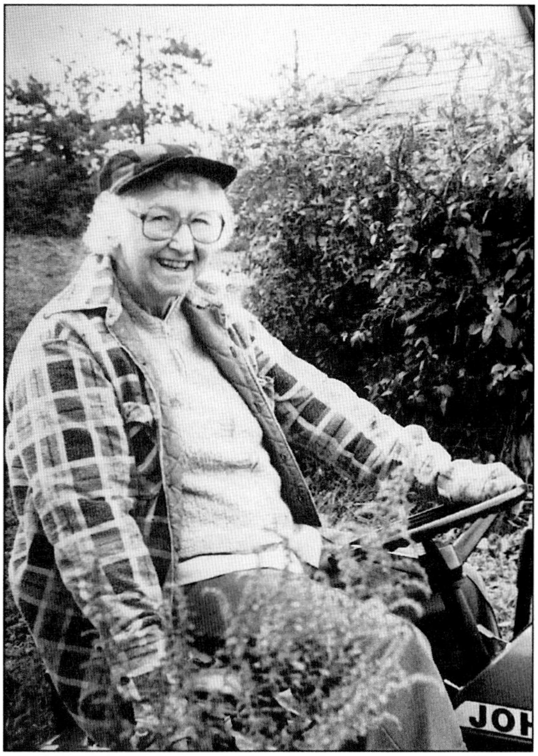

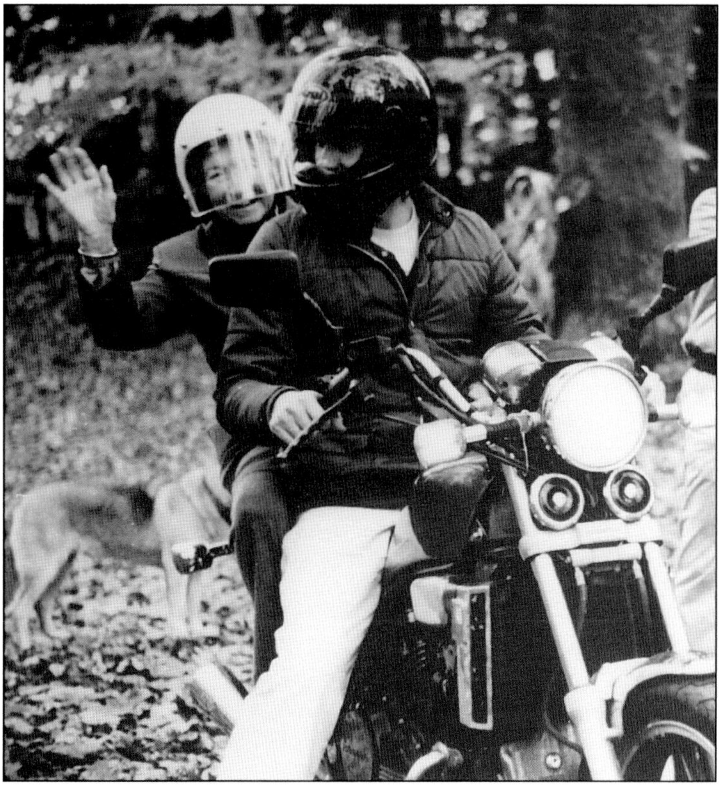

Julia takes a ride on the back of a motorcycle in the 1980s . . . while she was in her eighties. Way to go, Julia!

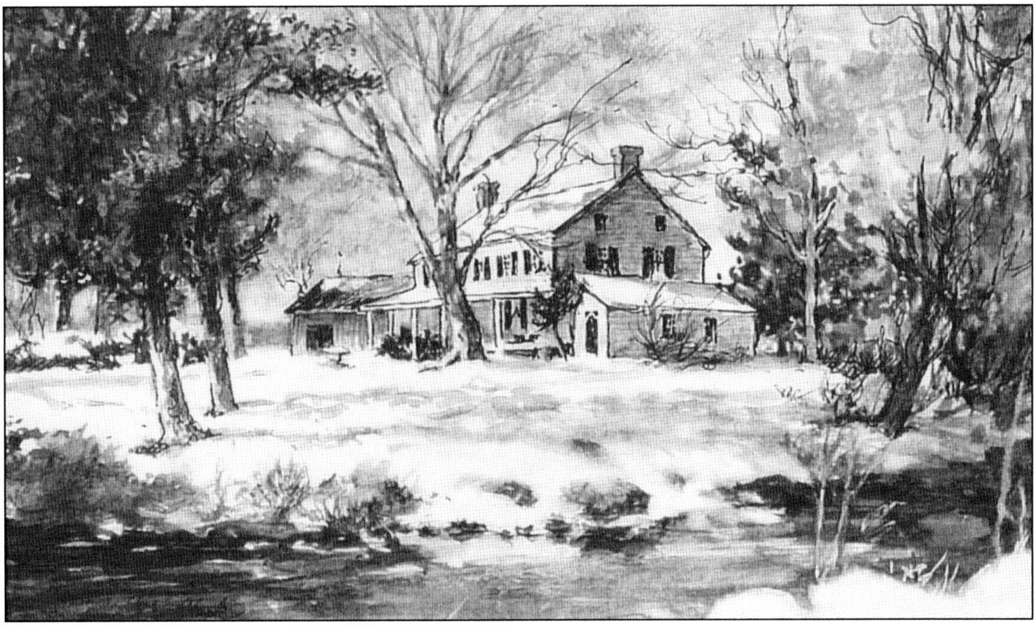

This contemporary watercolor of the Parker homestead is by well-known artist Roberta Carter Clark of Little Silver, who contributed her time and talent to create a series of scenes depicting the town's historic sites that were reproduced as prints and note cards. These and other commemorative items are sold by the Borough of Little Silver to benefit the Parker House Restoration Fund.

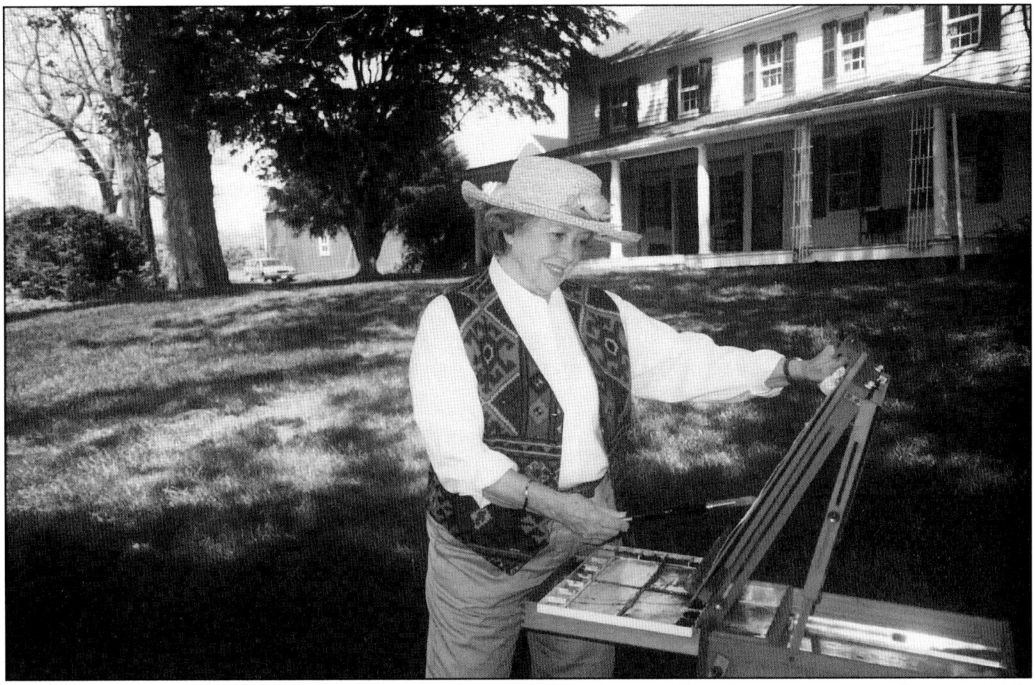

Roberta Carter Clark enjoys painting at the Parker homestead on a sunny spring day in 1998. To set the mood for this photo and recall a bygone era at the farm, the talented artist donned a charming straw hat. (Photo by author.)

Three

Houses, Great and Small

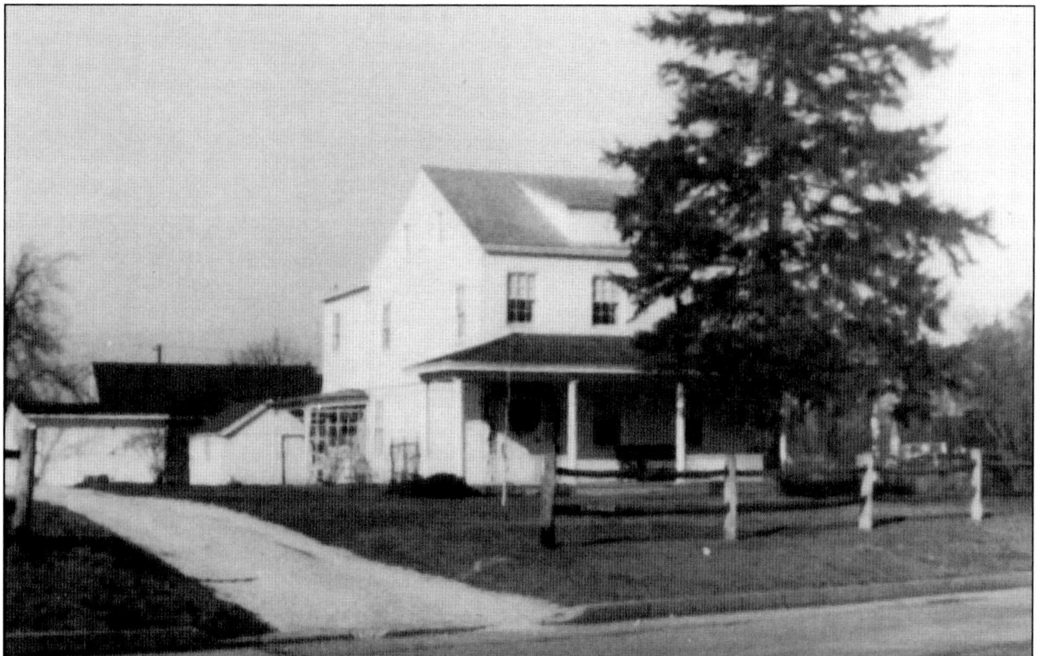

Built in 1848, this house on Church Street that belonged to Jacob Corlies Parker (grandfather of Julia Parker) is on the triangle of land that extends from Church Lane to Rumson Road. When Jacob became ill, he and his family moved back to the Parker homestead, where he died. The house was then sold to J. Hyer, who operated a general store (p. 59 of *Little Silver Vol. I*) next door. In the early part of the 20th century, the Edwards family lived here and sisters Allyne and Libby Edwards taught school in a small room of the house. Since 1974, the house (shown here *c.* 1956) has belonged to interior designer Cathy Oswandel and her husband, Bob, who have done extensive renovation and preservation. (C. Oswandel.)

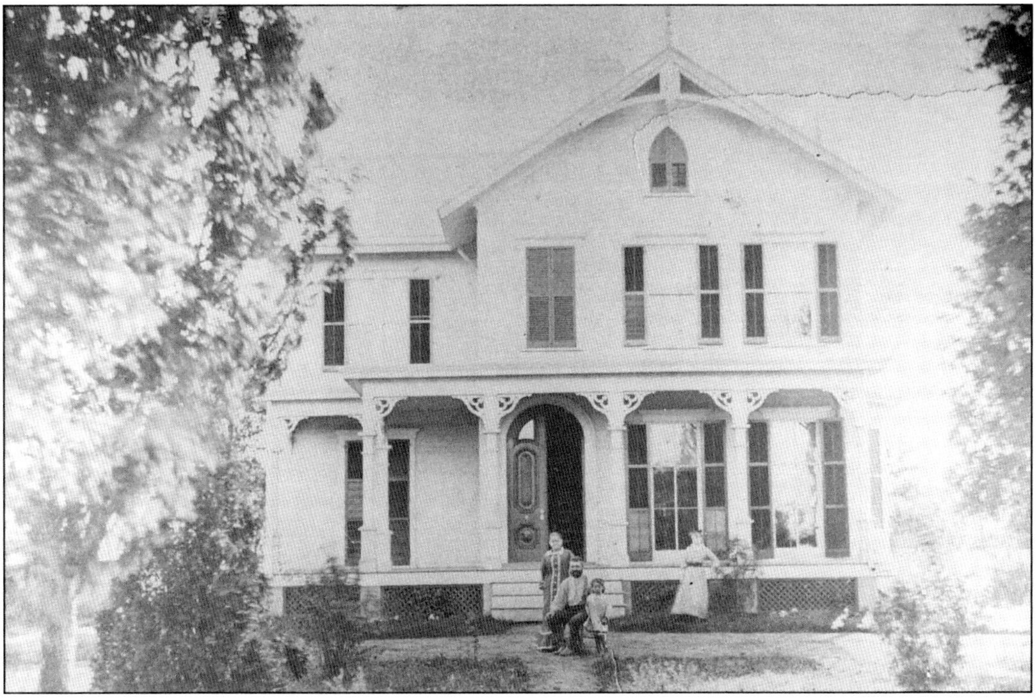

The William Parker homestead on Silverside Avenue was also the home of Richard and Agnes Parker, who are seen in this turn-of-the-century image with son Joseph and a maid. The reverse side of photo says: "Our home at Little Silver where I was born and lived until married—Father, Mother and Brother Joe and Maid in picture." (Little Silver Historical Society.)

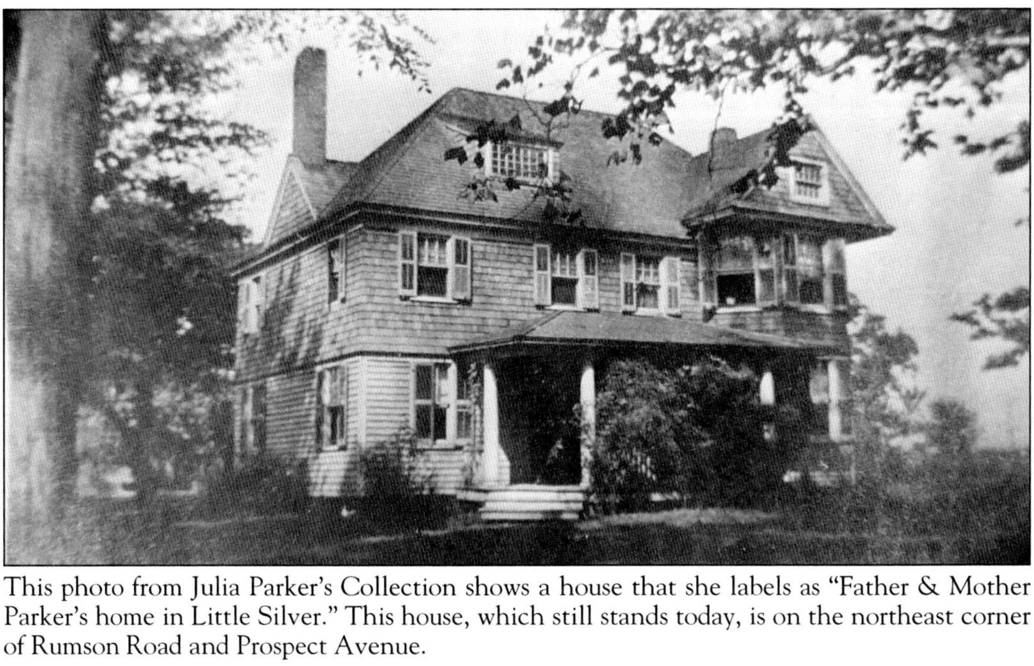

This photo from Julia Parker's Collection shows a house that she labels as "Father & Mother Parker's home in Little Silver." This house, which still stands today, is on the northeast corner of Rumson Road and Prospect Avenue.

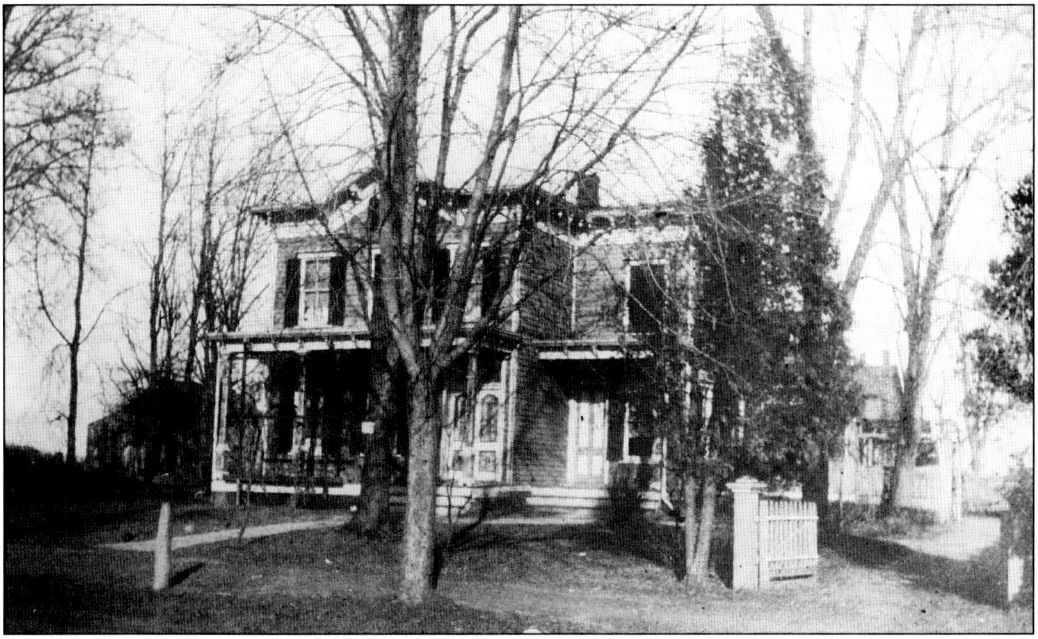

The house on the southeast corner of Rumson Road and Prospect Avenue, known as 140 Rumson Road, is a Little Silver landmark that stands today and has belonged to Donald and Jane Lux since 1969. Pictured here in the late 19th century, the house was the home of Julia Parker's grandfather, Lewis Smith, who was a Master Mason and died in 1897. Julia's parents, Susan Ella Smith and Michael Henry Parker, were married here on Nov. 13, 1884. (J. Lux.)

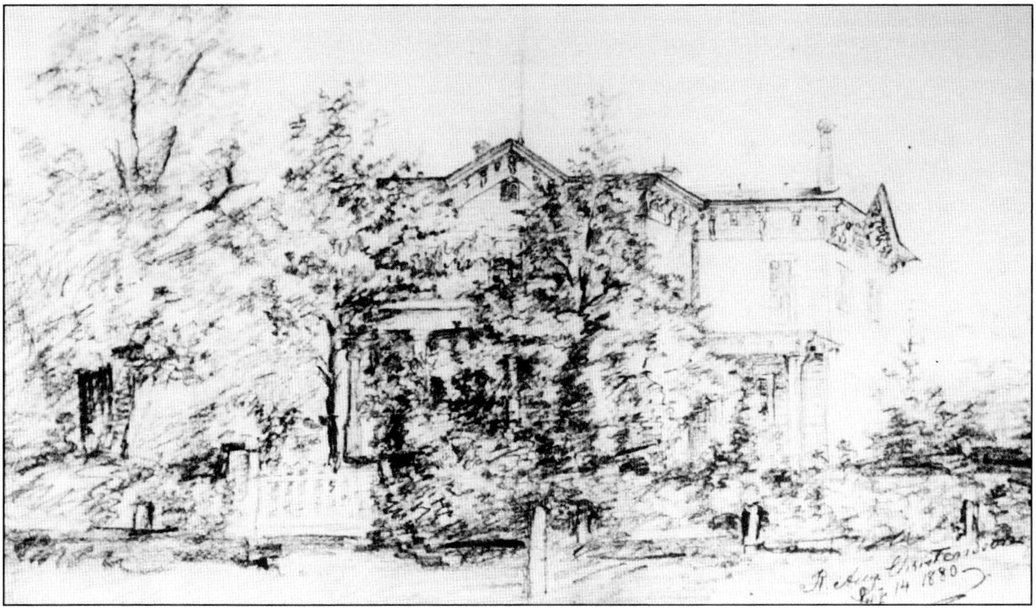

The signature, "R. Aug Christianson" and date, "Sept. 14, 1880," appear in the lower right-hand corner of this lovely charcoal sketch of the house known as 140 Rumson Road, seen in the photo at the top of the page. Although nothing is known about the artist who did this work, Jane Lux, current owner of the house and lender of a copy print of this drawing, is an artist who exhibits and teaches watercolor classes.

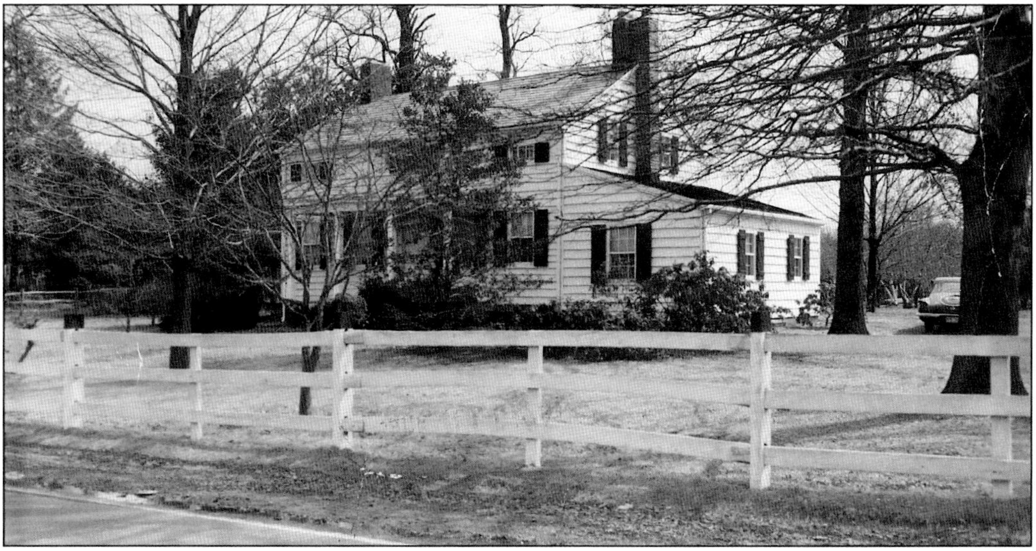

The ownership of this historic home at 174 Little Silver Point Road is well documented. George Lippincott Sr. purchased a tract of land from John Pintard in January 1845, and the front part (where the house was built) from Benjamin and Jane Airs (later spelled Ayres) in April 1845. In the early days, the only access to the property was a footpath across the marshlands. George Lippincott Jr. inherited the property when his father died. The present owners are Betty Jean and Karl Meyer, who purchased the home in 1966 and provided this 1970s photo.

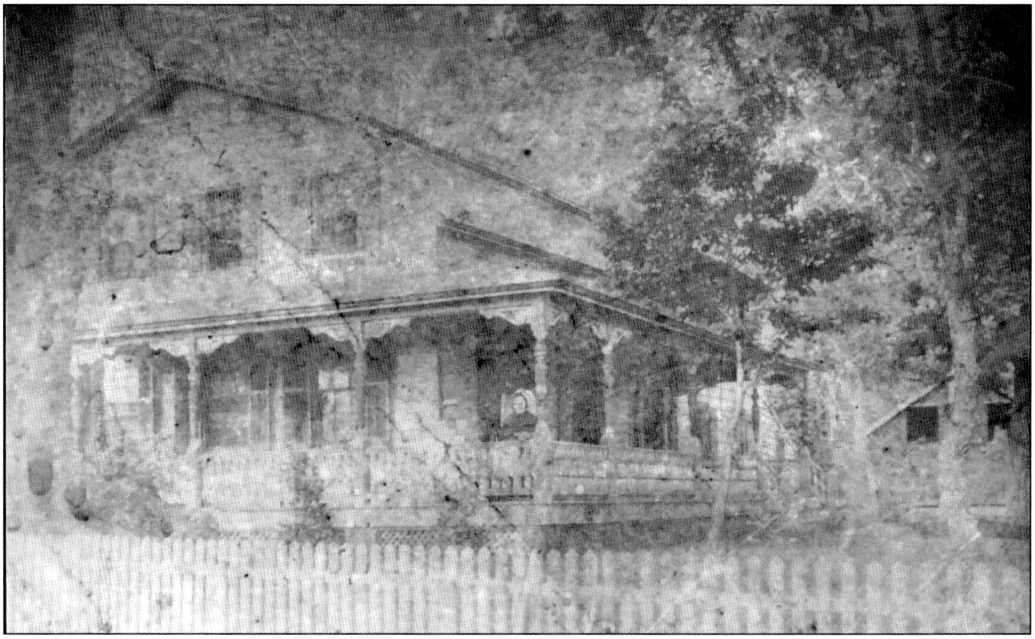

Although the quality of this faded image is poor, it is included because of its rarity and historic significance. The home with picket fence was the White homestead on Willow Drive where the Little Silver Board of Education offices are located. The family of Harrison Decatur White, who ran a "stage and carriage service," lived here. There were four children: William Harrison Jr. (born at the house in 1891), Mary, Theodore, and Augustus. (D. Ayers.)

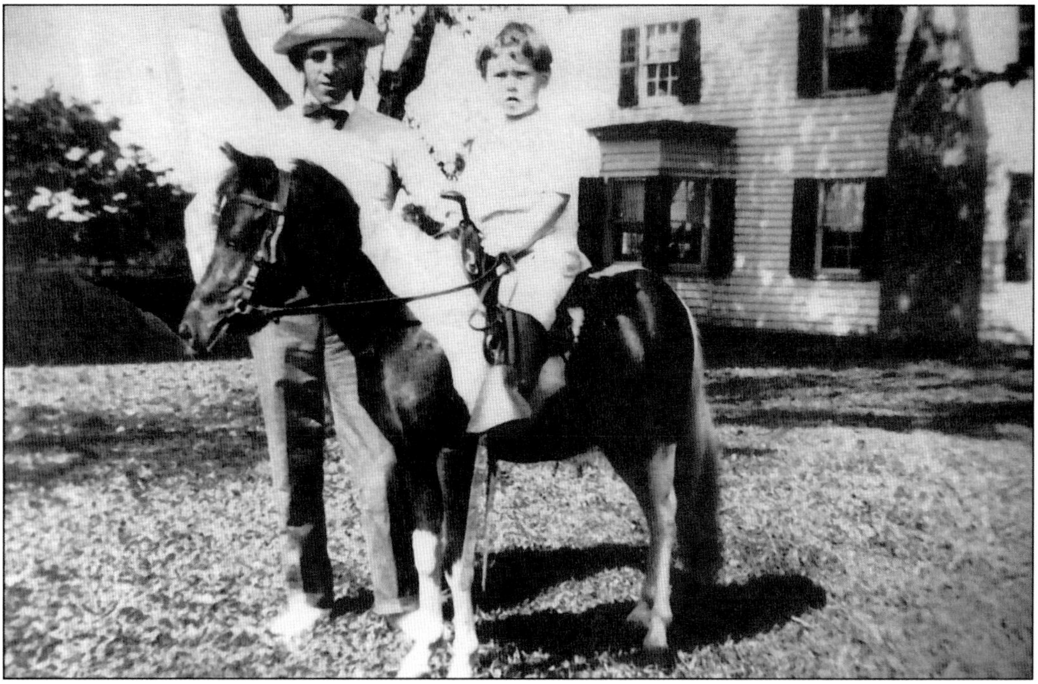

Four-year-old William Lippincott Jr., nicknamed "Champ," is pictured here in 1916 with one of his father's workers leading him on a pony. The rear of the Lippincott house at 635 Prospect Avenue is seen clearly in the background of this charming image. (W. Lippincott.)

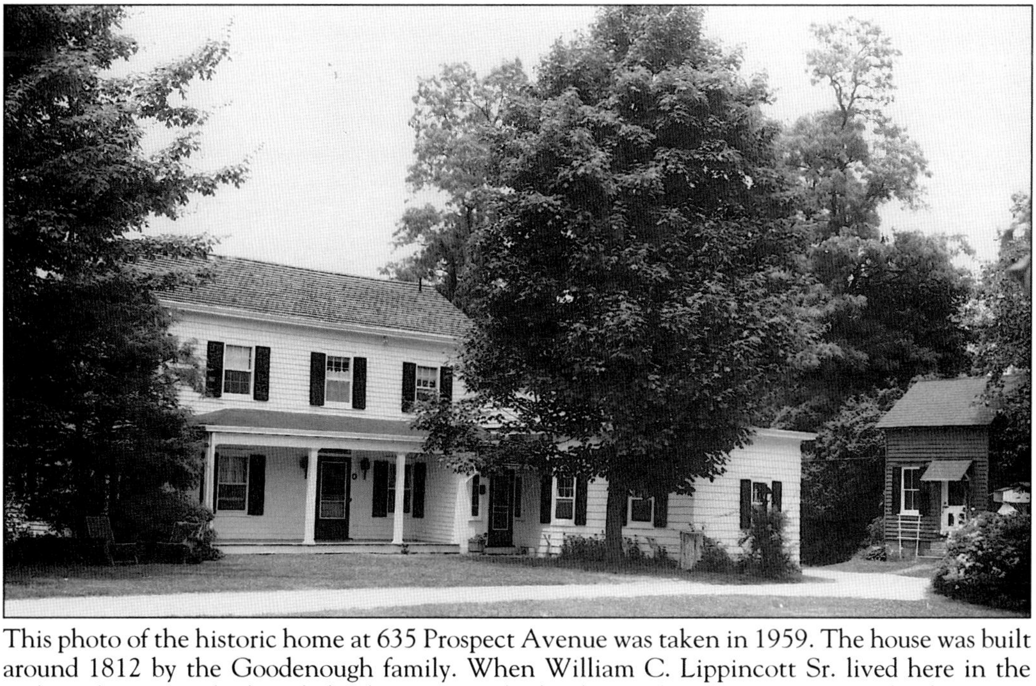

This photo of the historic home at 635 Prospect Avenue was taken in 1959. The house was built around 1812 by the Goodenough family. When William C. Lippincott Sr. lived here in the early 20th century, he boarded polo ponies and other horses from Rumson estates for the winter season. His farm extended south to the brook where there are now more houses. (Dorn's.)

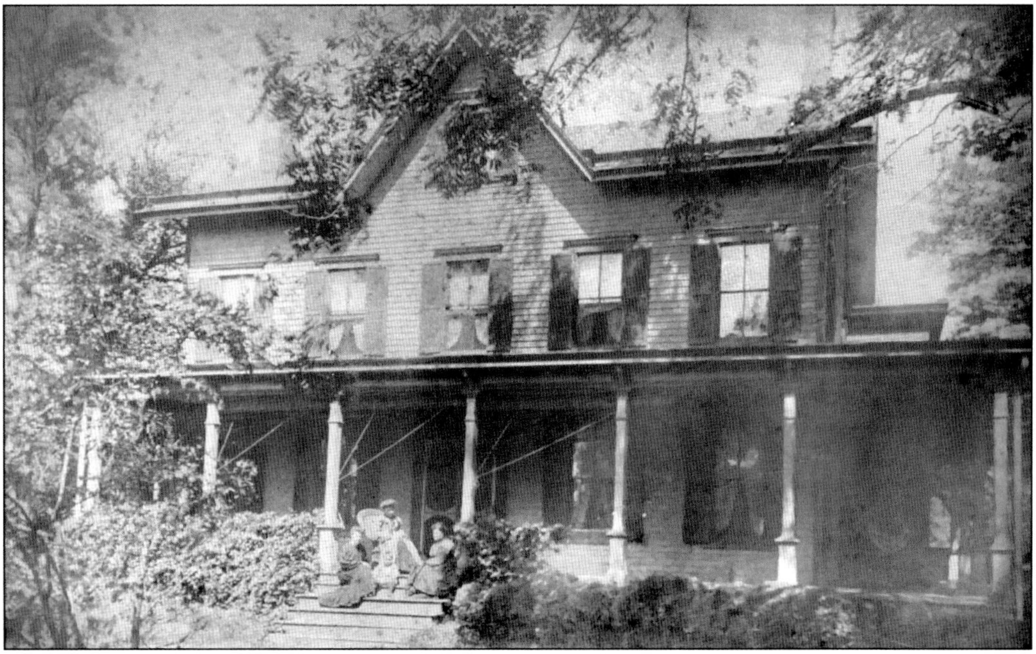

In 1865, sea captain William Robert Mulliner bought 23 acres of land for $8,300, and soon built this house that stands today at the corner of Little Silver Point Road and Willow Drive as a summer residence. In 1869, the family spent their first winter in the house. Much later, in this *c.* 1900 photo, the mother of the household, Ethel Mae Sarles Ericksen, is seated in a chair, and Mary Sophia Sarles is sitting on the right; the identities of the other woman and the child are unknown. (K. Pearson.)

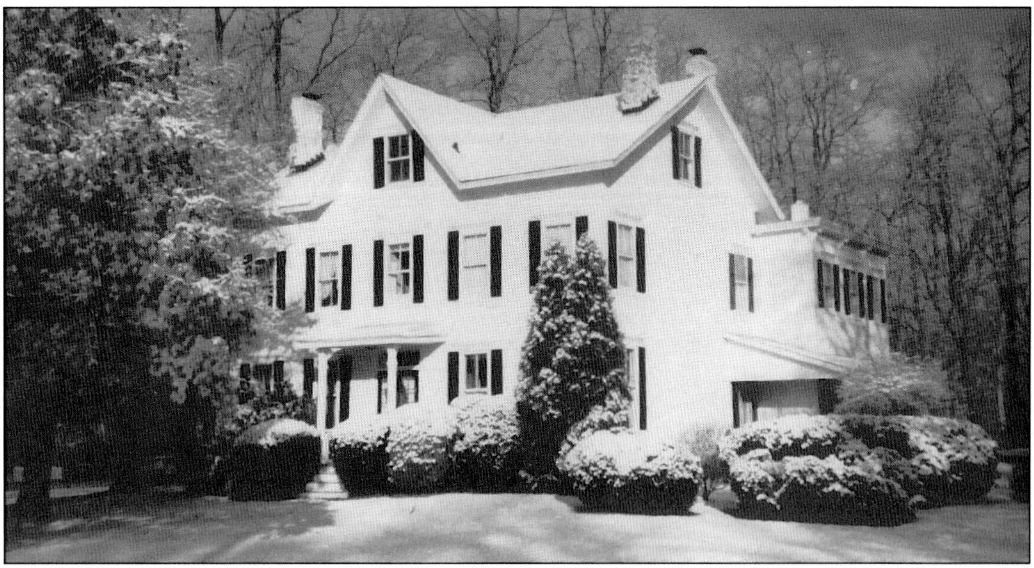

This house at 3 Little Silver Point Road, shown in earlier days at the top of the page, belonged to ancestors of Captain Mulliner until 1948, although the bulk of his land was sold off as building lots for many years prior. Today the home belongs to the Pearson family, who have made changes but with great respect for history and tradition. Now painted white, the house was originally gray. (K. Pearson.)

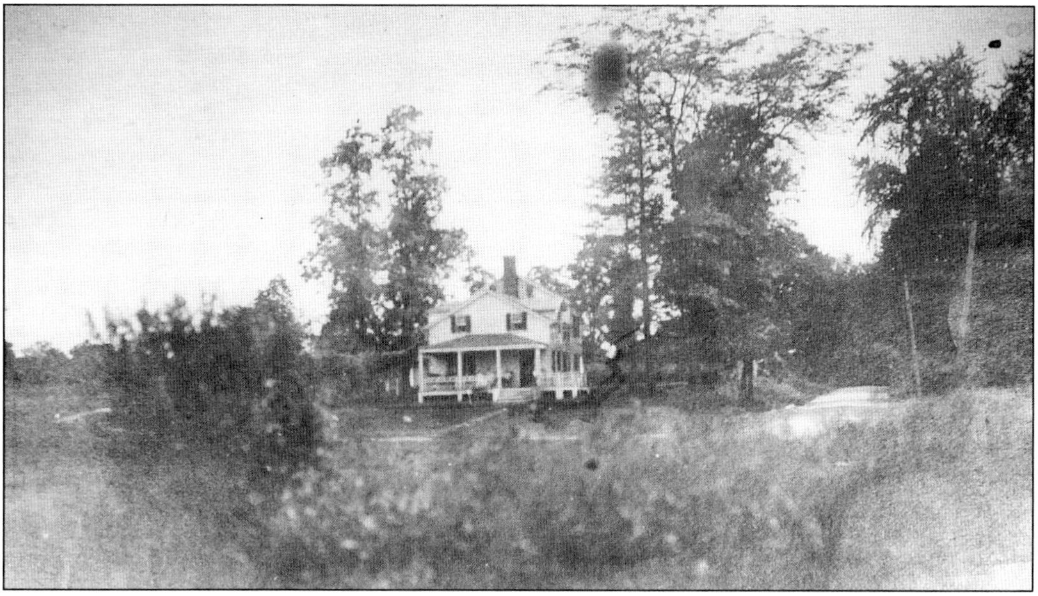

This 1918 view of Twin Pines, the Shampanore homestead at 26 Willow Drive, was taken at the "V" intersection where Prospect Avenue branches to the left and Willow Drive (which can be seen here) is on the right side. The Shampanore family's printing business was located in the building just behind the house that is not visible in this photo, which was provided by Doris Marcelli Shampanore Ayers (see pp. 61–63 of *Little Silver Vol. I*).

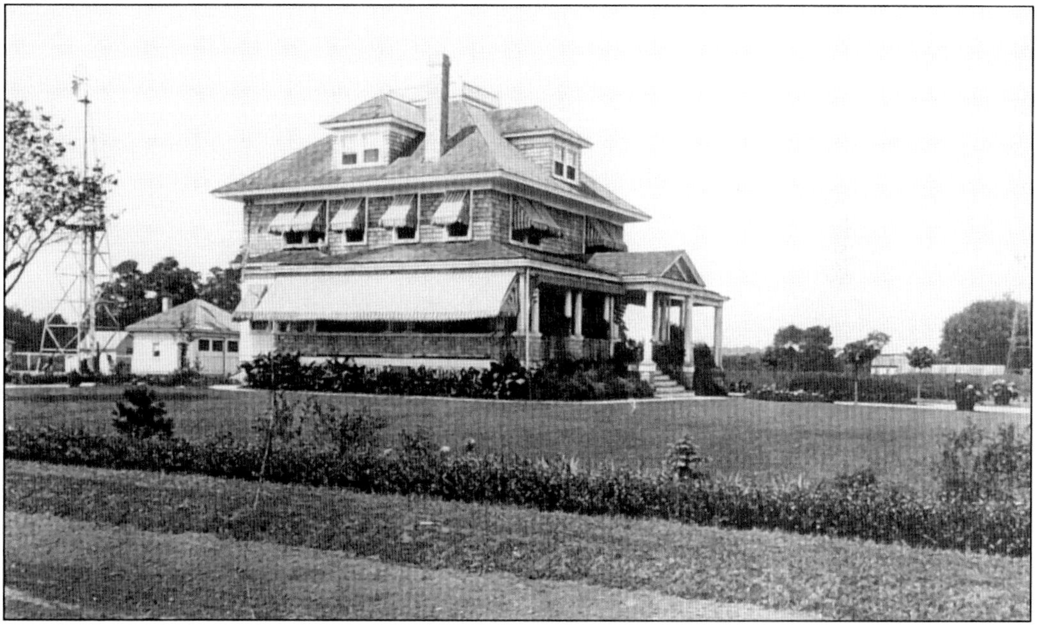

The attractive "Shore Colonial"-style house pictured here was built around 1904, and is located on the corner of Kings and Seven Bridges Roads. Many of the original trees remain but have grown very tall, making the property appear different from the way it looks in this photo, which was taken during the home's early years. Around 1930, a New York judge named Delahanty bought the house and added an addition. The Towers family purchased the property in the late 1940s. The Nishan Bogosians, the lenders of this photo, have lived here since 1972.

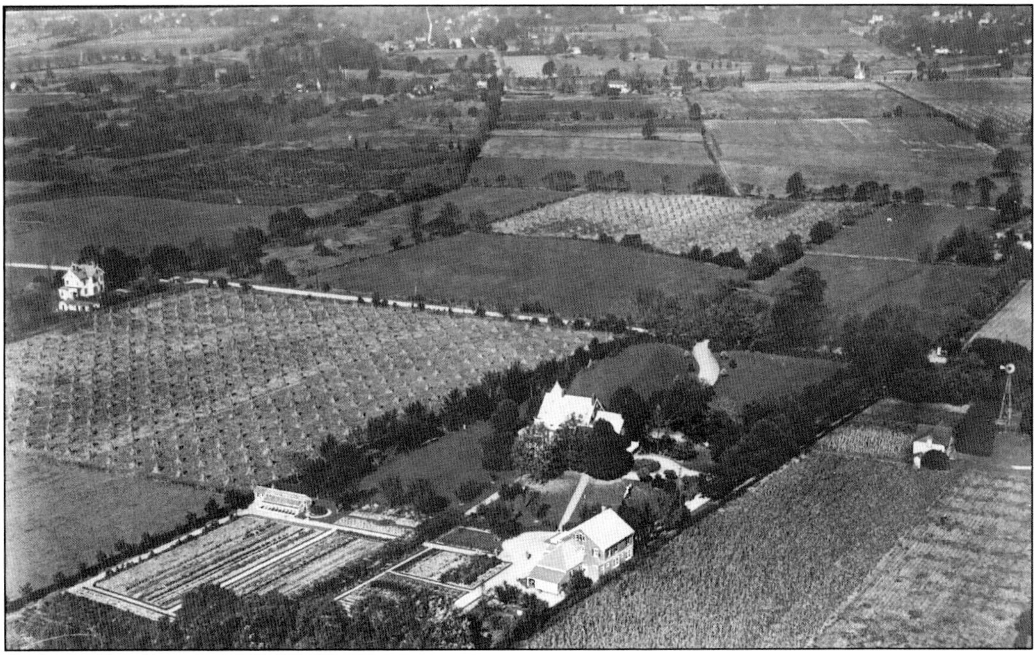

This dramatic 1920s aerial view of the Hasler estate and surrounding farms was taken from the south over the Shrewsbury River, looking north. The road in the center of the photo is Silverside Avenue. In the far distance, on the top right of the photo, you can see St. John's Chapel. (Dorn's.)

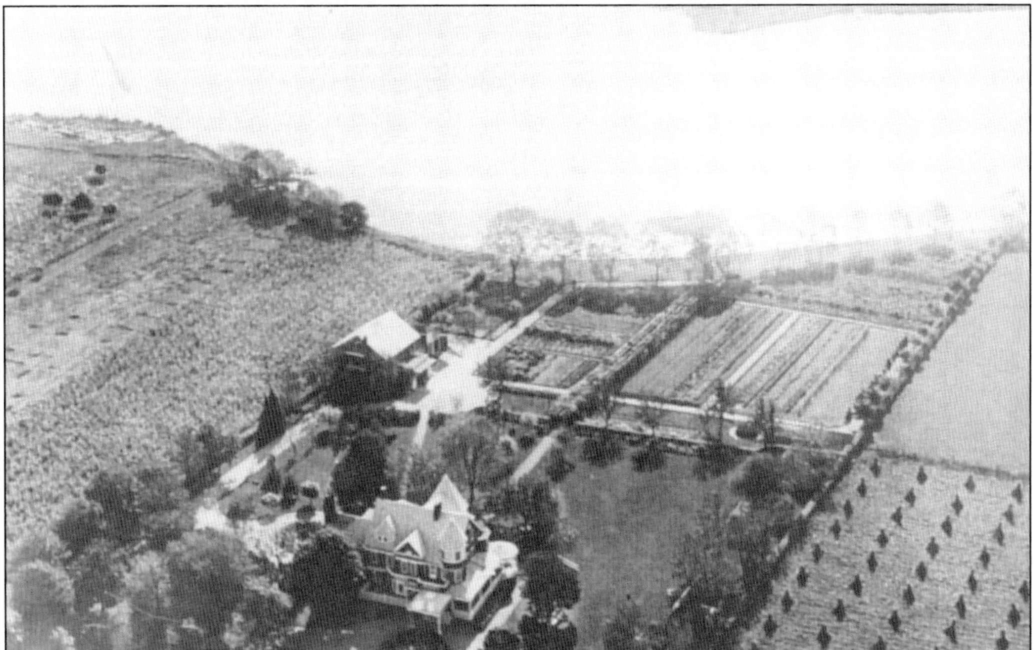

A closer 1920s aerial gives a clear view of the Hasler house, property, and gardens. The Shrewsbury River occupies the back of the photo. Notice the neatly stacked cornstalks in the field that is visible in the lower right-hand corner. (B. Pidel.)

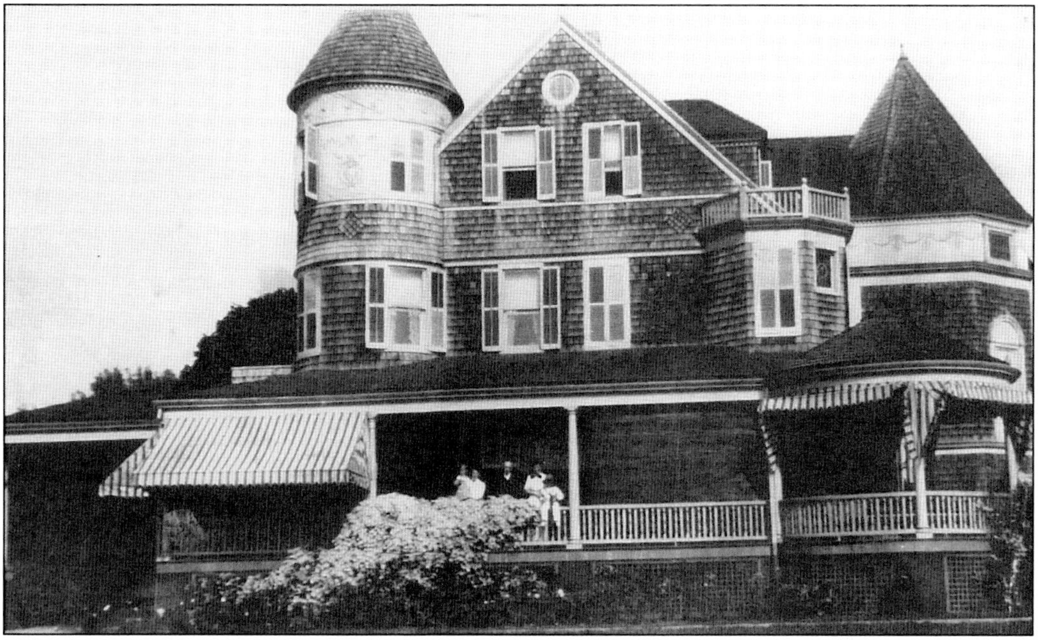

A shipbuilder named Philbrick purchased land from the Parkers on Silverside Avenue in the 1880s. When his daughter married Tom Hasler in the 1890s, he built this fabulous Queen Anne-style summer "cottage" as a wedding gift for them. Notice the wonderful bow-knot designs on the tower. (B. Pidel.)

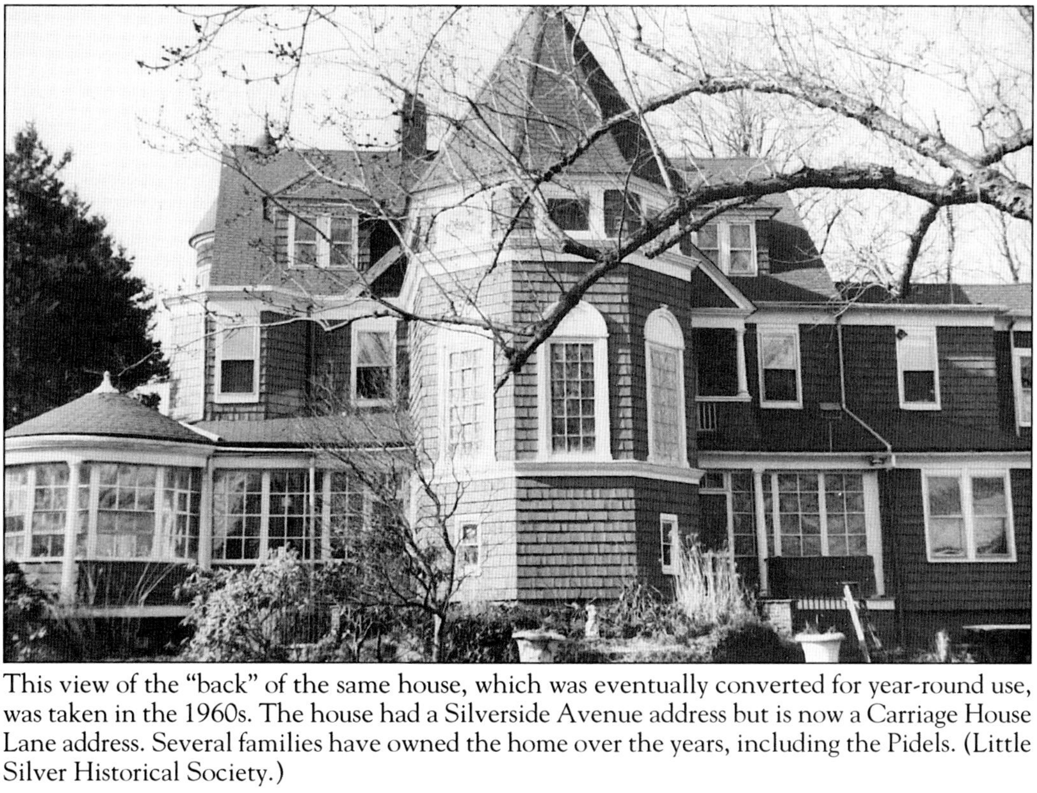

This view of the "back" of the same house, which was eventually converted for year-round use, was taken in the 1960s. The house had a Silverside Avenue address but is now a Carriage House Lane address. Several families have owned the home over the years, including the Pidels. (Little Silver Historical Society.)

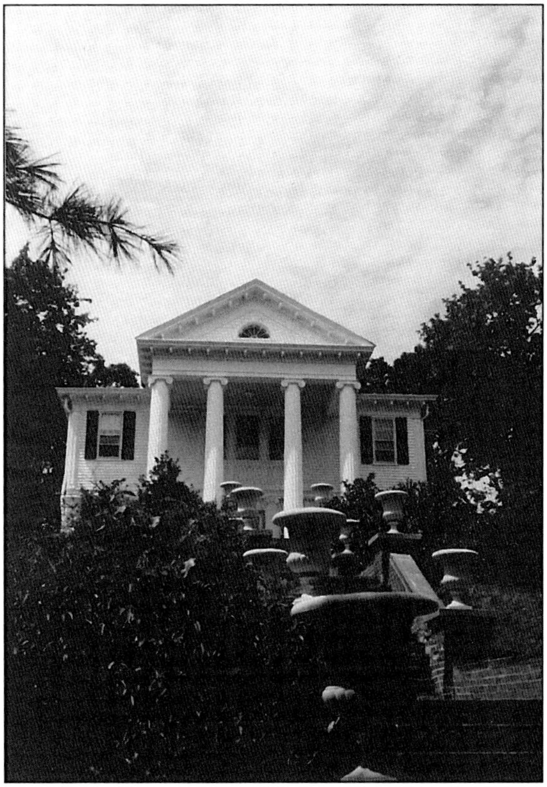

This lofty house on Fox Hill Drive commands a panoramic view of the Atlantic Ocean and the Shrewsbury River. Known as Sky High, it was originally owned by the Brooks family, and was built *c.* 1906. Theodore D. ("Ted") and Margaret Parsons purchased the home in 1935. Parsons, a prominent Red Bank attorney, called the home a retreat from the "cares that infest the day." In this recent photo, a steep set of brick steps flanked with stone urns leads to the front doorway. Since 1981 this home has belonged to Nancy and Obert Wood, who loaned this photo.

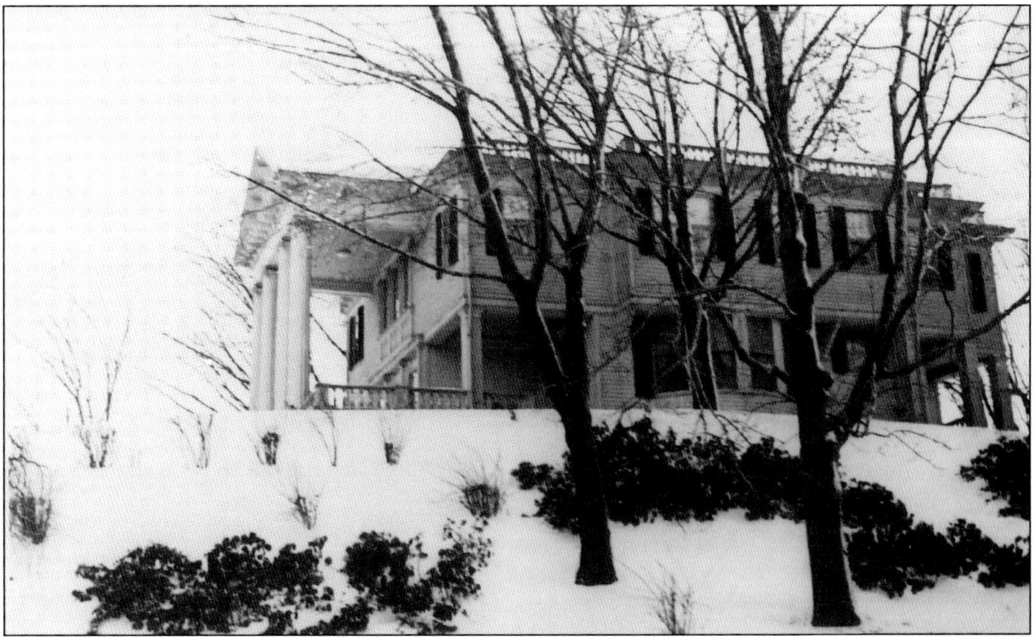

This view of Sky High during the 1930s, when Mr. and Mrs. Parsons lived here, was taken from the east side. Margaret Parsons initiated some structural changes, including the elimination of the two-story parlor that was surrounded by a gallery on the second floor. The second floor was enlarged to expand the bedrooms and to cover the high space over the parlor. (N. Wood.)

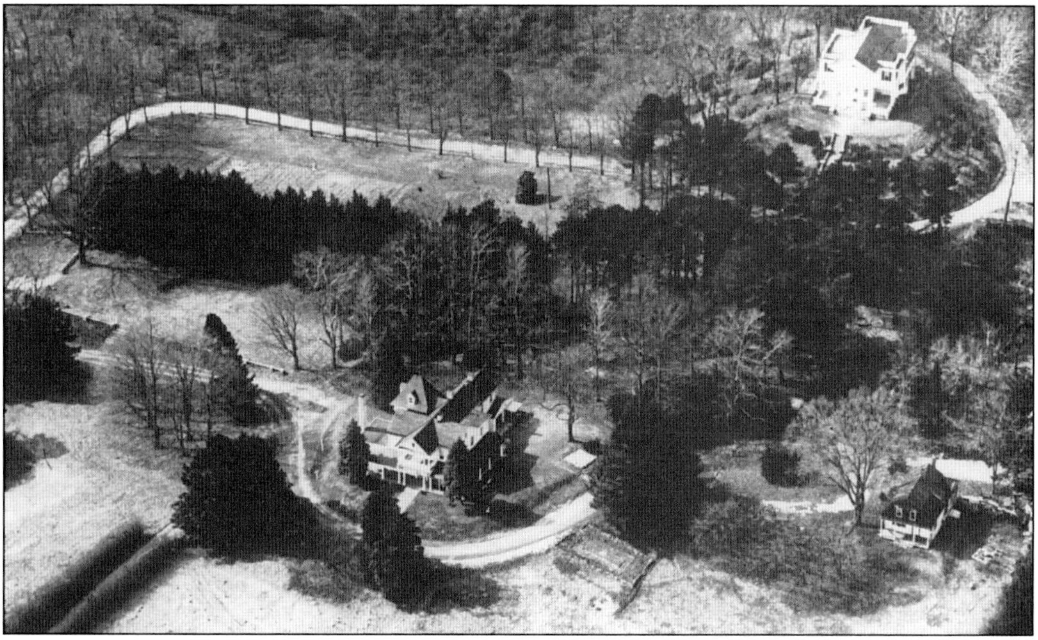

A 1930s aerial view clearly shows the Parsons's home Sky High at the upper right. Below is Grandview, the estate of Richard K. Fox, who was the publisher of the *Police Gazette*. (Grandview is pictured in *Little Silver Vol. I*, p. 111.) Both houses are still standing today, although other houses were built during the 1950s on the former grounds of these two estates. (N. Wood.)

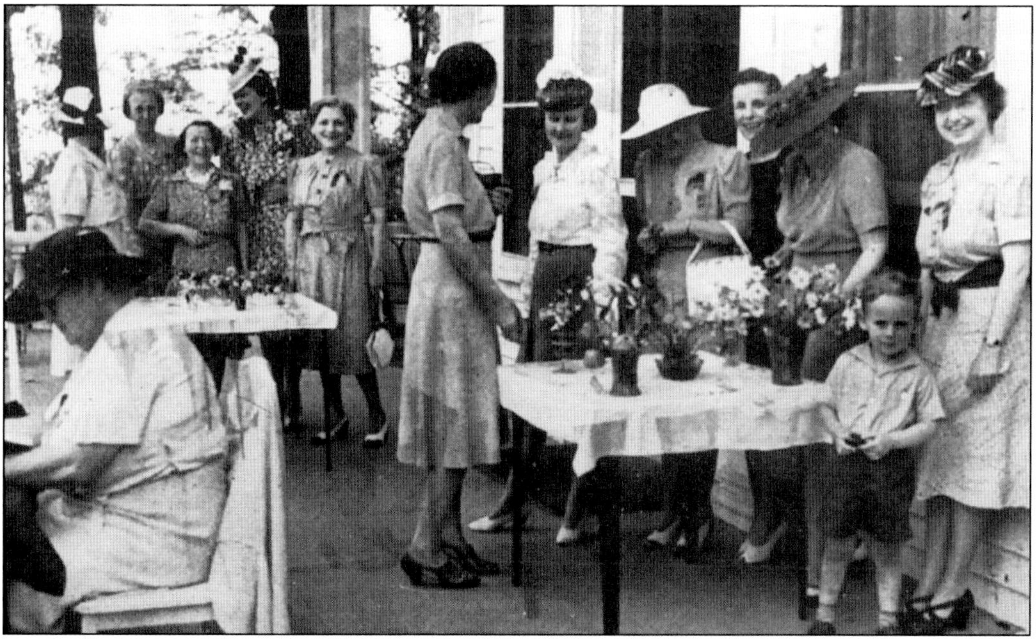

In the late 1930s, a flower show was given by the Neighborhood Garden Club at the Parsons's home. The copy to accompany this picture from a *Monmouth Pictorial* says, "This picture permits just a glimpse of Mrs. Parsons—third figure from right (without a hat)." (R.A. Schoeffling.)

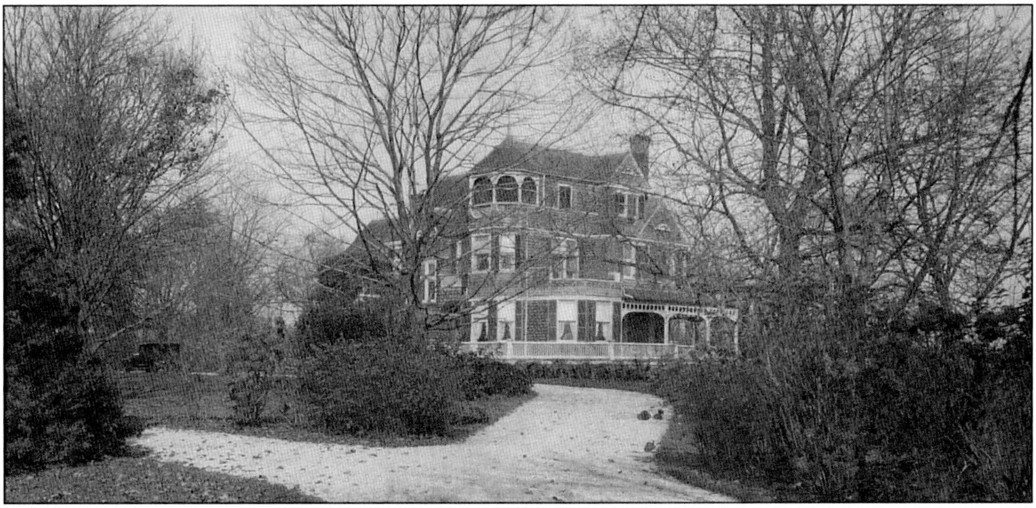

The original Lochmere on the southeast side of Seven Bridge Road near the Gooseneck Bridge was built in the 1890s as a summer residence by Edward C. Fiedler Sr. The land was purchased from the Parkers, who retained the right to clam along the river for many years thereafter. Pictured here in the late 1920s, the house featured a sweeping view of the Shrewsbury River from the third floor tower. The Fiedlers owned farmland in Eatontown that later became Fort Monmouth.

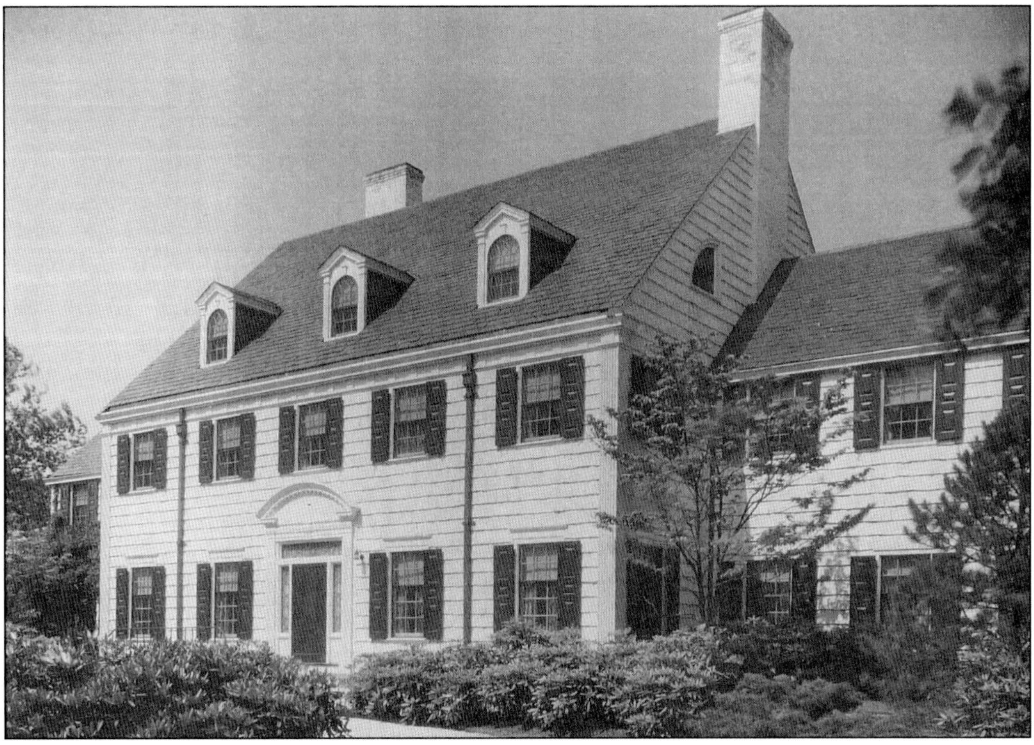

In 1930, the old Lochmere, a summer residence only, was demolished to make way for the new Loch Mere, which was suited for year-round living. This view shows the front of the house, designed to Mr. and Mrs. Edward C. Fiedler Jr.'s specifications by the New York architectural firm of Polhemus and Coffin.

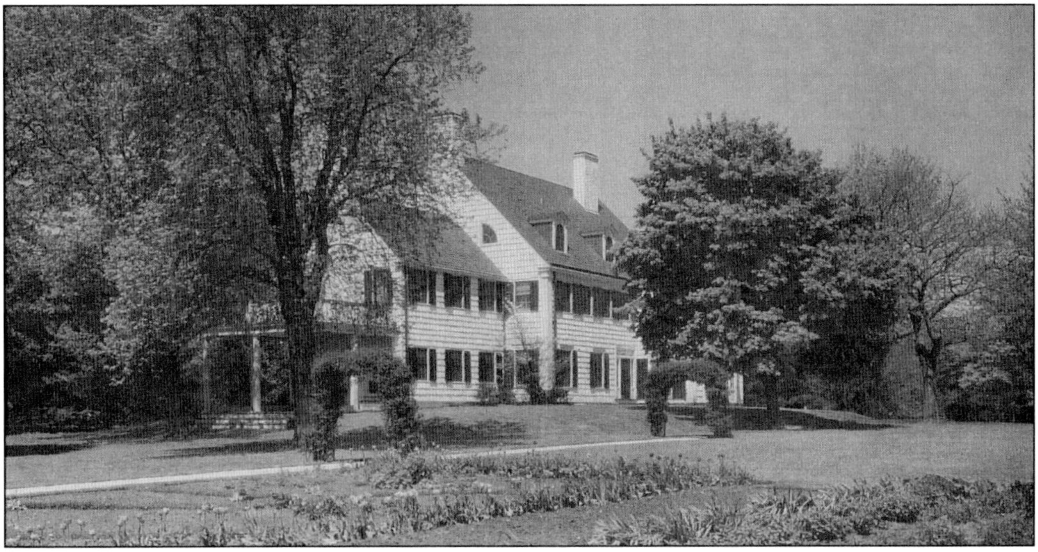

The back of the Fiedler house is just as attractive as the front. The open porch is on the south side by the river. This 1930s view when the house was new reveals many of the old trees and arches covered with vines on the garden path that led to the dock. The photographs and those on the preceding page were all taken by photographer Hubert Curtis of New York.

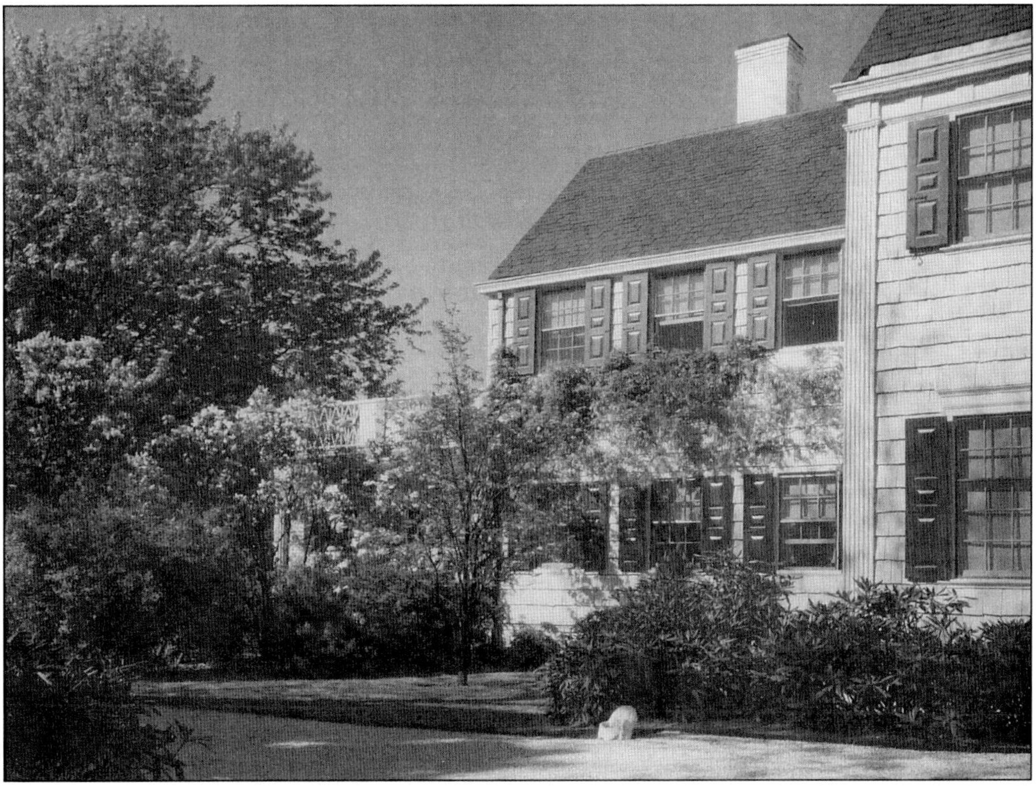

This closer view of the front of Lochmere displays many lovely shrubs and plants. Although the house was new in this 1930 photo, there are older wisteria plants climbing up to the second story! The wisteria was saved from the original house and placed upon the new one.

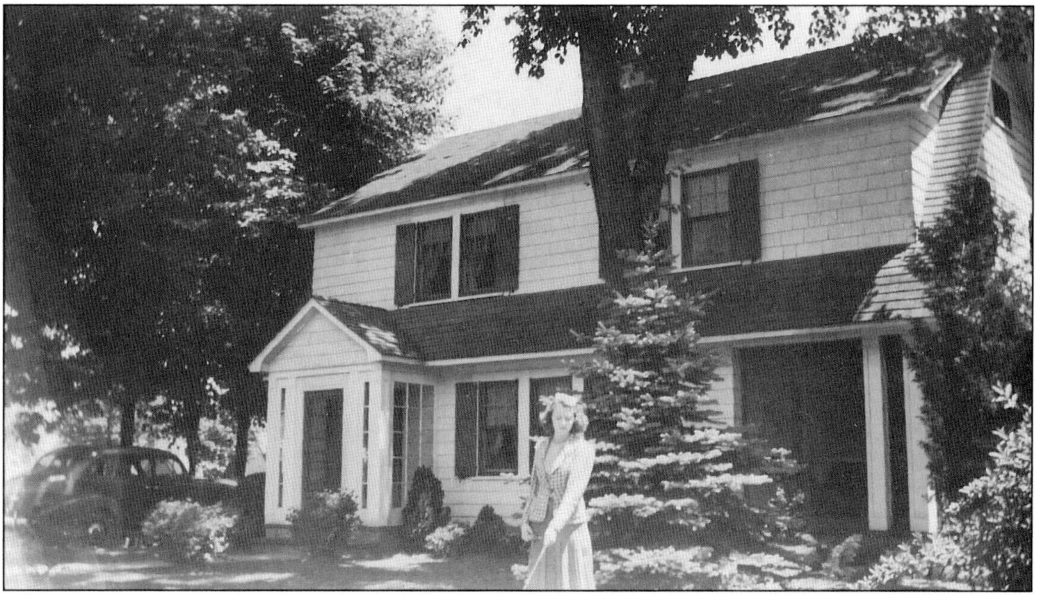

In 1926, the development known as Foxwood Park was built by Allen and Randolph in a previously wooded area. This Dutch Colonial-style house at 32 Woodbine Avenue was used as the "model home." The house has belonged to the Schnitzspahn's since 1976. The first owners were the Dunnell's, and the D'Amico family lived here for many years. Marion Dunnell is seen in this *c.* 1940 photo that is courtesy of her sister, Jeanne Little.

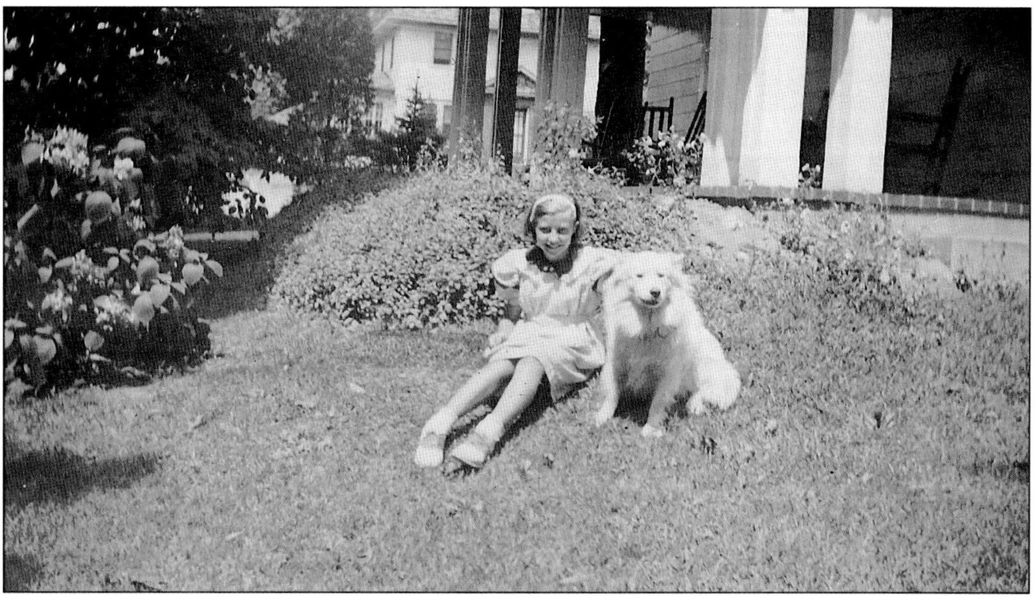

In the late 1930s, Marion Dunnell and "Bob" enjoy playing on the terraced garden on the side yard (west side) at 32 Woodbine Avenue. An unusual feature of the house that can be seen here is the open porch that is directly under the main structure of the house. The porch was completely closed in many years ago. The Cogan's house can be seen in the background across the street. (J. Little.)

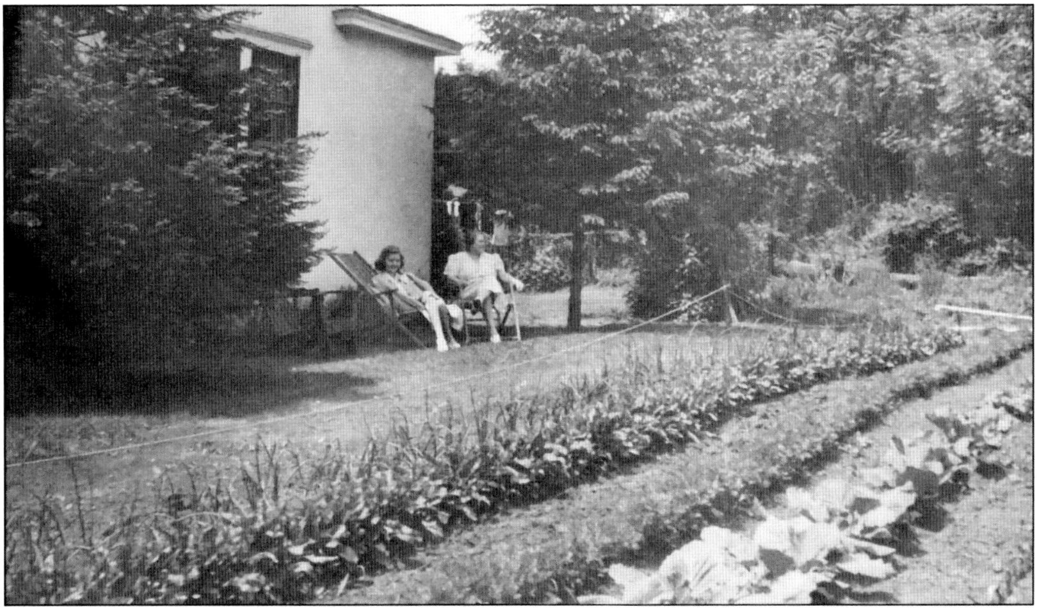

In the 1940s, during World War II, Mrs. Cogan and her daughter Marion sit on the east side of their home at 31 Woodbine Avenue that was built by Mr. Cogan in the 1920s. The plentiful garden on the east side of their property was a "victory garden," that was shared by neighbors and helped to alleviate food shortages during the war. (M. Cogan.)

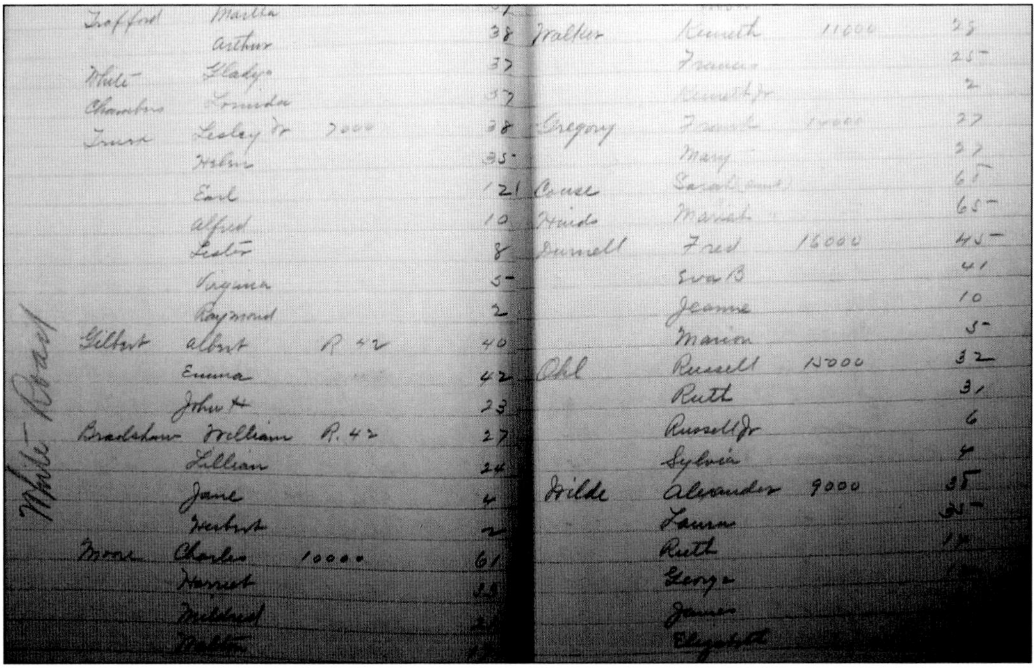

Trafford	Martha		[illegible]
	Arthur		38
White	Gladys		37
Chambers	Lorinda		37
Truex	Lesley Jr	7000	38
	Helen		35
	Earl		12
	Alfred		10
	Lester		8
	Virginia		5
	Raymond		2
Gilbert	Albert	R 42	40
	Emma		42
	John H		23
Bradshaw	William	R. 42	27
	Lillian		24
	Jane		4
	Herbert		2
Moore	Charles	10000	61
	Harriet		[illegible]
	Mildred		[illegible]
	Walter		[illegible]

White Road

Walker	Kenneth	11000	[illegible]
	Frances		25
	Kenneth Jr		2
Gregory	Frank	[illegible]	27
	Mary		[illegible]
Couse	Sarah		65
Hinds	Mariah		65
Dunnell	Fred	16000	45
	Eva B		41
	Jeanne		10
	Marion		5
Ohl	Russell	15000	32
	Ruth		31
	Russell Jr		6
	Sylvia		4
Wilde	Alexander	9000	35
	Laura		[illegible]
	Ruth		[illegible]
	George		
	James		
	Elizabeth		

These handwritten pages are from the official 1930s Little Silver Borough Census. Shown here is a page for White Road, listing the Moore family, among others, on the left; Woodbine Avenue residents, including the Gregory family (Mr. Gregory was mayor of Little Silver from 1947 to 1949) and the Dunnells, are on the right-hand side. The values of the homes are listed and the ages of the people are to the right. (D. Ayers.)

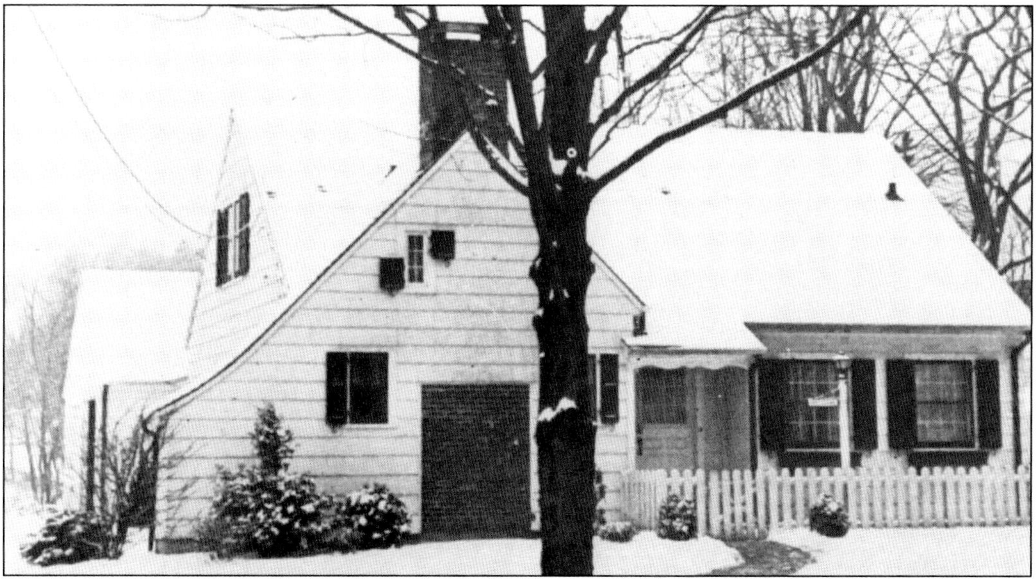

In 1940, this Fox Hill home at 330 Prospect Avenue was owned by Mr. and Mrs. Ross E. King. The house was featured in an advertisement for the Jersey Central Power & Light Company that appeared in the *Monmouth Pictorial* spring issue. The street across from their home, Rosslyn Court, was named for their daughter Rosslyn. (R.A. Schoeffling.)

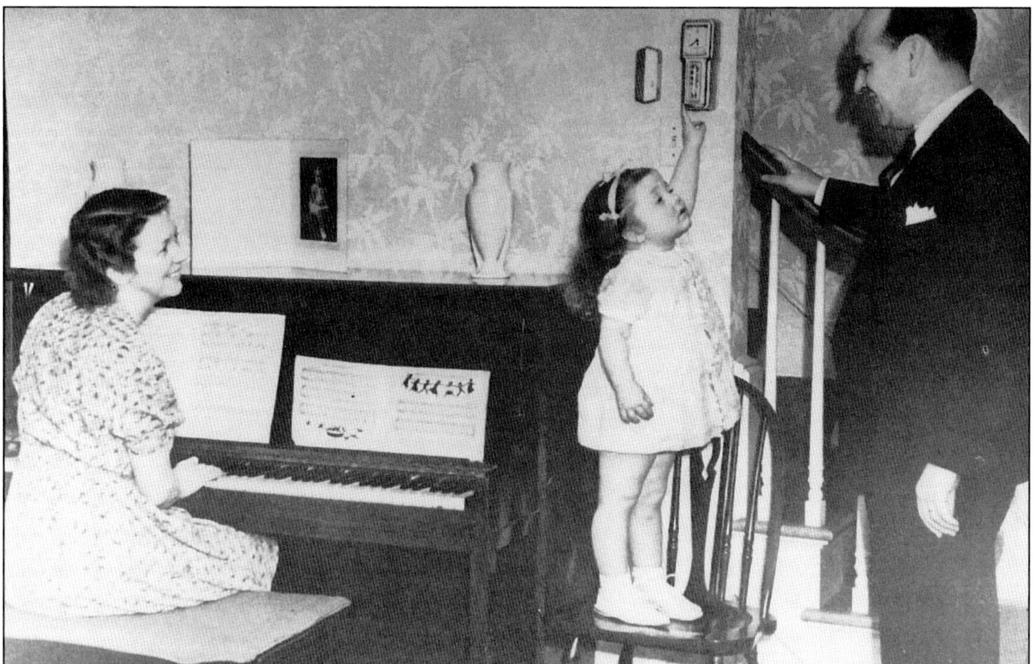

The 1940 Jersey Central Power & Light Company ad featured this photo of the King family and caption: "Yes, my darling daughter, that little thingamajig regulates the heat of the entire house. It's a thermostat—you just turn the indicator to the desired temperature and presto!... Mrs. King smiles tolerantly as this imaginary conversation takes place between Mr. King and his daughter, Rosslyn." (R.A. Schoeffling.)

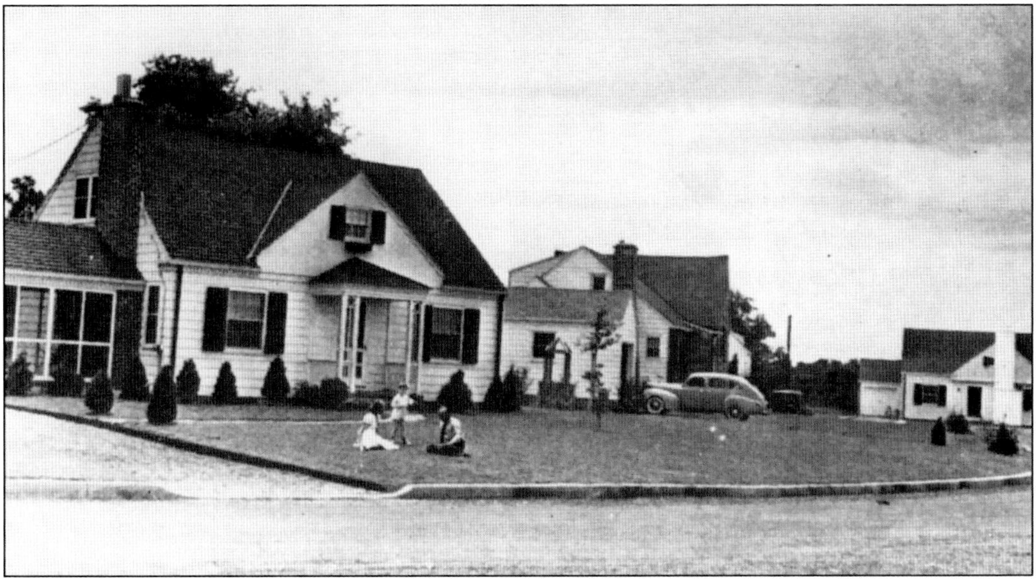

In 1939, the development known as Sunnycrest was built by Maimone Brothers upon former farmlands and open space. Maimone also built many ranch homes on the south side of Little Silver. The home seen above on North Sunnycrest Drive was featured in a *Monmouth Pictorial* during the summer of 1940. FHA mortgages were available with low downpayments and monthly payments of only $33.50 per month including taxes. (R.A. Schoeffling.)

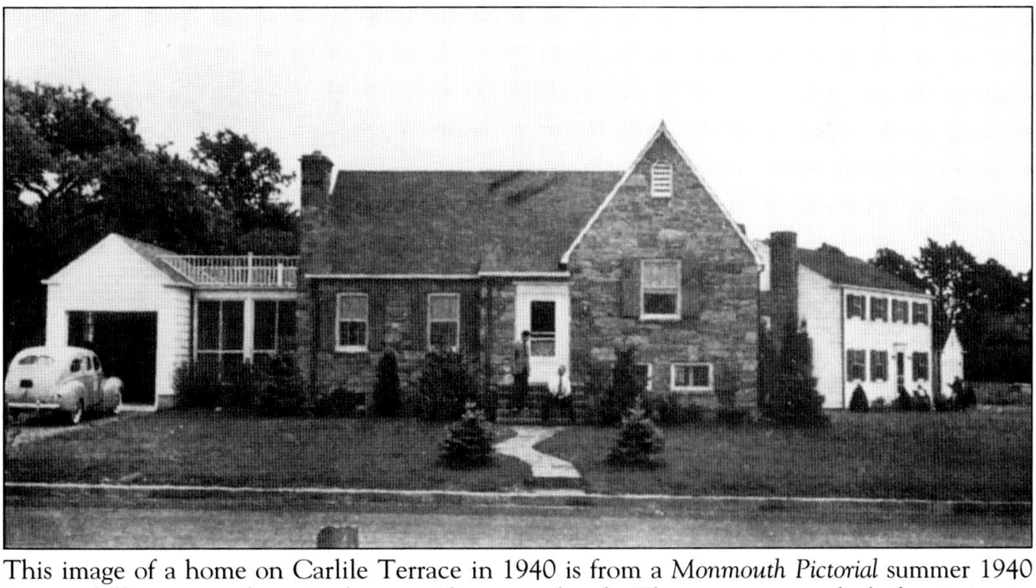

This image of a home on Carlile Terrace in 1940 is from a *Monmouth Pictorial* summer 1940 issue and illustrates a charming house with a stone facade. There was a great deal of variation in the style and details of the small "new country homes" in the Sunnycrest development. Prices started at $4,990, quite a difference from today's prices! (R.A. Schoeffling.)

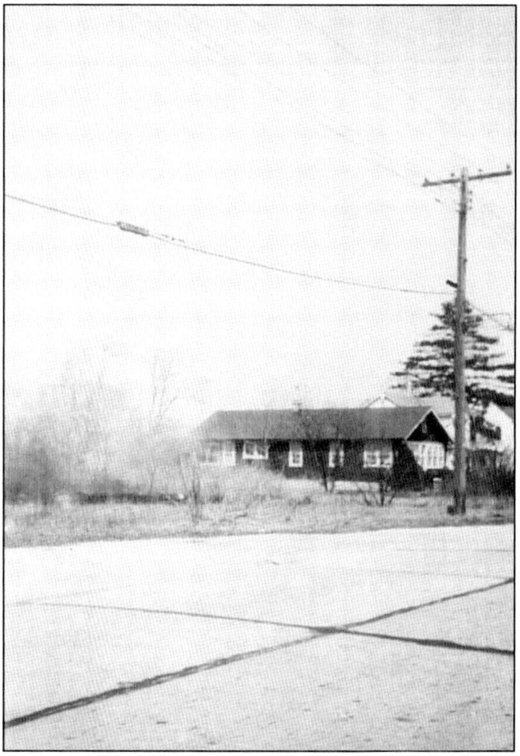

A 1940s view of the bungalow at 179 Rumson Road shows the undeveloped land on the west side of the property where Laurelwood Drive is now located. Harold and Hazel Tetley (parents of Richard Tetley, who provided this photograph) purchased the house in about 1925 and it remained their family home for many years.

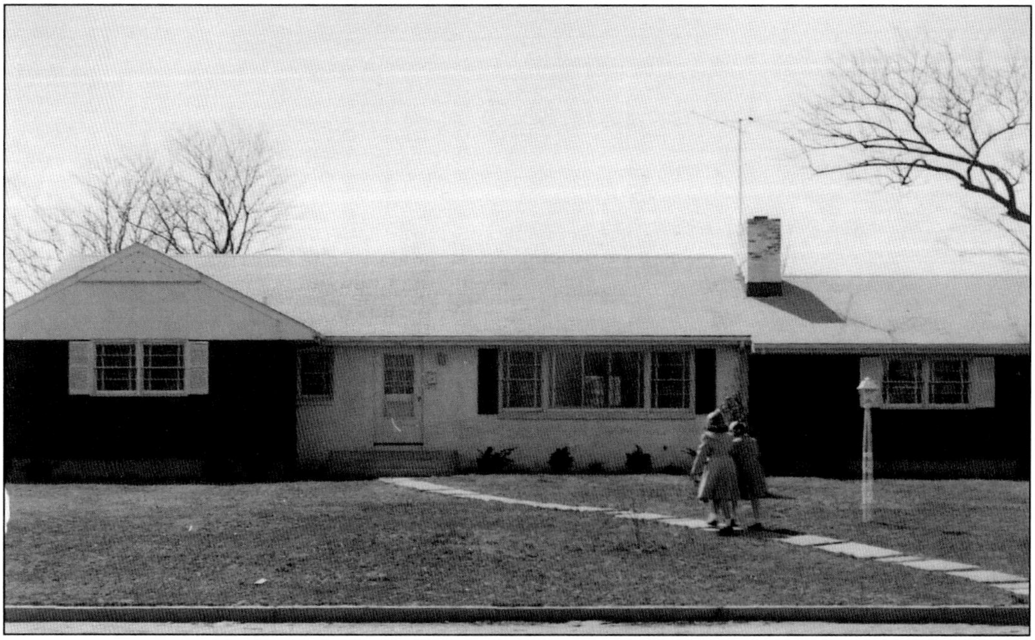

Many ranch-style homes cropped up in Little Silver during the postwar construction boom of the 1950s. The home of Mr. and Mrs. Hibbard Christian at 25 Laurelwood Drive, built by Frank J. Patock Construction Company, is seen here when it was new, *c.* 1955. The two little girls on the walk are the Christian's daughter Mary and her friend, Nancy Liddell, who lived at 8 Laurelwood Drive. (M. Christian.)

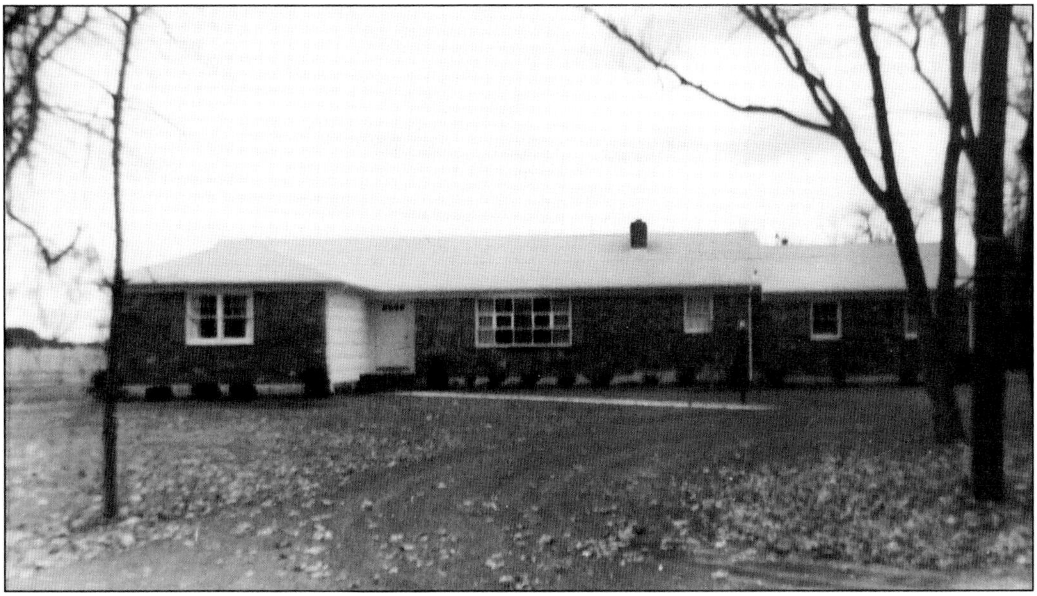

This photo appeared in the *Red Bank Register* on Dec. 13, 1962, with a caption reporting that executive Carl V. Giersch purchased this new brick-and-frame ranch house built by Carmelo Maimone on Point Road, Little Silver. At their first party in 1963 at the new home, Mr. and Mrs. Giersch entertained famous Green Bay Packers coach Vince Lombardi and his wife, Marie. (J. Giersch.)

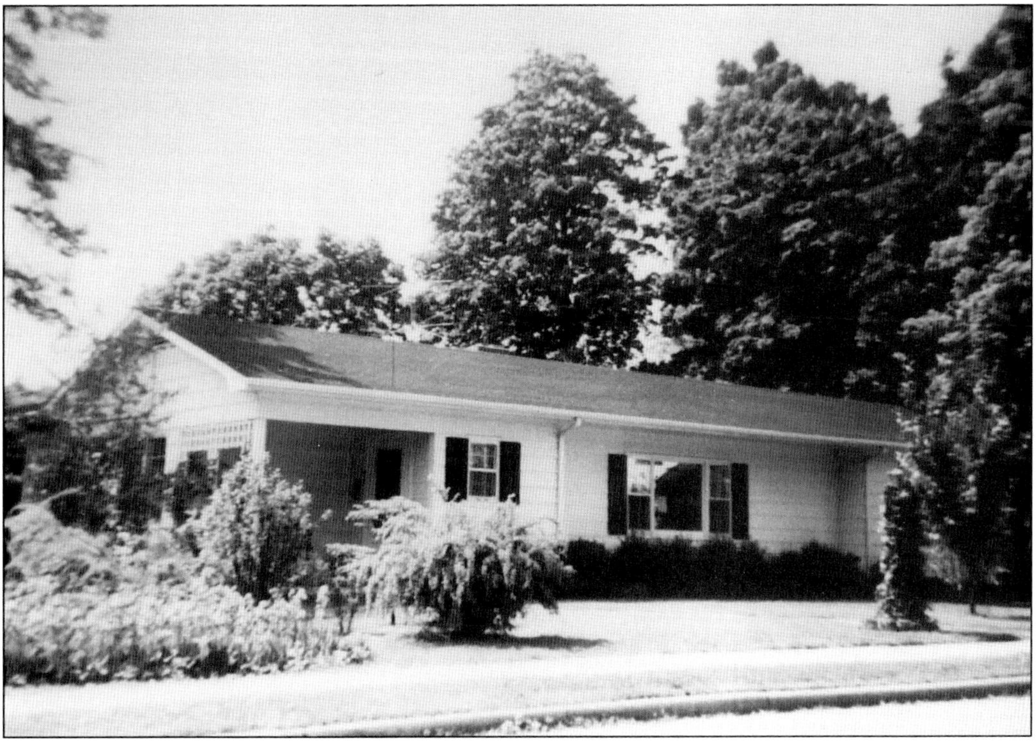

This well-designed custom ranch home at 36 Woodbine Avenue was built by Johnson Brothers for George Inman in 1950. The Inman family lived here until 1962. (E. Pope.)

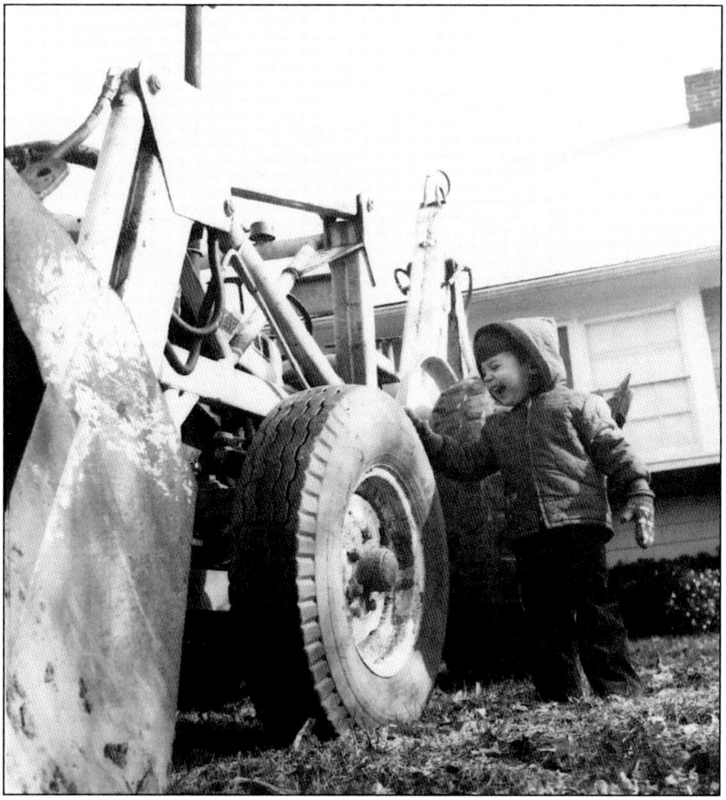

Heavy equipment and tractors were a familiar sight on front lawns in Little Silver while the sewer system was being installed in the early 1970s, replacing septic tanks. Here Doug Schnitzspahn is seen with a giant new "toy" at 45 Salem Lane in a 1972 photo that was taken by his dad, Leon.

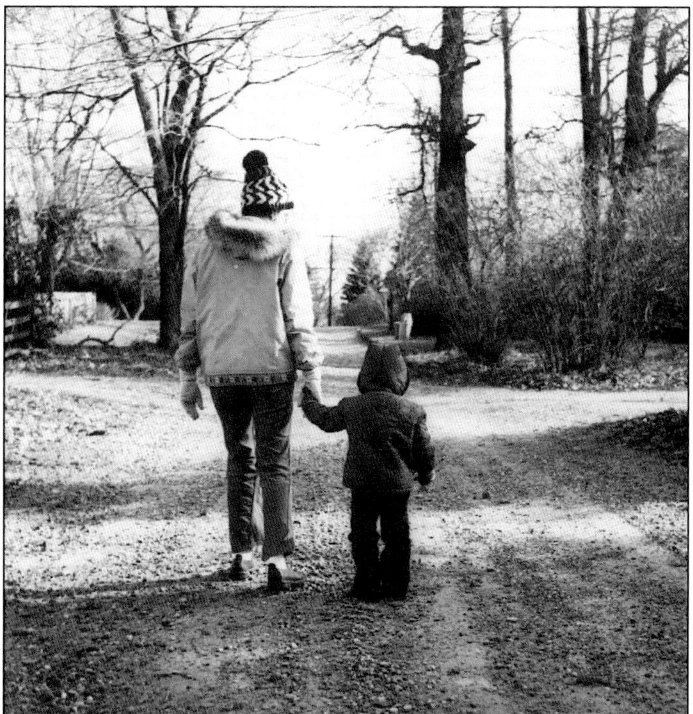

Walking on Bennett Lane in 1972 when it was a rustic dirt road where you could see horses in a corral (out of photo, on the right), the author and her son Doug are headed towards Salem Lane on a chilly day. (Photo by L. Schnitzspahn.)

Four

Business, Transportation, and Weather

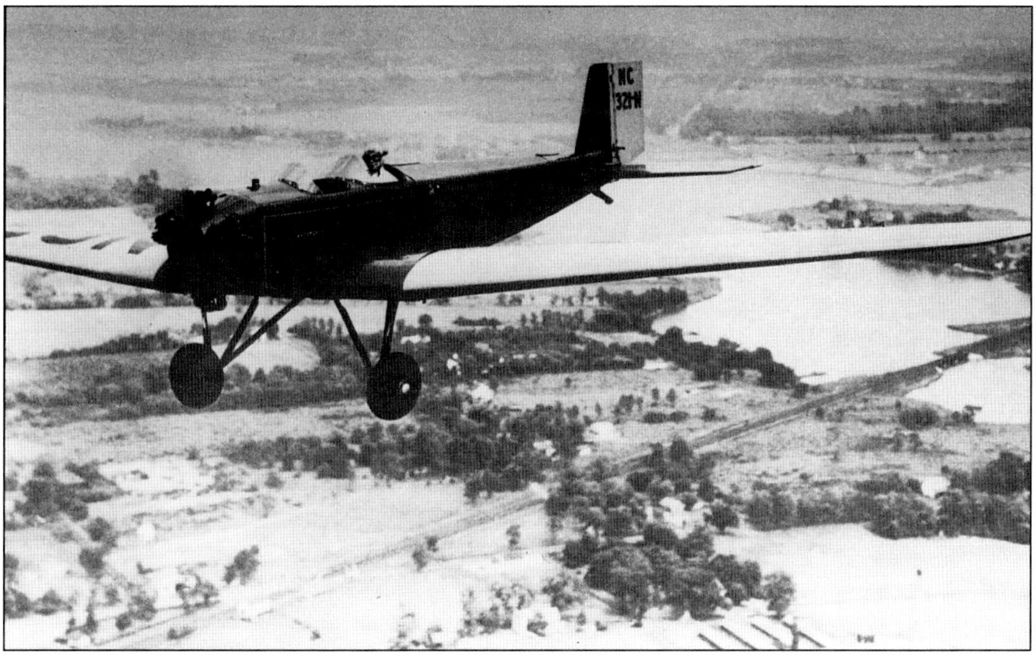

Aerial photos provide documentation for both business and residential development of an area, are useful to historians and fascinating to study. In 1936, a Klemm monoplane (made at Aeromarine in Keyport) from Red Bank Airport flies over Little Silver. Dean's greenhouses are in the foreground. The Shrewsbury River and Oceanport Avenue bridge are on the right. (R.A. Schoeffling.)

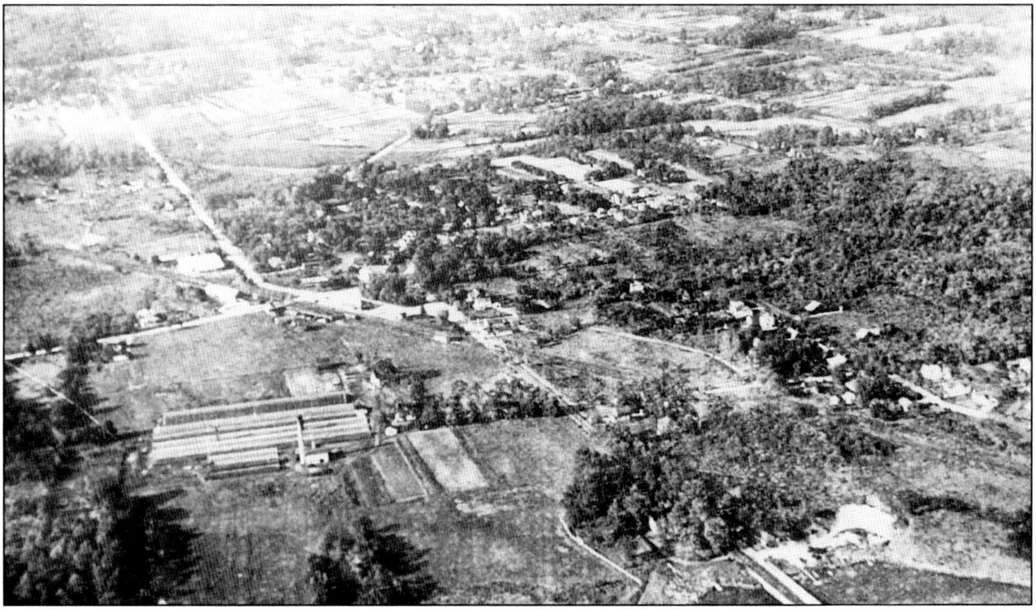

From the Autumn 1940 issue of *Monmouth Pictorial*, this aerial view of Little Silver, looking north from Fort Monmouth, shows Branch Avenue, Dean's greenhouses, and the railroad station. The caption states that Little Silver has about 600 homes and "During recent years there has been a definite trend toward building new homes in this Borough where the tax rate is one of the lowest in the State." Times have changed! (R.A. Schoeffling.)

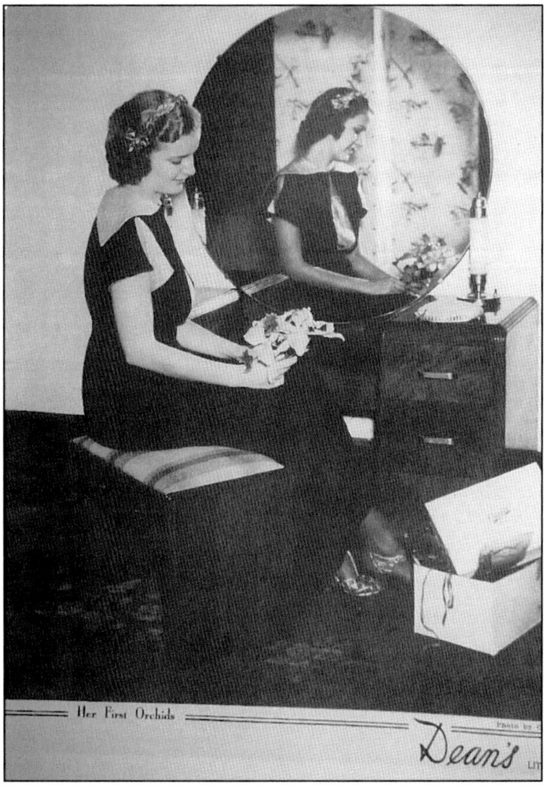

"Her First Orchids," a charming 1936 *Monmouth Pictorial* advertisement for Dean's Flowers in Little Silver, reflects the art deco look of the times. Although Dean's no longer exists in Little Silver, Dean's Flowers, a shop in Red Bank, continues the family tradition. (R.A. Schoeffling.)

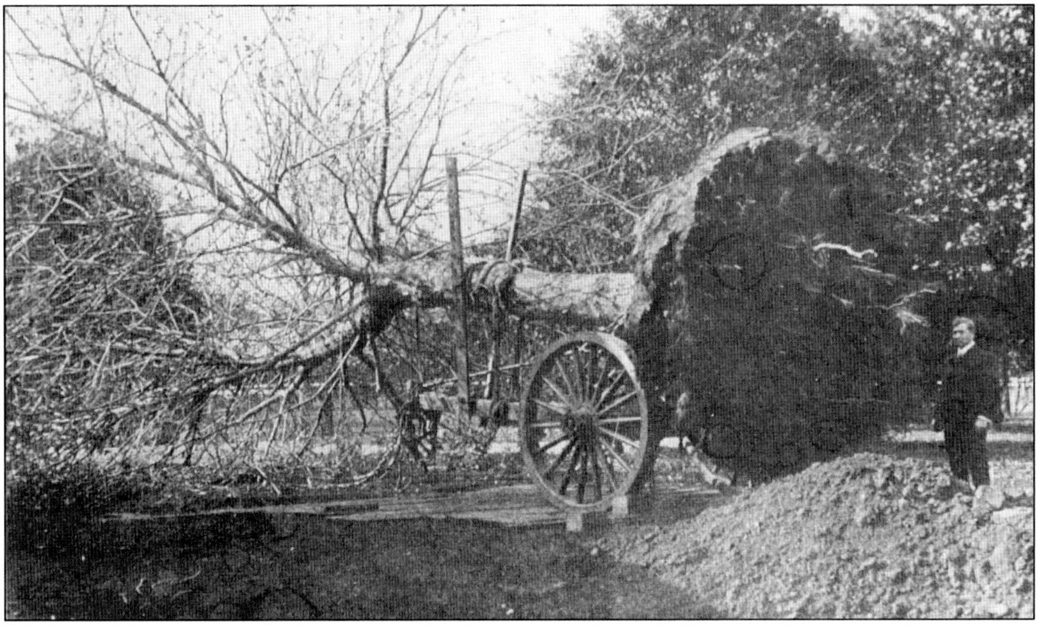

Moving huge trees is quite a feat! John T. Lovett's Monmouth Nurseries provided expert tree carting services using an apparatus as seen in this July 1911 photo from the Monmouth County edition of *American Suburbs*. (R.A. Schoeffling.)

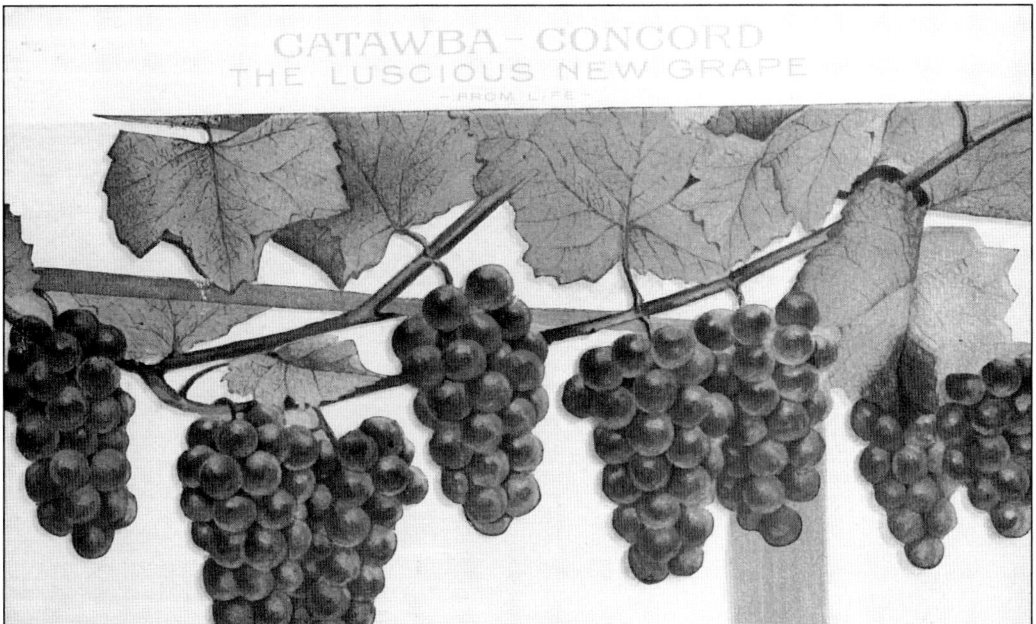

"The New Grape For Everybody Everywhere," is the motto printed on the back of this Lovett's advertising postcard from 1913. Also described as "the ideal grape for you," the luscious Catawba-Concord introduced by John T. Lovett was sold by mail order for $1.00 per vine (see *Little Silver Vol. I* for more about J.T. Lovett and his nurseries).

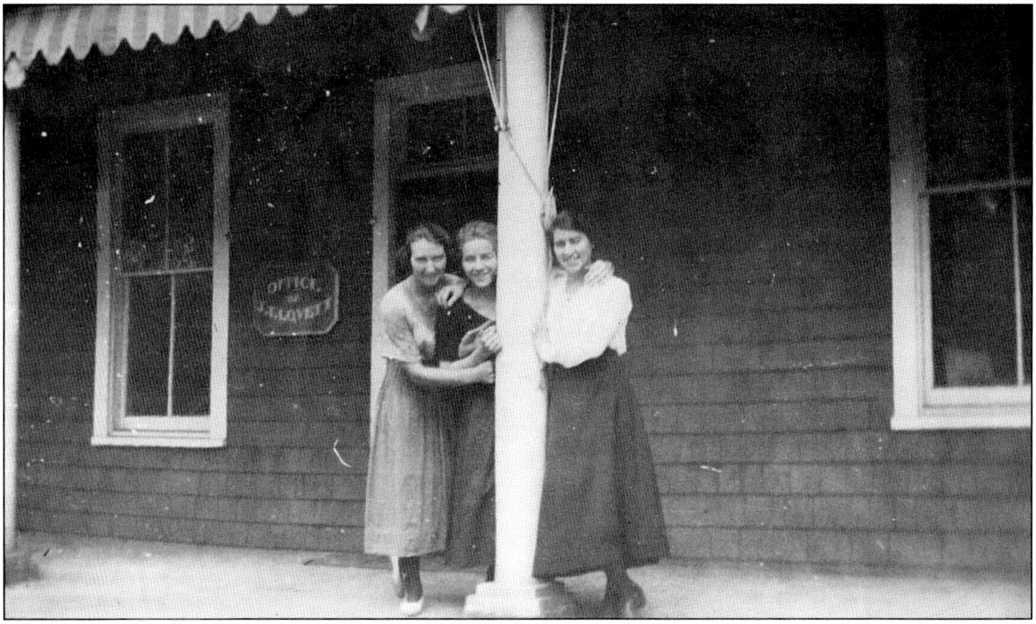

In a c. 1917 photo that belonged to Julia Parker, the J.T. Lovett's office employees are taking a break outside. A striped awning is visible above them. Julia, who worked as secretary to Lester Lovett, is on the left. (Borough of Little Silver.)

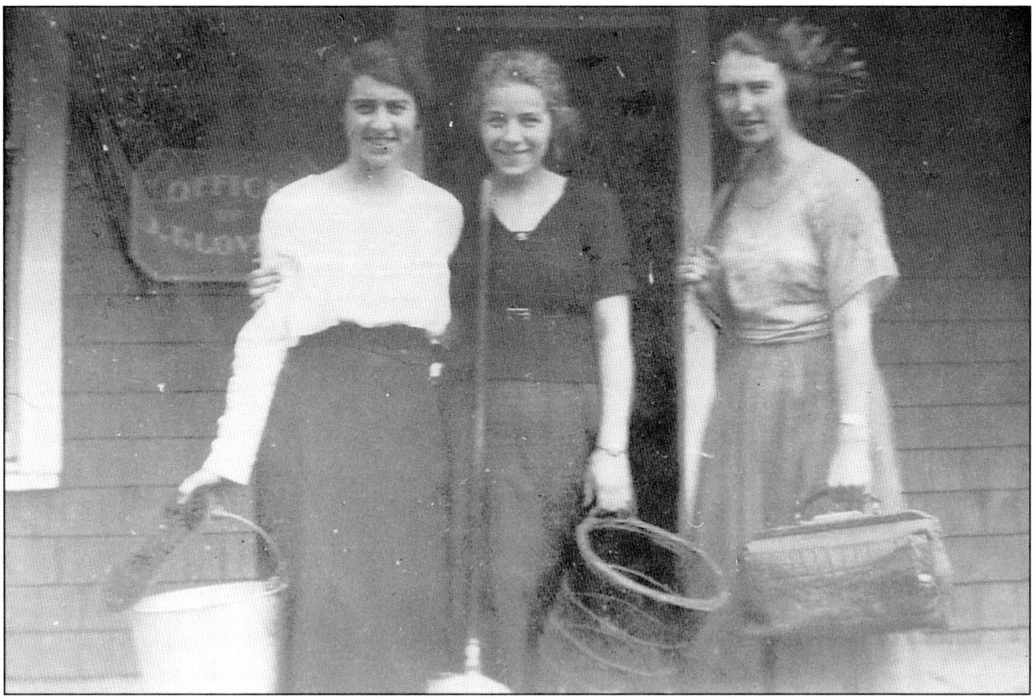

In this photo of three of the same Lovett's office workers, Julia Parker is on the right. The three young women appear to be having some fun by posing with a bucket, wastebasket, broom, mop, and valise. (Borough of Little Silver.)

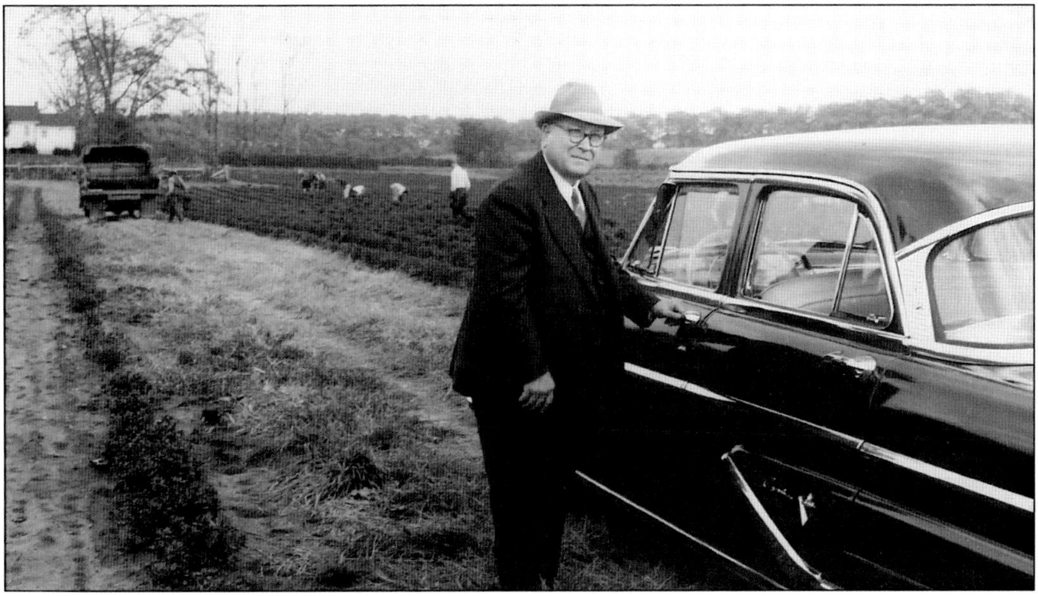

Lester Lovett, son of John T. Lovett, and his brothers ran the nursery business after their father's death in 1922. Here Lester, who was well known to everyone in Little Silver, is seen by his car while visiting workers in the fields in 1955. (Dorn's.)

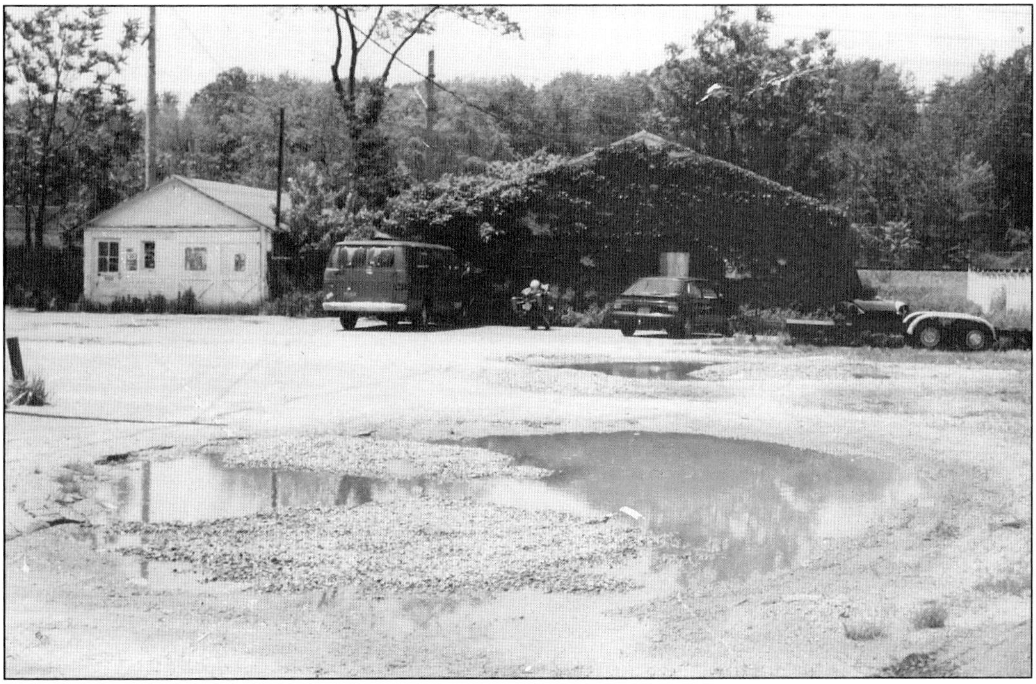

This property on Branch Avenue, next to the 7-11 Store, once belonged to the Lovett Nursery. The structure seen in this photo was ivy-covered because it was a cooling building that stored flowers for the nursery, *c.* 1917, that could then be shipped via the nearby railroad. The building, demolished in 1993, is the site of Robert Wichmann's R.W. Auto Repair. Wichmann's father was postmaster in Little Silver for many years. (D. Santelle.)

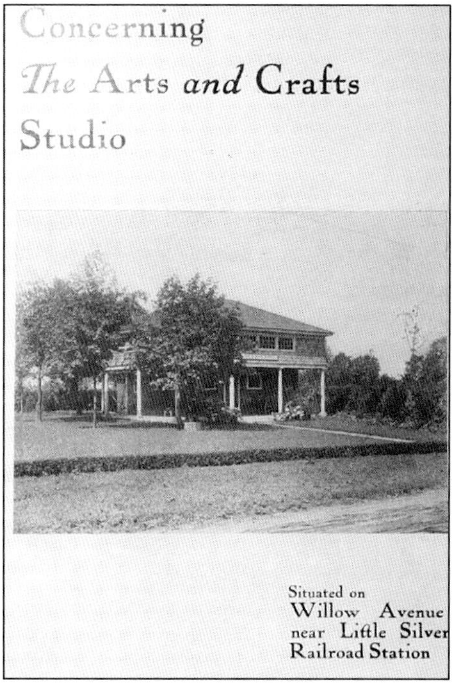

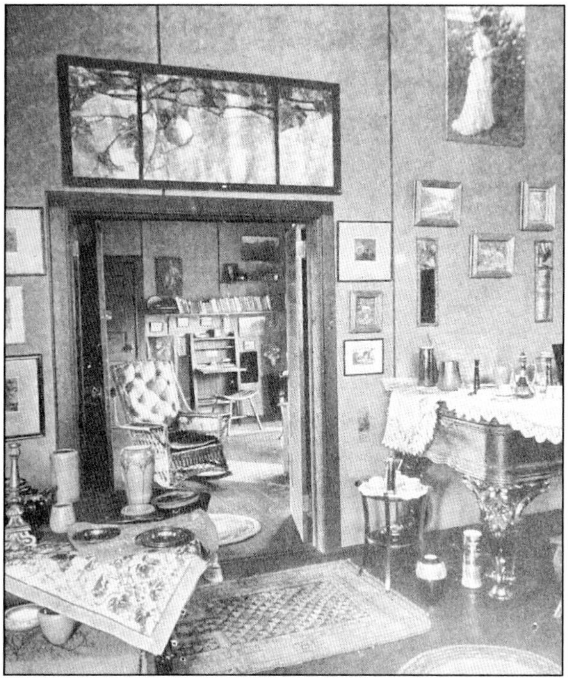

Left: A 1913 brochure promotes the Arts and Crafts Studio on "Willow Avenue near Little Silver Railroad Station" that was managed by Alida Lovett, a daughter of nurseryman John T. Lovett. The cooperative shop, open only in summer, displayed and sold handicrafts made by women and was located in back of the Lovett house on Branch Avenue. *Right*: An interior view reveals a light and airy room displaying pottery, etchings, jewelry, and stained-glass panels. Alida's specialty was handpainting on china.

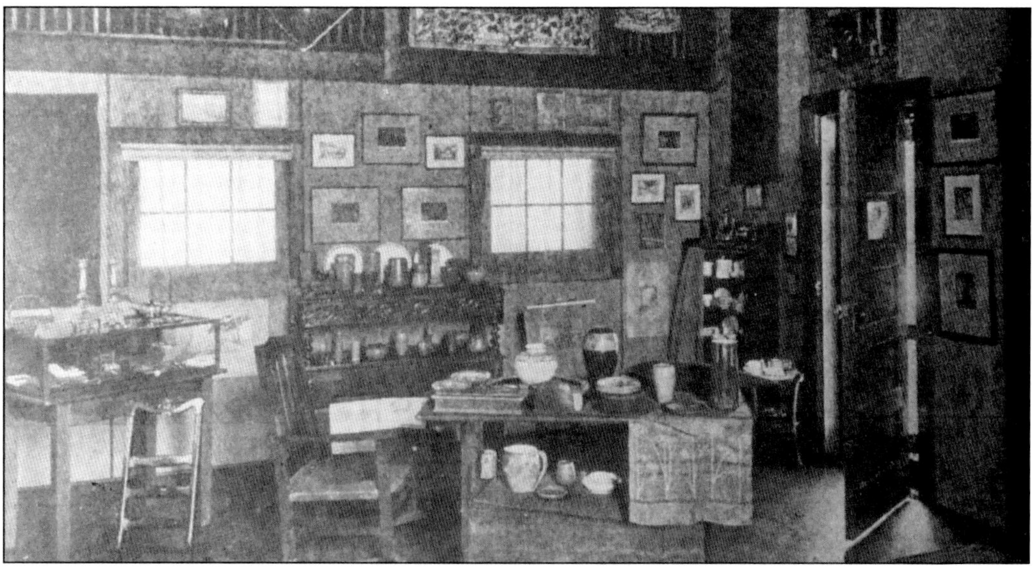

Another interior view of the Arts and Crafts Studio of 1913 reveals pottery, metal work, paintings, and rugs. Lillian E. Childs, a painter of miniatures on ivory, ran the studio with Alida Lovett. The 1913 brochure shown on this page is from the collection of the Little Silver Historical Society.

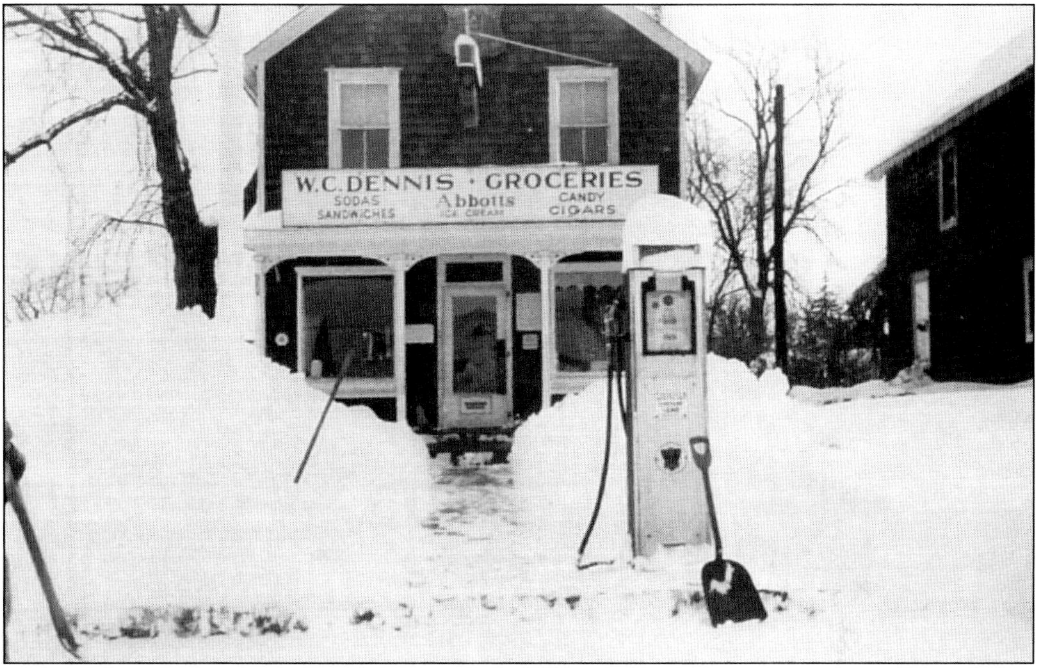

The W.C. Dennis general store (formerly Mechanics' Hall) featured a gas pump. Located on Rumson Road, it opened in 1928. After Walter Dennis's death the business was run by his two daughters as Dennis's Luncheonette. The store, pictured here shortly after the blizzard of 1947, is known today as Edie's, a popular place for breakfast or lunch. Richard Tetley, who has lived in Little Silver all his life, is the lender of this photo of his grandfather's store.

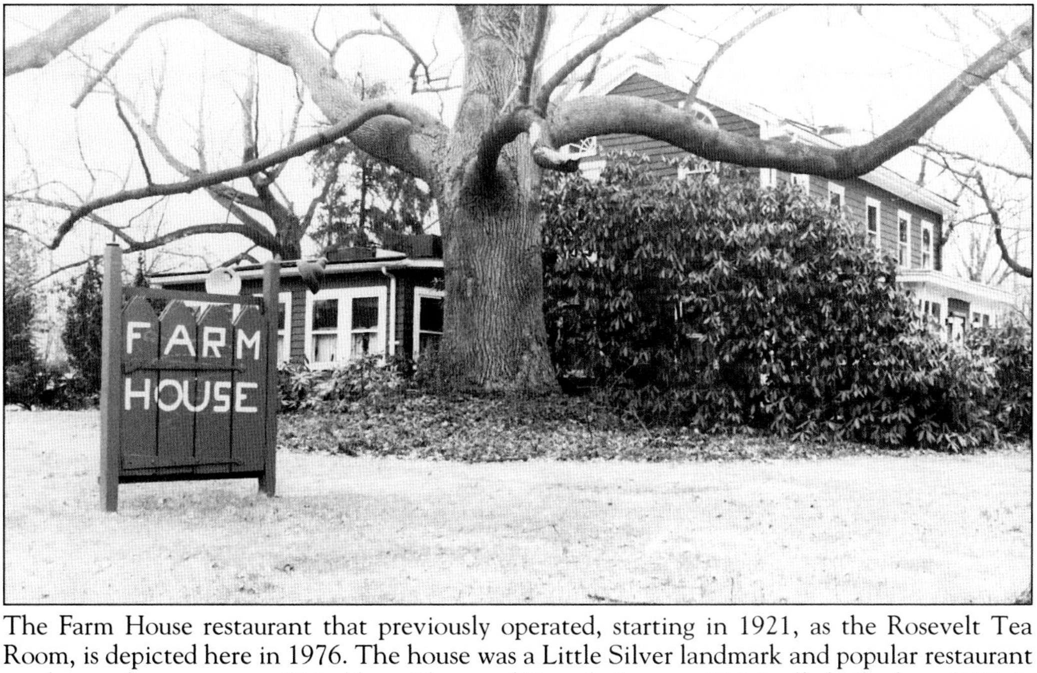

The Farm House restaurant that previously operated, starting in 1921, as the Rosevelt Tea Room, is depicted here in 1976. The house was a Little Silver landmark and popular restaurant on the northwest corner of Markham Place and Branch Avenue. Originally built about 1820, it was tragically destroyed by fire in 1995 and has since been replaced by a private residence.

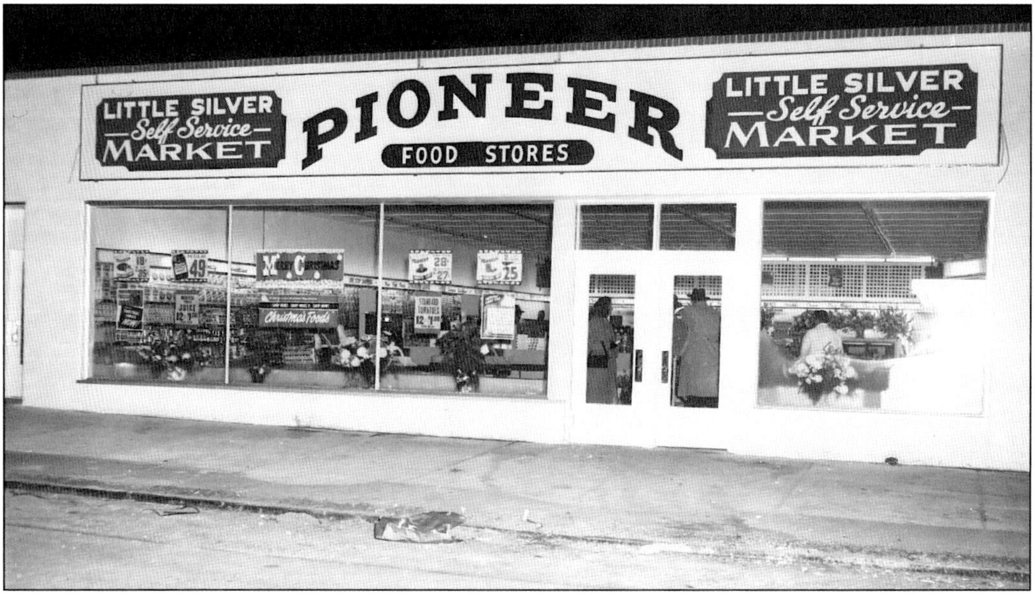

The first Little Silver Market, opened in 1945 by Anna and Henry Scaccia on land that was previously all wooded, was on the southeast corner of Prospect Avenue and Church Street. This photo is of their second location, where the store was moved to in 1950. Located on Prospect Avenue across from the Borough Hall, the market offered home deliveries besides the self service and in its early days featured the "Pioneer" brand name. (Dorn's.)

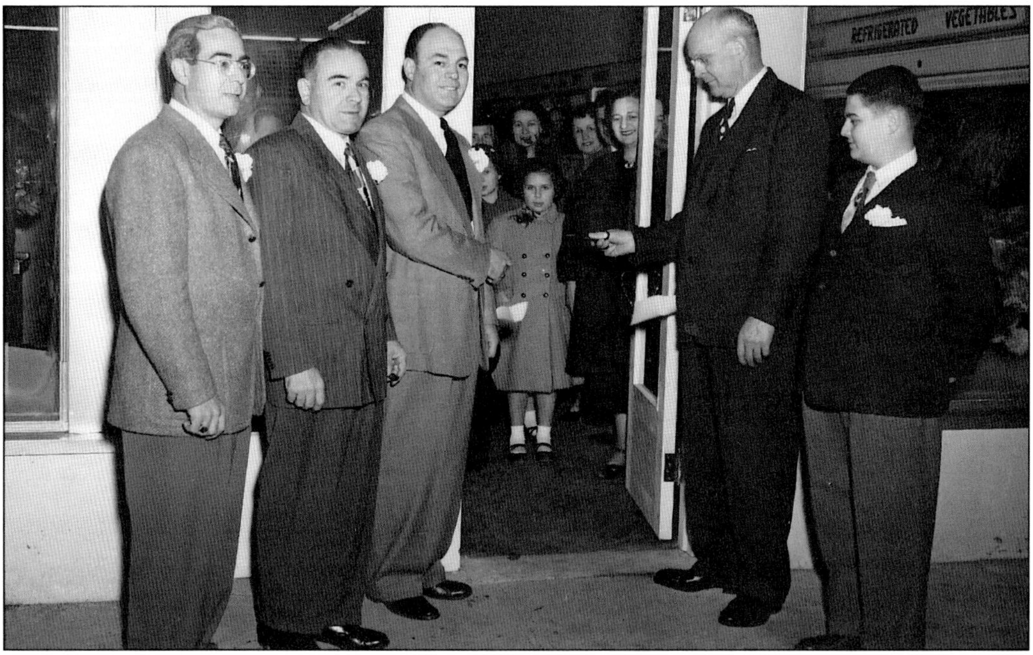

Little Silver Mayor Davison cuts the ribbon to open the new Little Silver Market on December 20, 1950. On his right is 12-year-old Henry Scaccia Jr. (who would eventually run the store), and on the left closest to the door is his father, Henry Scaccia Sr. The other two men worked in the store. Inside, by the door, is Anna Scaccia, the only woman of the business, who managed the groceries while her husband, Henry, was in charge of the meats. (Dorn's.)

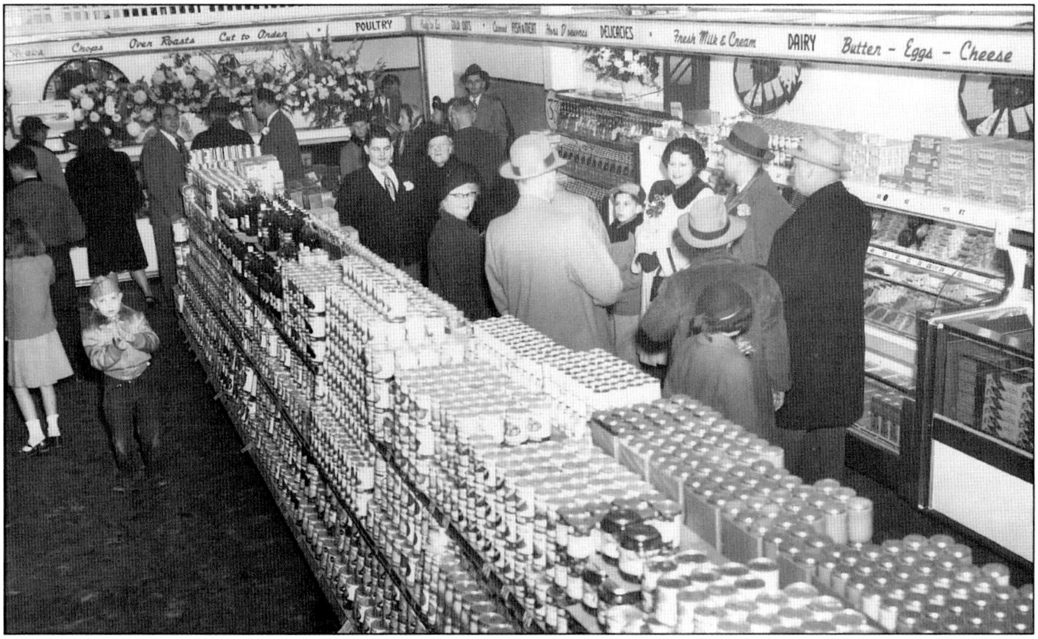

Neatly stacked rows of canned goods fill the center aisle inside the Little Silver Market on opening day in 1950. Anna and Henry Scaccia retired from the business in 1974, leaving Henry Jr. to operate the market, which became a gourmet shop. The new store is in a converted barn at the rear of the Scaccia property that consists of five stores and a house. The Little Silver Market today carries on the tradition of good service started by the Scaccias and is operated by Dale and Jon Bitman. (Dorn's.)

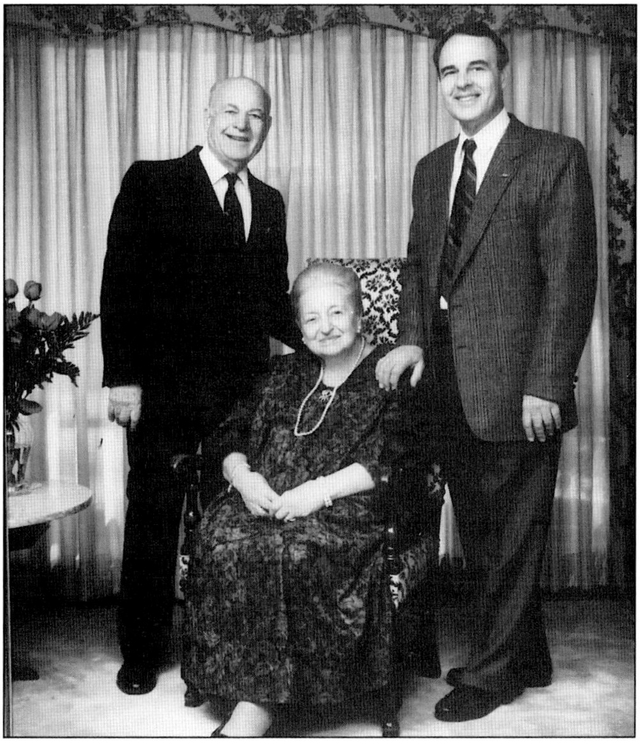

This engaging 1993 portrait of Anna Scaccia with her husband and son, Henry Sr. and Henry Jr. (now both deceased), was taken on the Scaccia's 60th wedding anniversary. In memory of her husband and son, Mrs. Scaccia generously donated the large Little Silver Bulletin Board that displays important announcements in front of the Borough Hall. (A. Scaccia.)

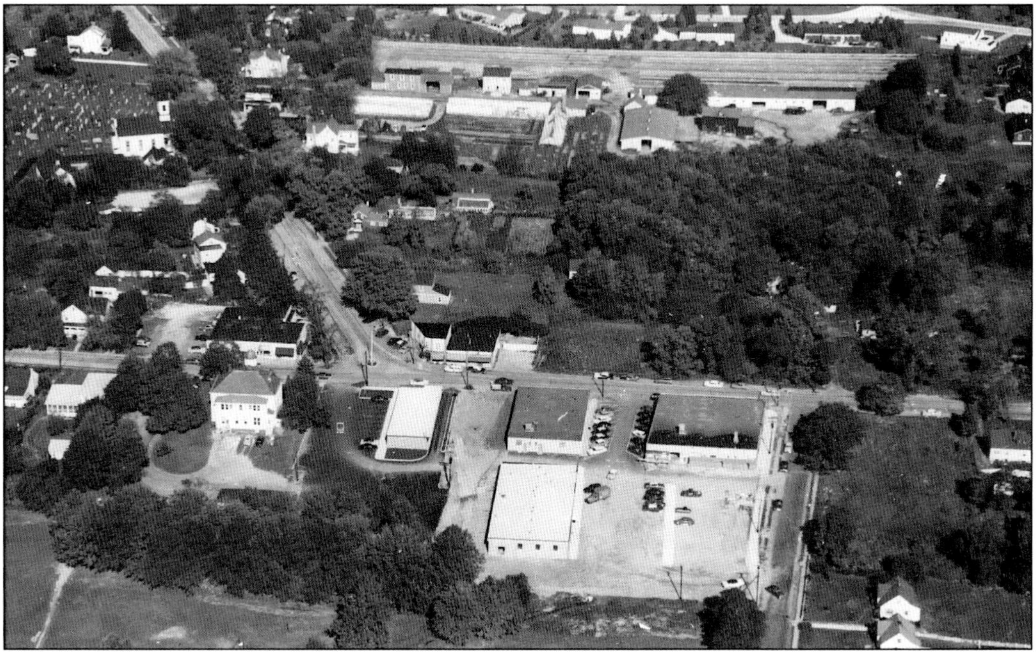

This aerial view from the early 1950s shows the intersection of Prospect Avenue (horizontal across center of photo) and Church Street (diagonal on upper right) with the flagpole in the middle. Markham Place is on the left side. Lovett's nurseries are in the top of the photo and the large wooded area just below is where the A&P shopping center is now. The white building on the left side is the old Borough Hall. (Dorn's.)

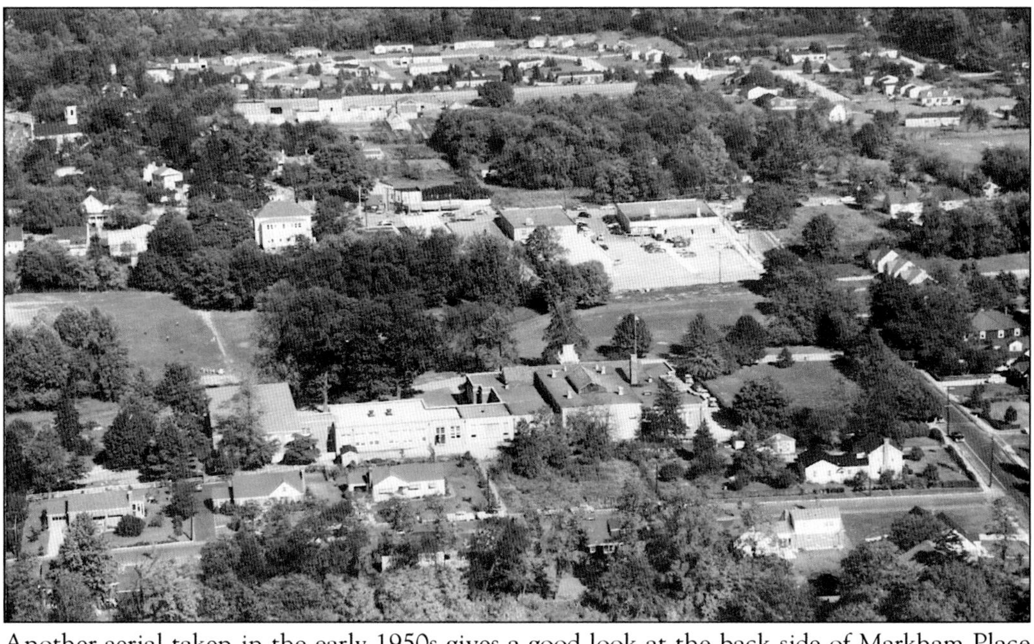

Another aerial taken in the early 1950s gives a good look at the back side of Markham Place School and Lovett Avenue. Again, the wooded area is the vicinity of the A&P shopping center that is now on Prospect Avenue. The houses in the top section of the photo are on Prince Place, and Kings Road, which was cut through not long before this, is on the left. (Dorn's.)

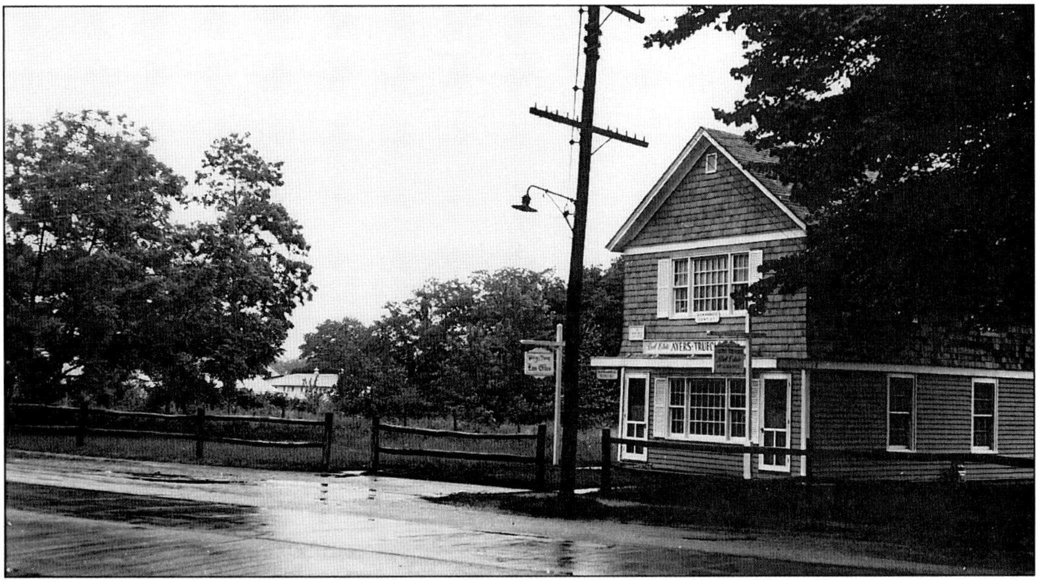

This building at 16 Church Street was once the Little Silver firehouse (see p. 88). In 1948, the fire company purchased its present location on Prospect Avenue and sold this building to attorney Harry Green, who turned it into an office complex. The second floor was occupied by Dr. Victor Marascio, dentist, and by Mr. Green's law office. In 1953, the downstairs offices became the Ayers-Trufolo Agency, run by Fred L. Ayers (Little Silver tax assessor & borough clerk) and Anthony F. Trufolo (a Red Bank High School teacher). (A.F. Trufolo.)

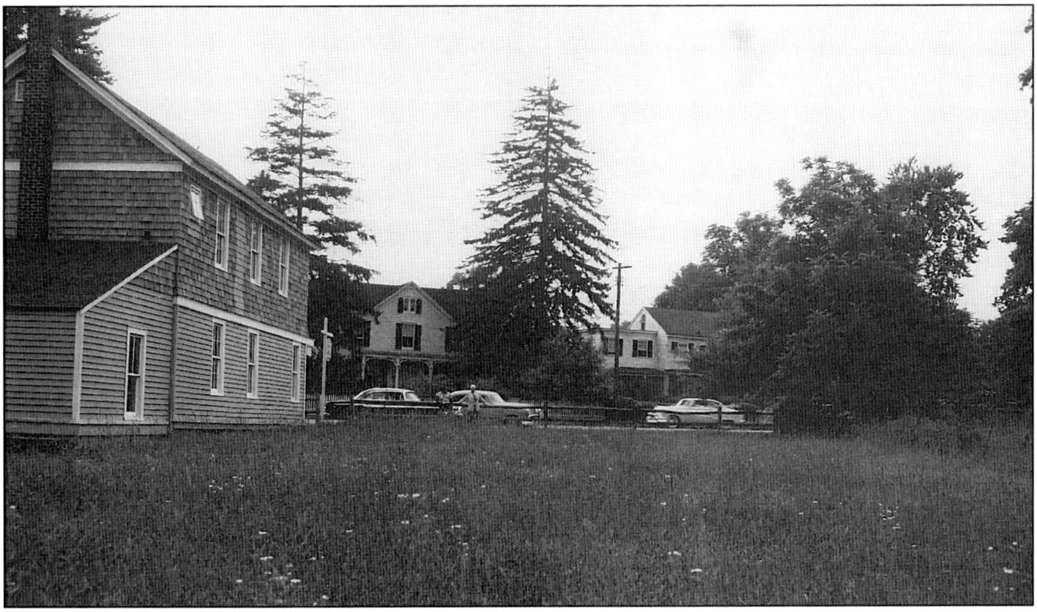

This early 1950s view reveals what Church Street looked like from the back of the old firehouse, which was at the time an office building. Today, only the top half of this old building is recognizable. The vacant lot is the site of the present Little Silver Post Office. In the image at the top of the page, you can see how the lot looked from Church Street with some of Lovetts' Nurseries' buildings visible. When the A&P was built in the mid-1950s, a road was cut through this field that leads to the A&P parking lot. (A.F. Trufolo.)

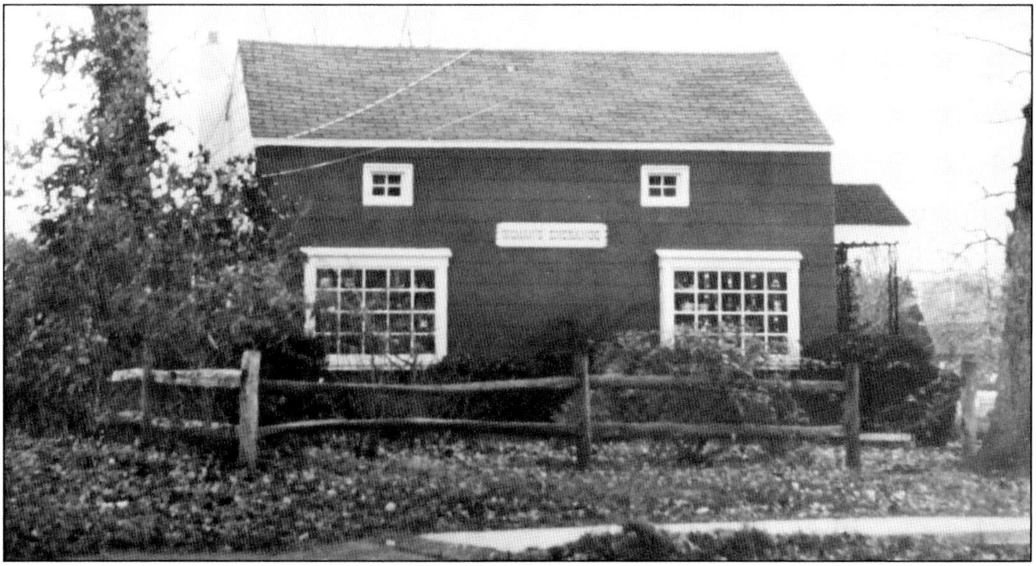

The Woman's Exchange of Monmouth County, a non-profit organization, provides a center for the sale of crafts, artwork, and food items. The exchange began in Rumson in 1934, and soon moved to Red Bank. As seen in this photo, c. 1970s, "The Little Red House" on Church Street was the exchange's home from 1950 to 1985, when it was demolished to make way for a larger building, where the shop continues its tradition of selling fine handcrafted goods. (Little Silver Historical Society.)

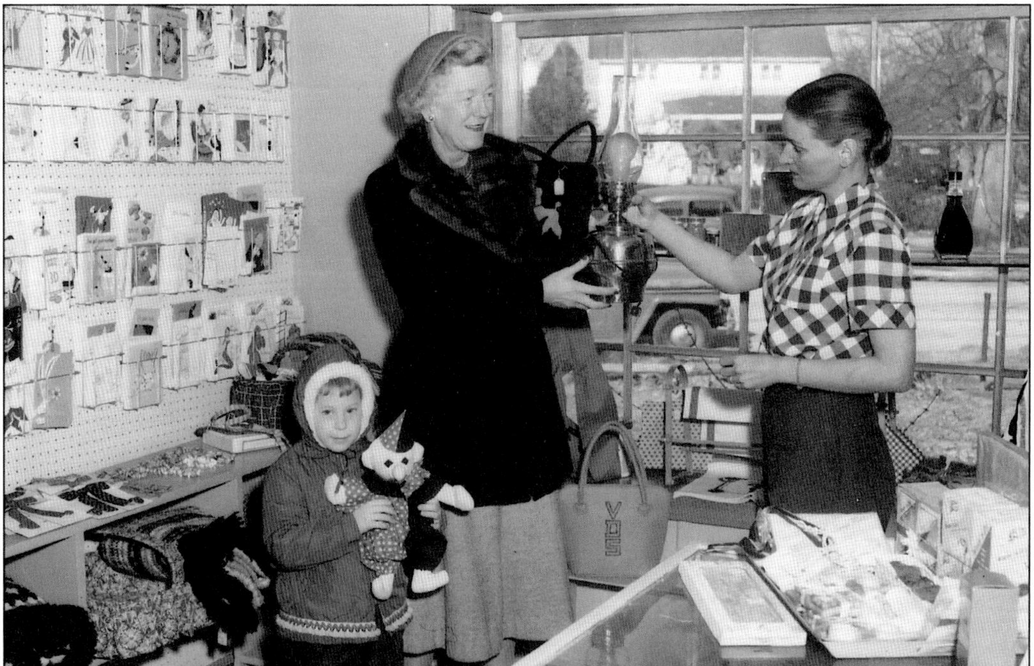

Inside the Woman's Exchange during the early 1950s, a woman and a child (who fondly clutches a clown doll) shop for handcrafted items. The view on Church Street can be seen through the panel glass windows. (Dorn's.)

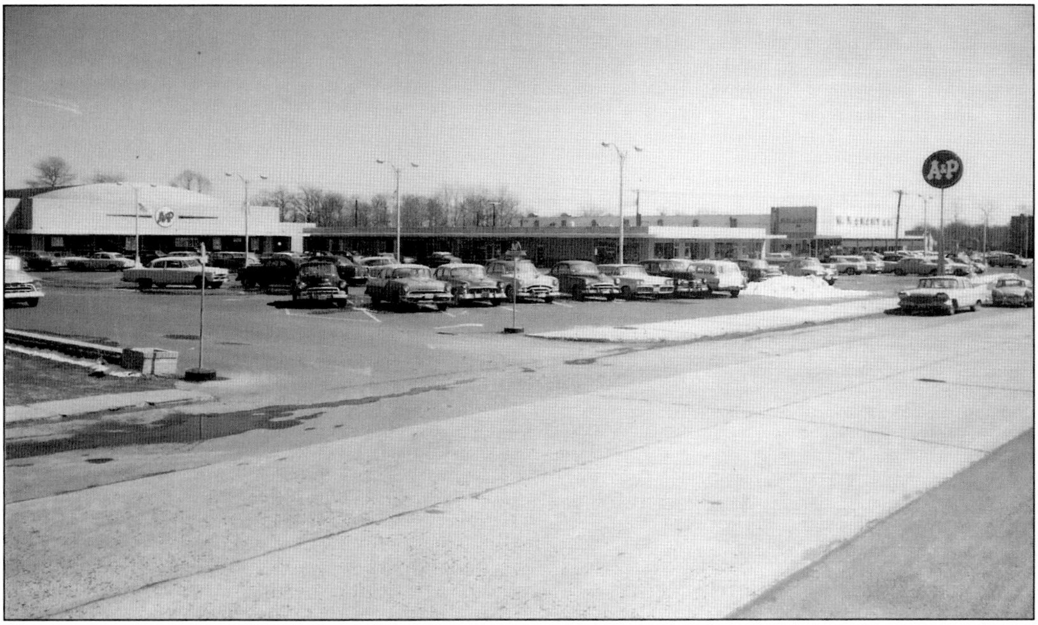

This is how the Prospect Avenue A&P shopping center looked in 1960. The W.T. Grant store, now the site of Walgreens and Gift Winds, is visible on the right. Those parked cars are considered classics today! (Dorn's.)

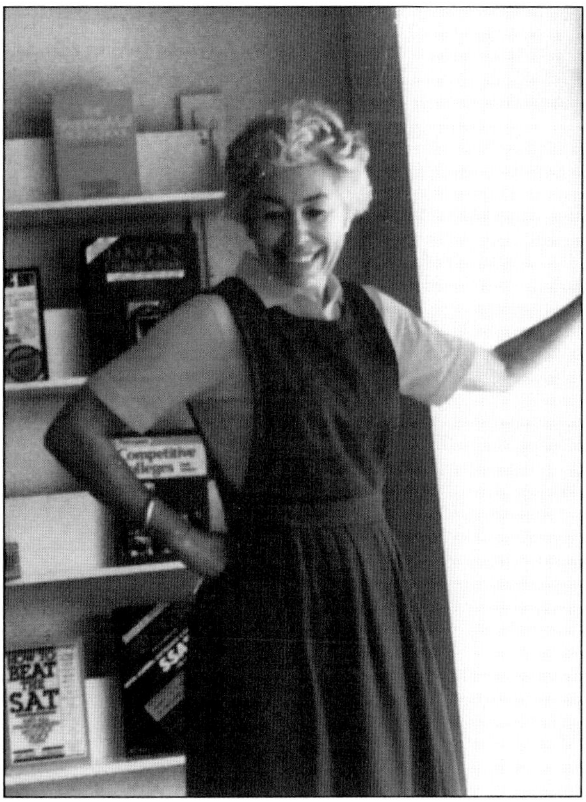

The Little Silver Bookshop, located in the Prospect Avenue A& P shopping center, was truly an institution in the town for many years until its closing in 1993. The late Sally Hetzler, who is pictured here, was a friendly and knowledgeable proprietor of the shop and well respected by local booklovers. She is pictured here in one of the Hetzler family's favorite photos. (J. Hetzler.)

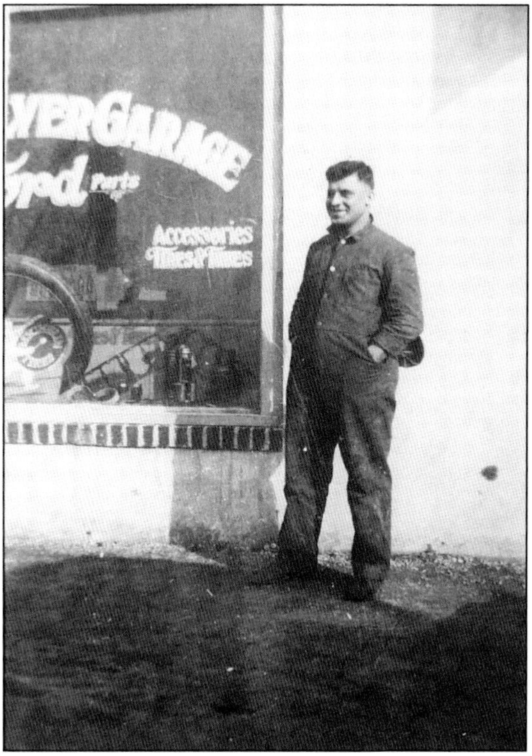

James Annarella, seen here in the 1920s, operated Little Silver Auto Body on the corner of Eastview and Branch Avenues. In 1933, after the repeal of Prohibition, James and his wife, Agnes, applied to the State for a wholesale liquor license, received one at the end of that year, and began selling Schaefer beer to local taverns in 1934 as the Shore Point Distributing Company.

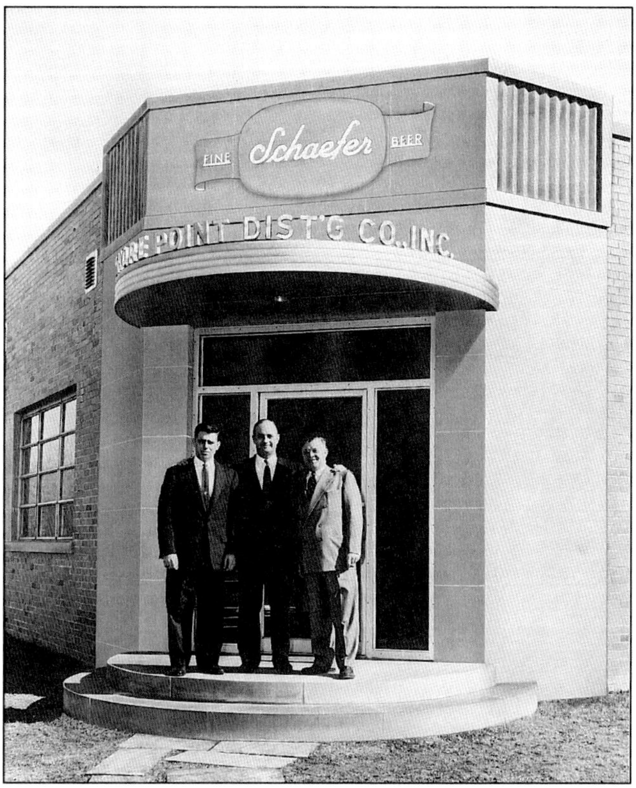

In the early 1950s, "Shore Point Dist'g Co. Inc.," as the sign reads on the semi-circular portico above the entrance, opened their new offices on Eastview Avenue. Standing proudly in front of the doorway are R. James Annarella (left), Rudy Schaefer (center), and James Annarella, company founder, on the right. The photos on this page and the aerial on the opposite page were provided by James Annarella of the Shore Point Distributing Company.

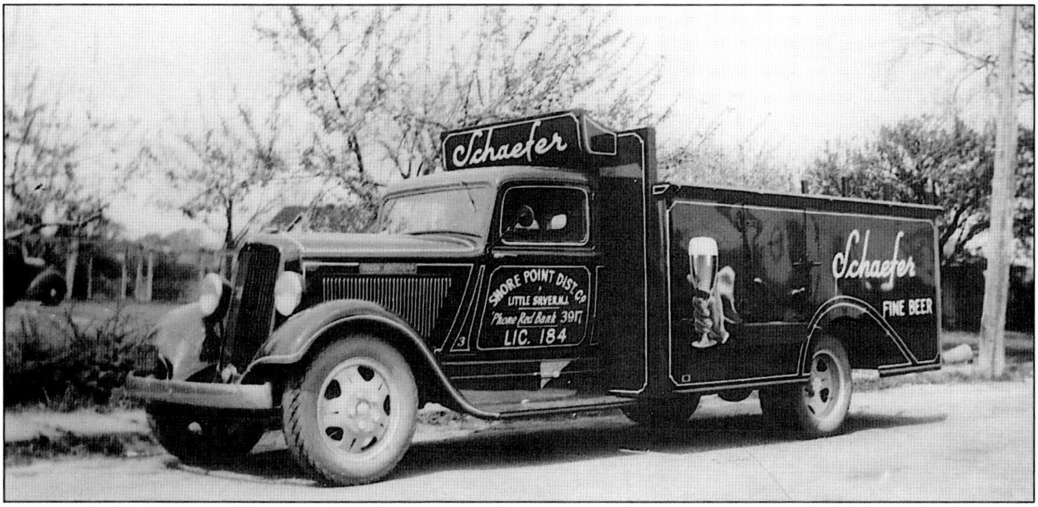

This Dorn's photo of a "Shore Point Dist'g Co." beer delivery truck made by "Dodge Brothers" is marked "3/7/56."

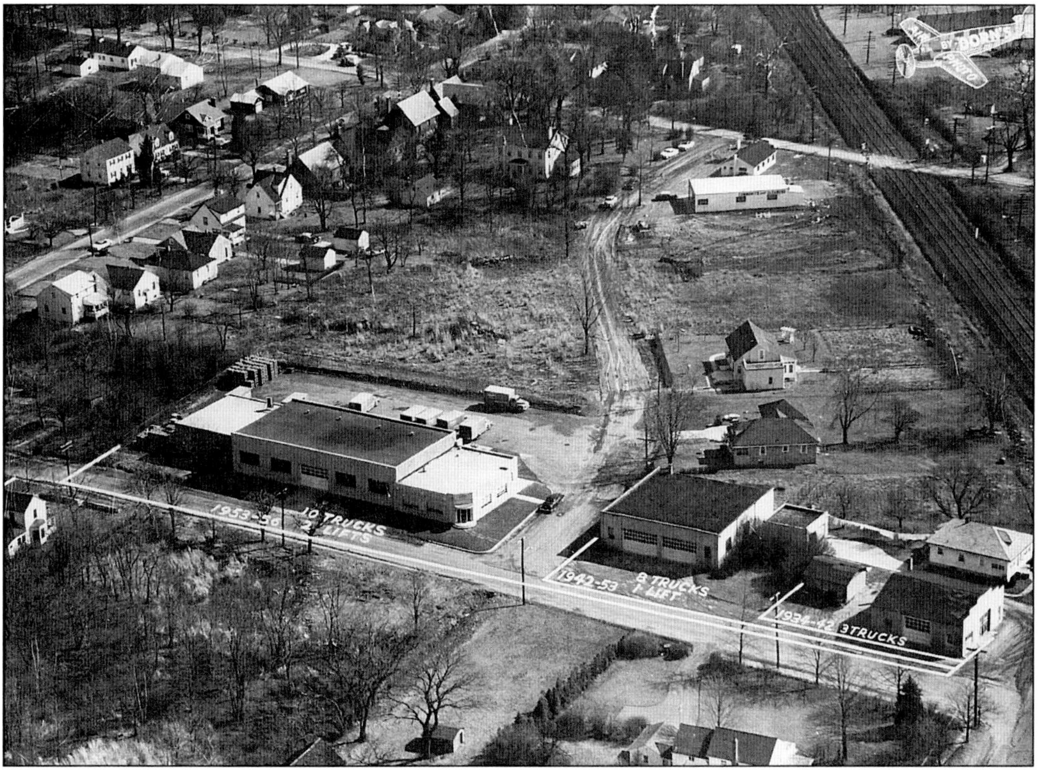

Using a 1950s aerial view taken by Dorn's, the Shore Point Distributing Company prepared a history of the company's growth and development that is marked directly on the photograph. Eastview Avenue was then a dirt road. The street at the top of the photo is Silverside Avenue. The company continued to grow and added additional distribution territories and brands. In 1987, they acquired the Coors brand and constructed a new facility in Freehold, where the company operates today. The Little Silver property is currently the home of a few local businesses and is still owned by the Annarella family.

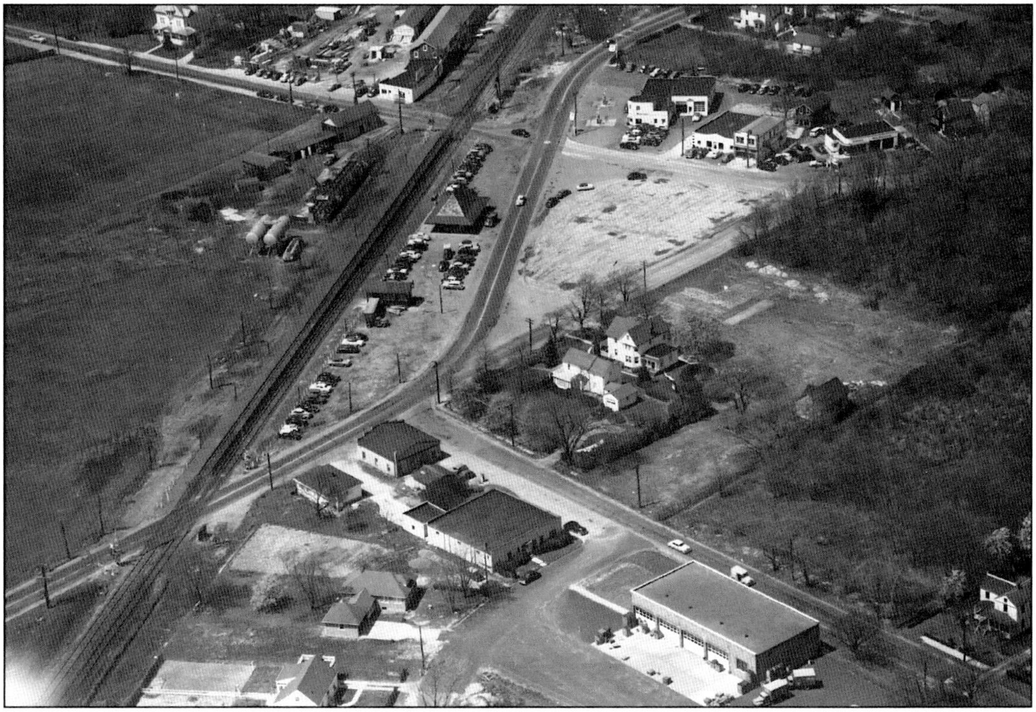

An early 1950s bird's-eye view of the Little Silver railroad station shows evidence of many changes. Some differences from today that will be noticed immediately are the empty lot across from the station, where the Exxon station is situated, and the open field on the left where the commuter parking lot is located. There were no electronic R.R. crossing gates then. See how many other changes you can find! In the front of the photo is the Shore Point Distribution Company, which is depicted on the previous two pages. (Dorn's.)

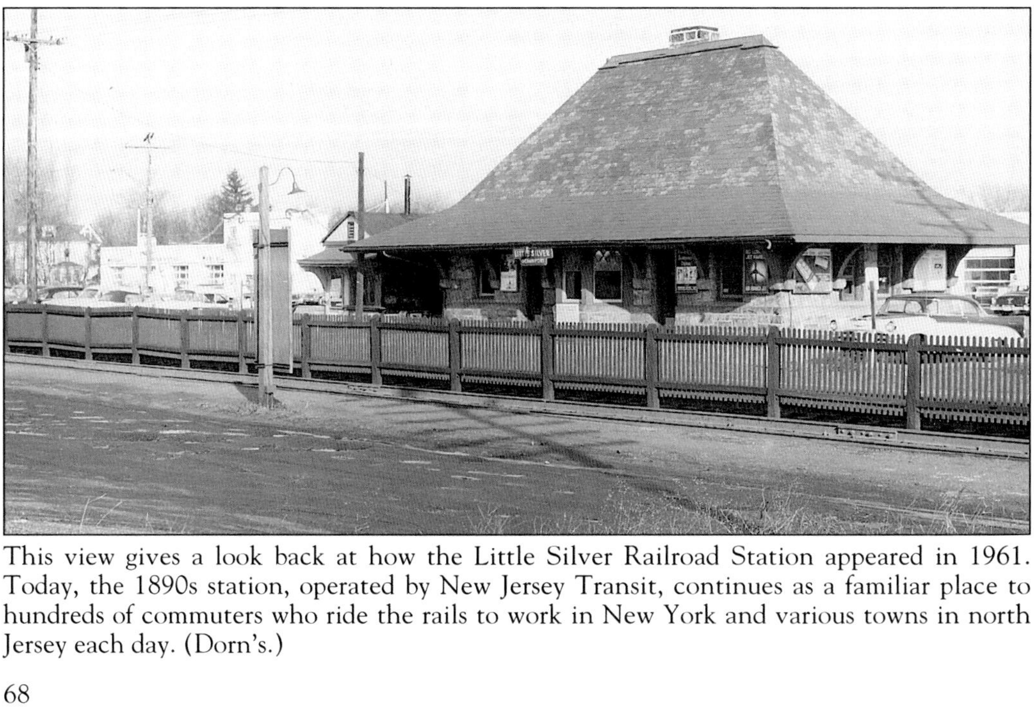

This view gives a look back at how the Little Silver Railroad Station appeared in 1961. Today, the 1890s station, operated by New Jersey Transit, continues as a familiar place to hundreds of commuters who ride the rails to work in New York and various towns in north Jersey each day. (Dorn's.)

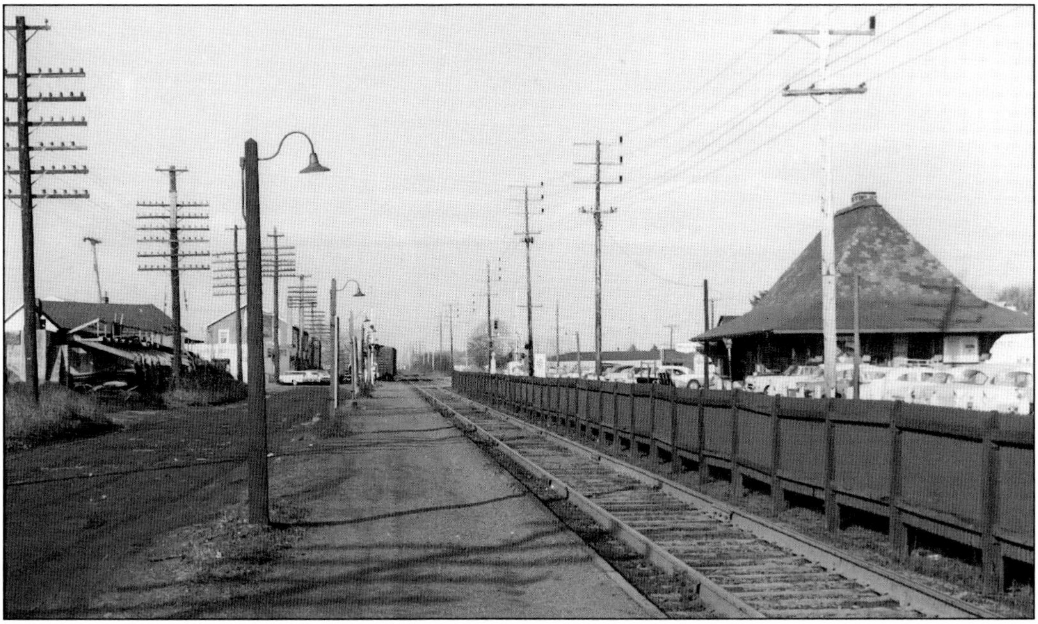

The historic Little Silver Railroad Station, built in 1890 and still in use, is depicted here as seen from the southbound side of the tracks in 1961. The solid wooden fence seen here between the tracks was replaced by an iron one that is now around the Post Office Museum next to the Little Silver Public Library. (Dorn's.)

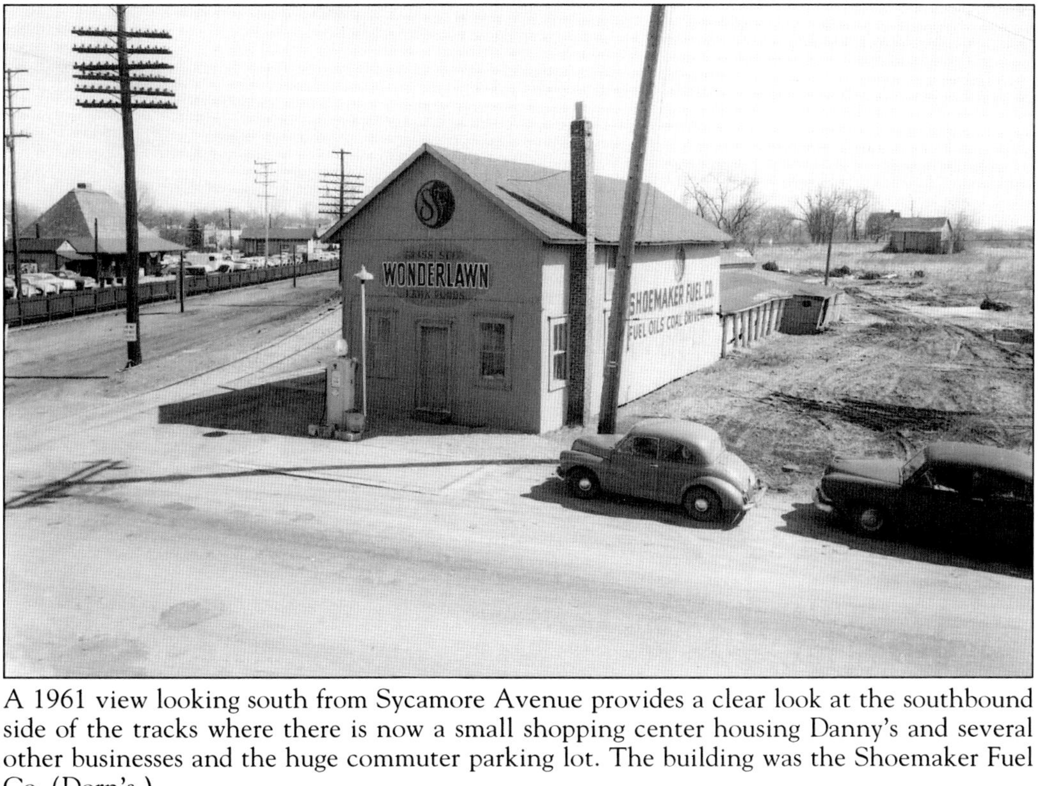

A 1961 view looking south from Sycamore Avenue provides a clear look at the southbound side of the tracks where there is now a small shopping center housing Danny's and several other businesses and the huge commuter parking lot. The building was the Shoemaker Fuel Co. (Dorn's.)

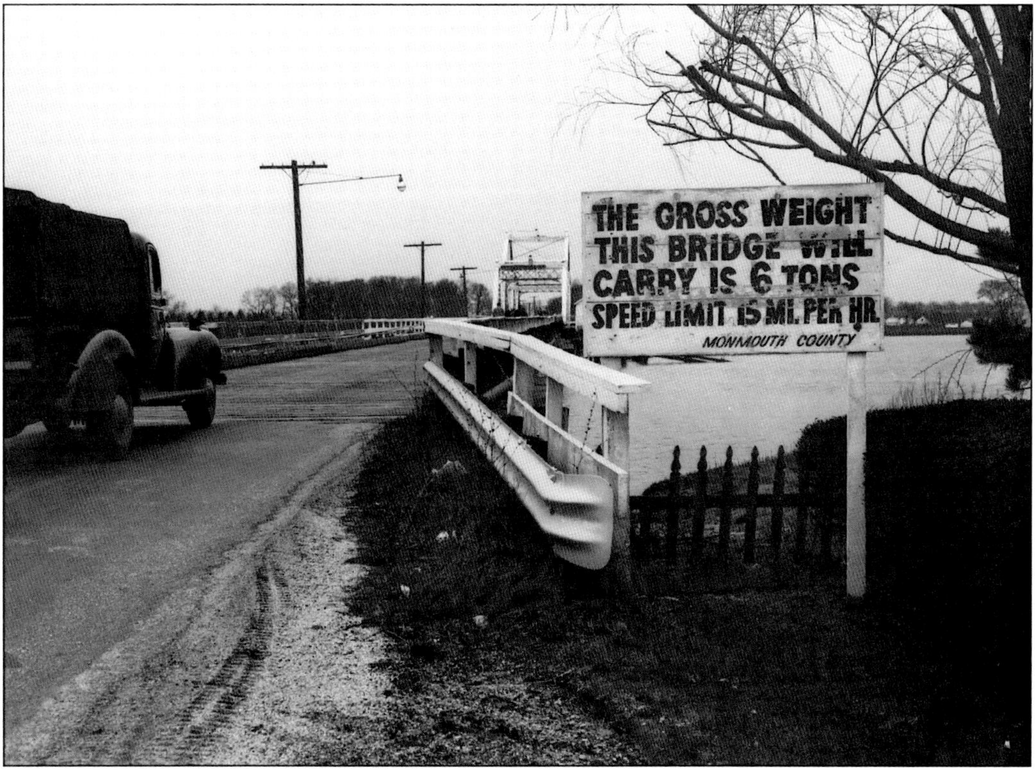

A photo dated April 13, 1950, shows the old Gooseneck Bridge, owned by Monmouth County on Seven Bridges Road (or Seven Bridge Road as the old timers call it!) connecting Little Silver and Oceanport. According to the sign, the swing-type drawbridge could hold no more than 6 tons and the speed limit was only 15 miles per hour. The timber-and-steel structure was built in 1898. (Dorn's.)

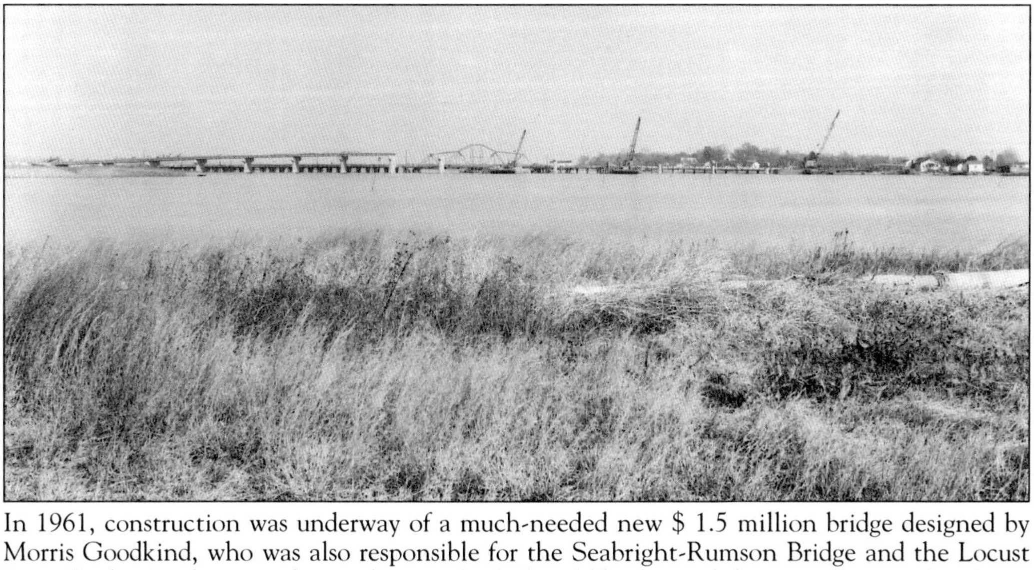

In 1961, construction was underway of a much-needed new $ 1.5 million bridge designed by Morris Goodkind, who was also responsible for the Seabright-Rumson Bridge and the Locust Point Bridge. In this view from a distance both the old bridge and the partially completed new one can be seen. (Dorn's.)

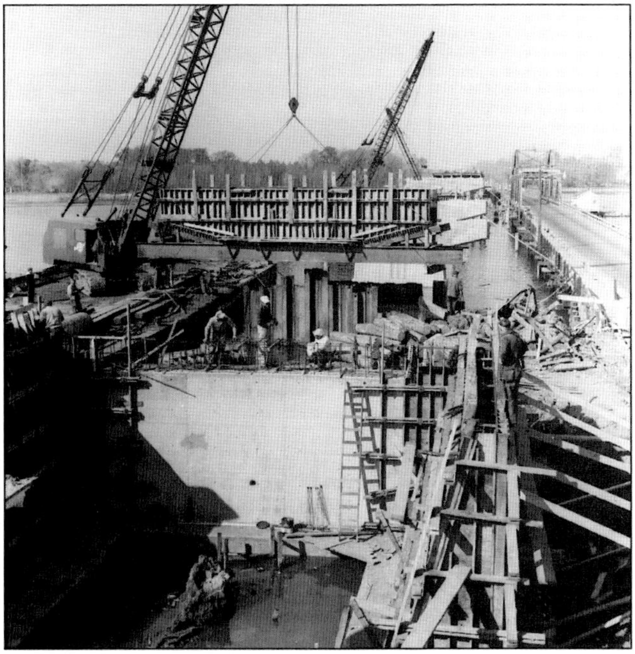

This photo gives a good look at the construction of the new Gooseneck Bridge during 1961. The fixed concrete-and-steel span was made by Public Constructors Inc. under the supervision of its designer, Morris Goodkind. About 150 men labored to build the 1,100-foot-long span, which is 25 feet high at high tide. (Dorn's.)

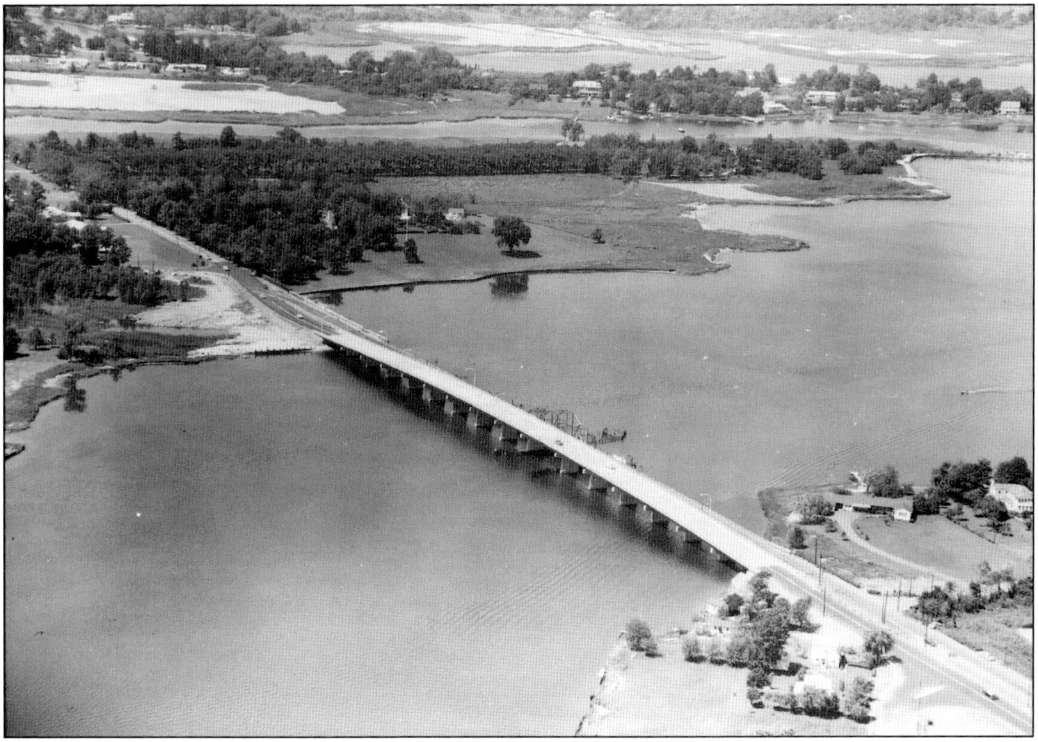

A spectacular aerial view displays the new Gooseneck Bridge soon after it opened on July 10, 1962. Monmouth County Freeholder Joseph C. Irwin presided at the opening ceremony and called the structure "a thing of beauty." Both Little Silver Mayor Charles W. Stephens and Oceanport Mayor Edward C. Wilson Sr. were on hand as Freeholder Abram D. Voorhees cut the red ribbon to let the first traffic cross. (Dorn's.)

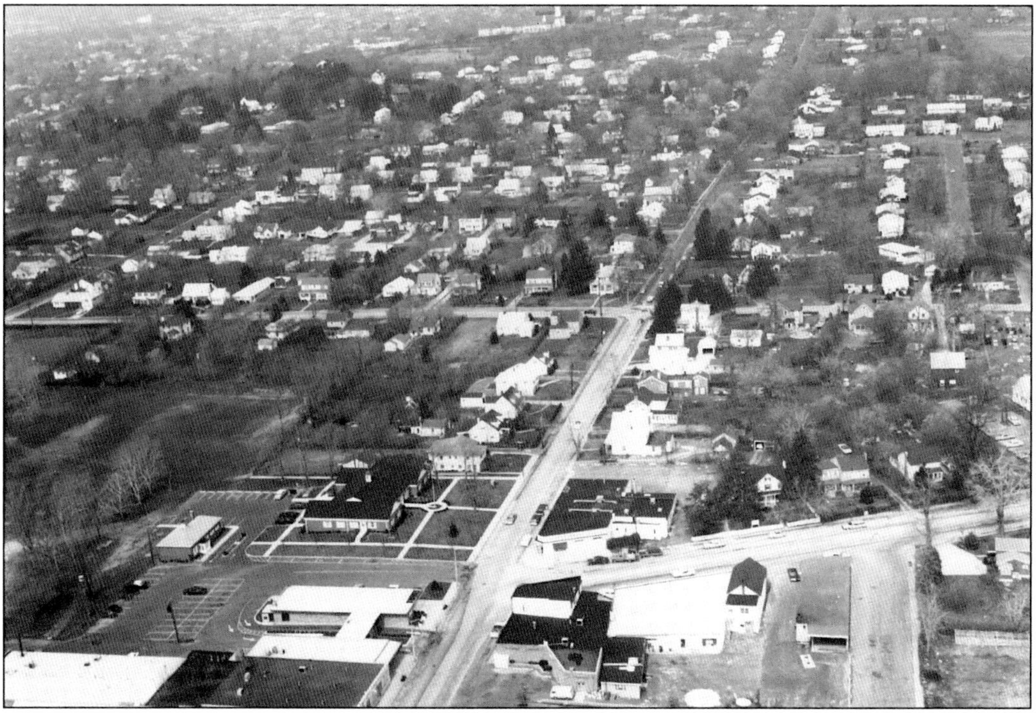

David A. Kennedy, retired Little Silver police captain, took some great aerial photos in the late 1960s. This one is looking toward the north on Prospect Avenue. The Borough Hall and public library just behind it (on the left) were new at the time. The Tower Hill Church in Red Bank can be seen in the far distance. (D.A. Kennedy.)

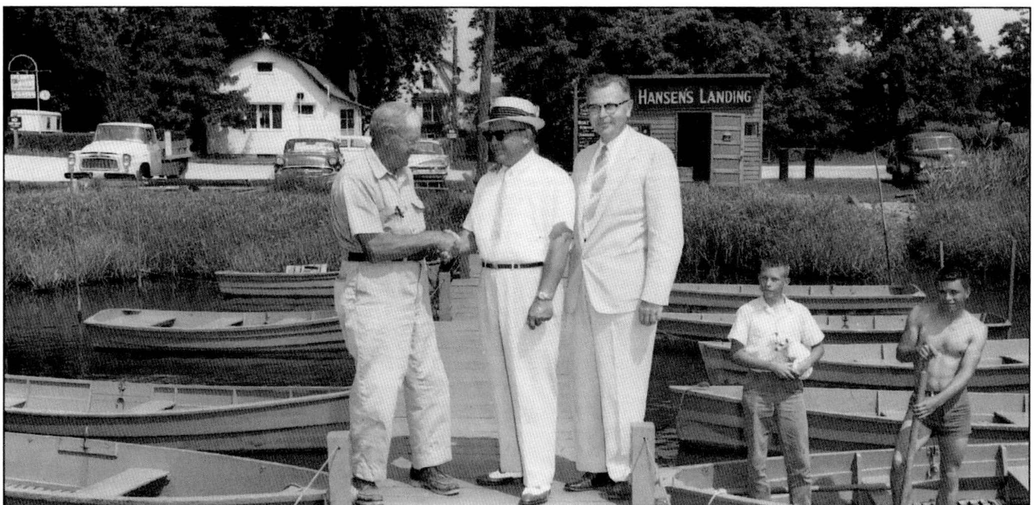

This 1961 photo shows a dock called Hansen's Landing that was located just before the Oceanport Avenue Bridge on the southeast side of Branch Avenue, across from Fort Monmouth. Little Silver's Bob Fritsche (not in the photograph), who now lives in Florida, worked there as a teen in the 1960s. He recalls how people would come from all over and rent rowboats to go crabbing in the Shrewsbury River. The people in the photo are not identified but the man on the left is probably Mr. Hansen. (Dorn's.)

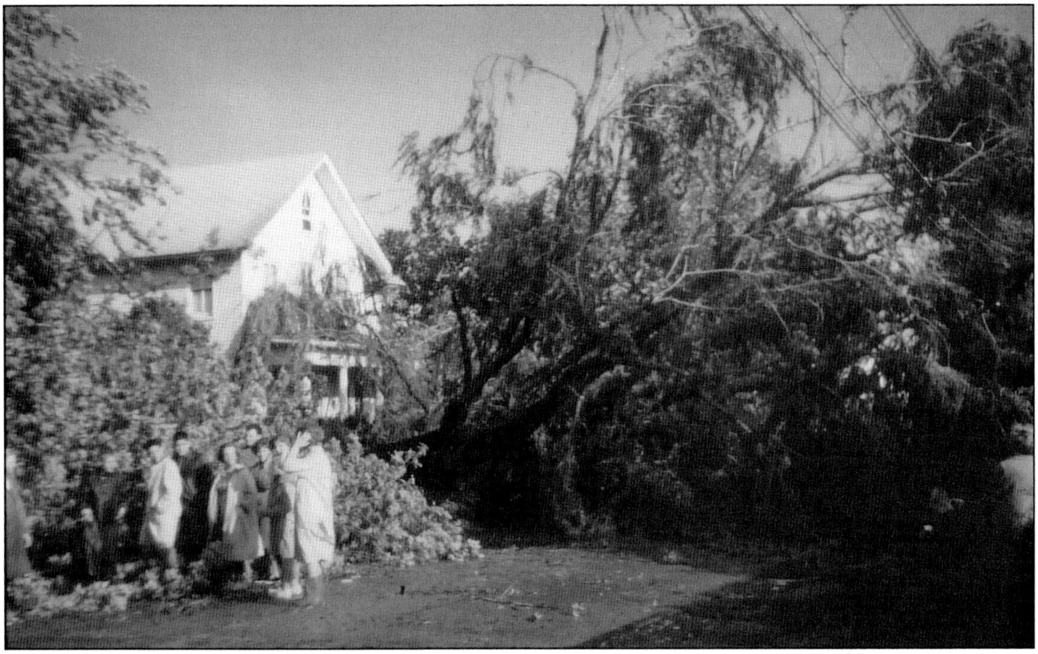

Sandy Ferrogiari Wells writes about this photo that belongs to her: "On September 12, 1960, Hurricane Donna blew through Little Silver with maximum wind speeds of 108 mph. My sister and I were home by ourselves when the Police Department called and said that the large willow tree in our front yard (463 Prospect Ave.) looked like it was going to fall and we should get out of the house. We did and the tree fell, mostly across Prospect Ave. In the photo, a group of neighbors stands together, assessing the damage as our willow tree lay across Prospect Ave."

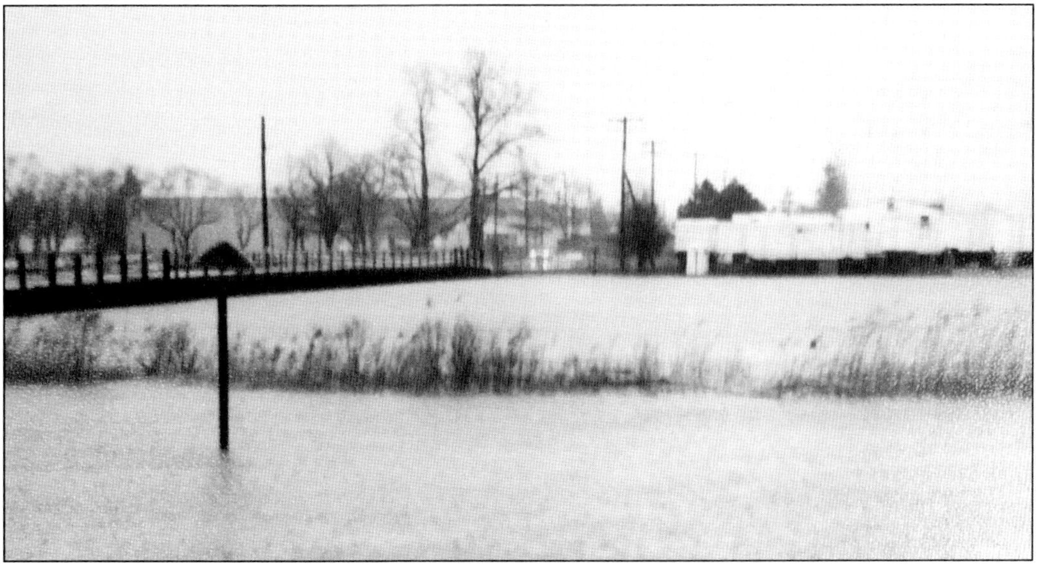

The parking lot of the Monmouth Animal Hospital on Oceanport Avenue, looking south toward Fort Monmouth, has turned into a giant swimming pool in a photo from the summer of 1984. The Shrewsbury River has swelled almost to the road that goes over the Oceanport Bridge. This photo was loaned by Dr. and Mrs. Robert Nelson of Little Silver, who recall a scene similar to this during Hurricane Donna in 1960.

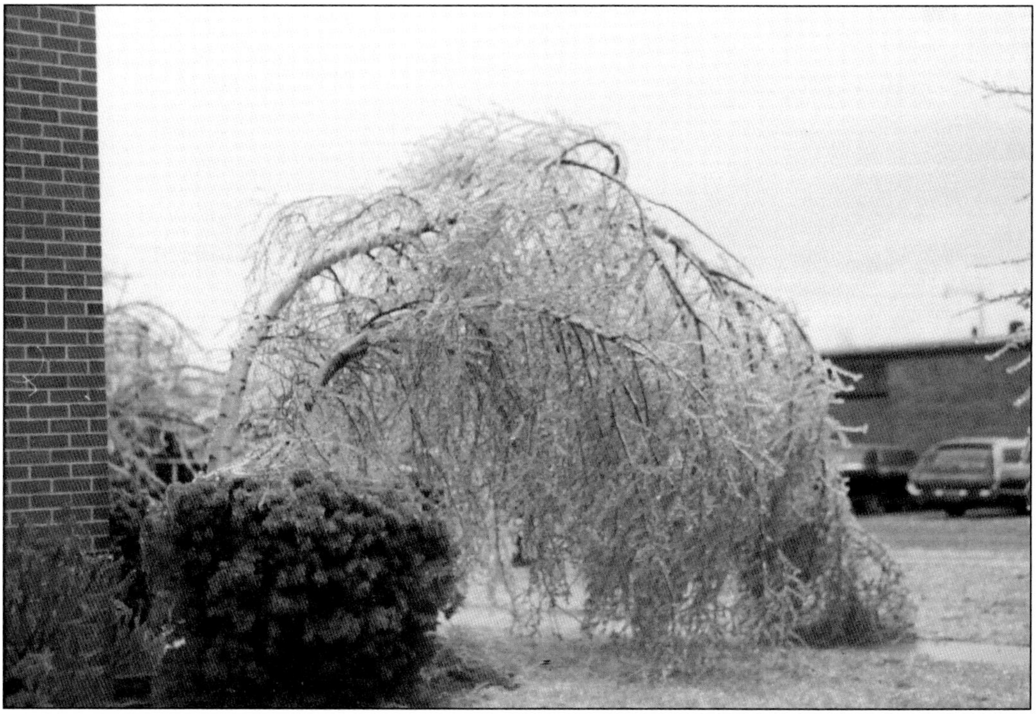

In December 1973, Assistant Borough Administrator Peggy Henneberry (now retired) photographed the terrible ice storm that knocked down power lines and left the New Jersey shore area crippled for days. Although the storm was treacherous, the beauty of the fantastic shapes formed by the glazed trees as they bent over, such as this one by the Borough Hall, was exquisite.

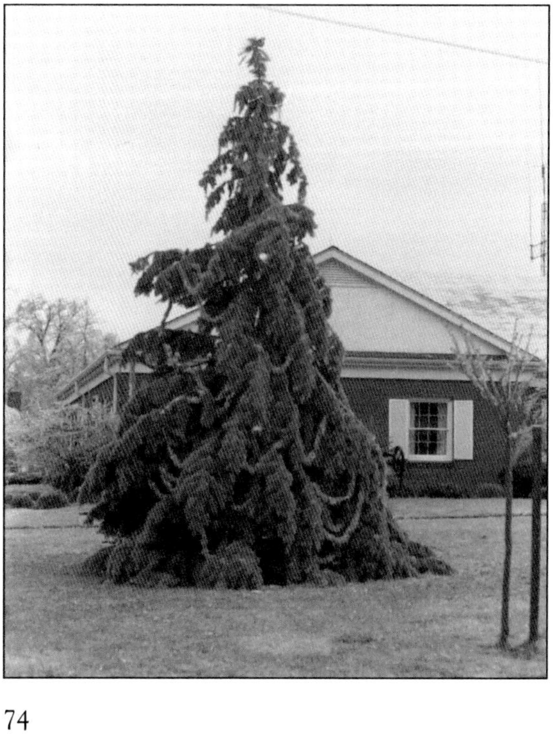

In this image, the annual town Christmas tree in front of the Borough Hall on Prospect Avenue is sadly drooping from the weight of the ice during the never-to-be-forgotten ice storm of December 1973. (Peggy Henneberry.)

Five

Some Little Silver People

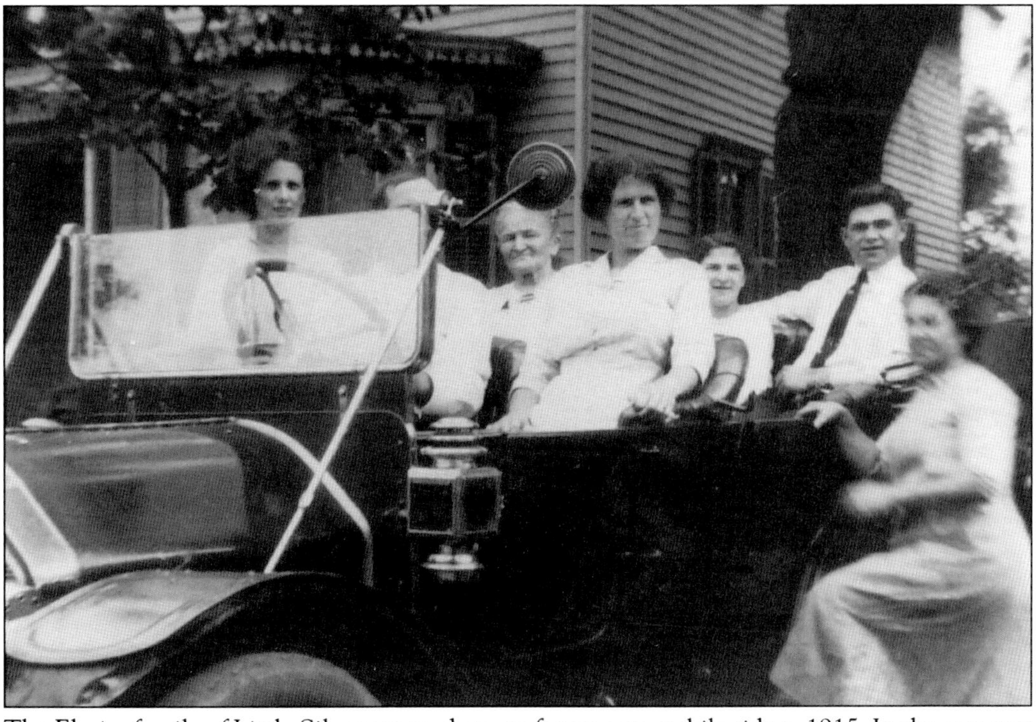

The Elgrim family of Little Silver are ready to go for an automobile ride *c.* 1915. In the rear seat are Mrs. Elgrim and her grandchildren, Anna and Eugene. The woman standing outside the car is their mother, Alice Buckley Elgrim. (D. Elgrim.)

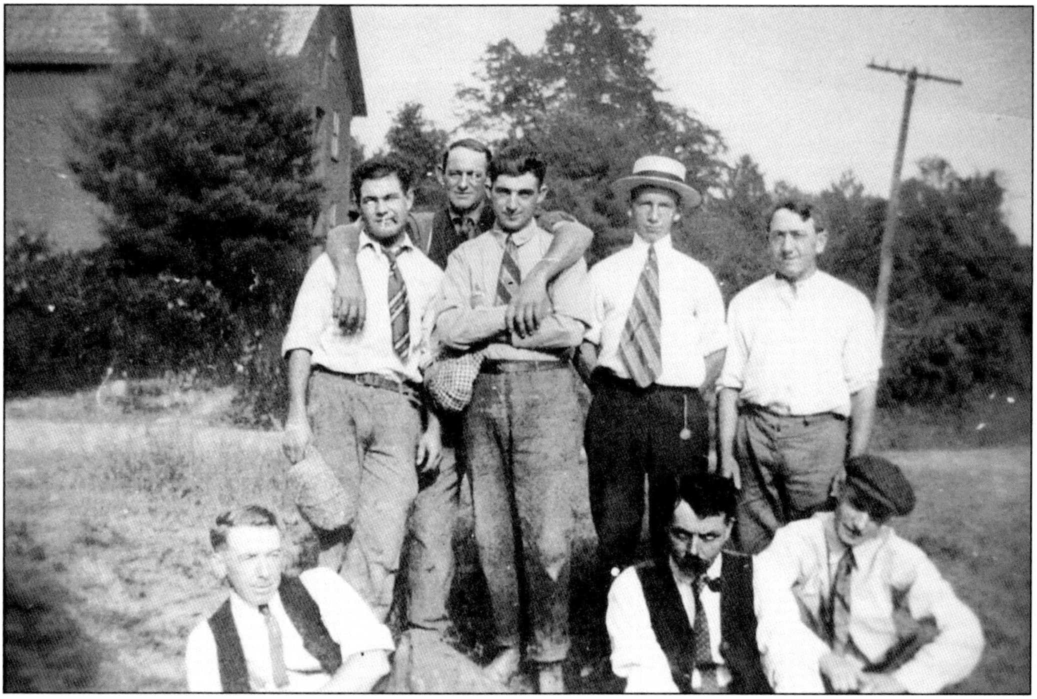

A group of Little Silver men, *c.* 1918, pause for a casual portrait, probably taken in the vicinity of Rumson Road. Eugene Elgrim is standing on the far left with a cigar. (D. Elgrim.)

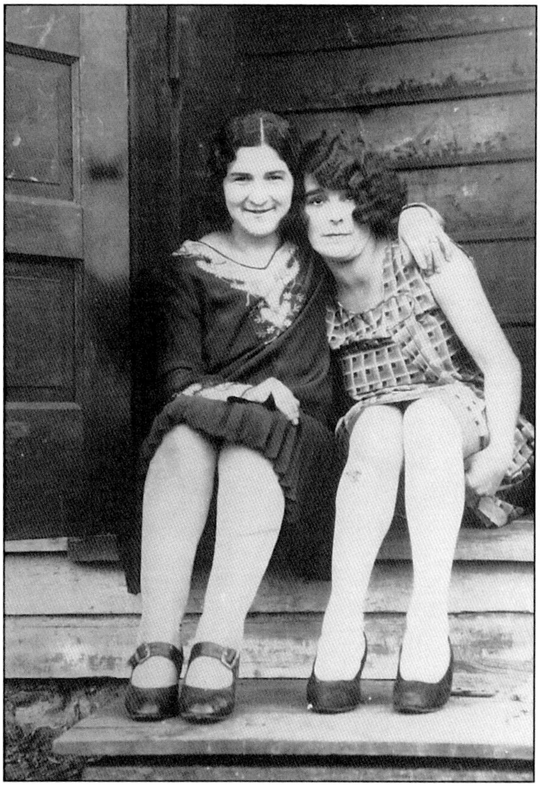

In about 1918, Anna Elgrim (left) poses playfully with an unidentified friend whose bobbed hair represents a daring new look at that time. Also, until this time (right after World War I), young women would not have revealed their stockinged legs so boldly! The styles and times were changing. (G. Kingston.)

Eugene Elgrim lived on Rumson Road, worked at Lovett's nurseries, and was a chauffeur for people who owned well-to-do homes and estates. This handsome portrait *c.* 1918 shows Elgrim in his driving uniform with leather leg coverings that extend from the tops of his shoes to his knees. This photo and several others belong to his son, Dennis Elgrim.

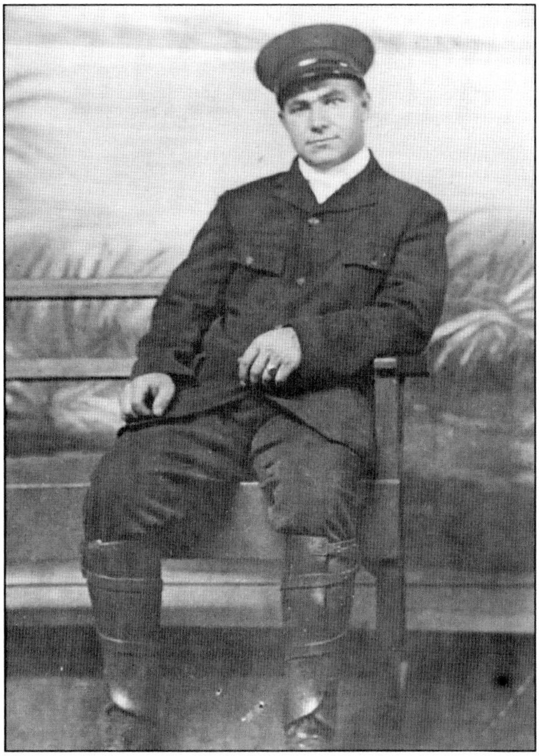

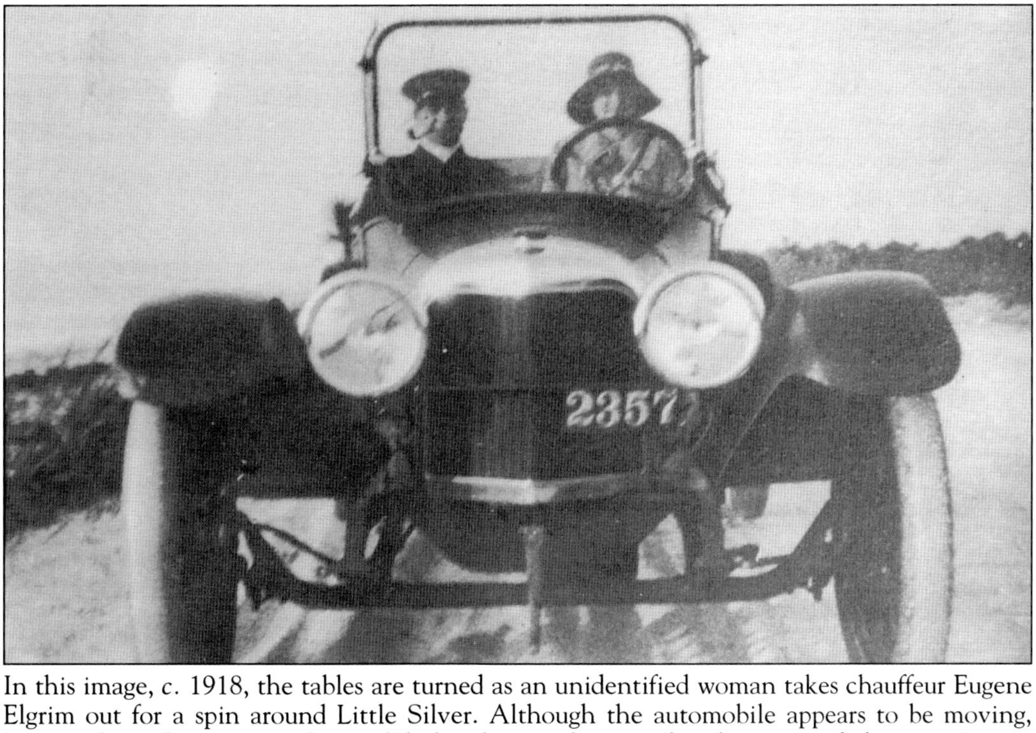

In this image, *c.* 1918, the tables are turned as an unidentified woman takes chauffeur Eugene Elgrim out for a spin around Little Silver. Although the automobile appears to be moving, it must have been stopped—or did the daring photographer hop out of the way just in time? (D. Elgrim.)

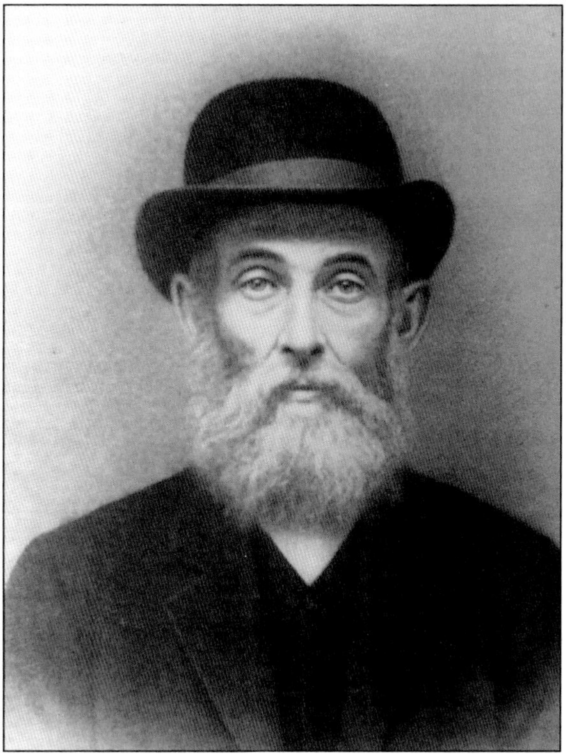

This gaunt-looking man in the hat is Michael Ayres, who was a well-known contractor and builder from Little Silver. According to *The New Jersey Coast in Three Centuries, Vol. II* (1902), Ayres was the first master mechanic to successfully introduce the 10-hour work day system to the region in 1856. On an 1889 map of Parkerville, his property is shown at 160 Rumson Road, adjacent to the Embury Methodist Church property. (Moss Archives.)

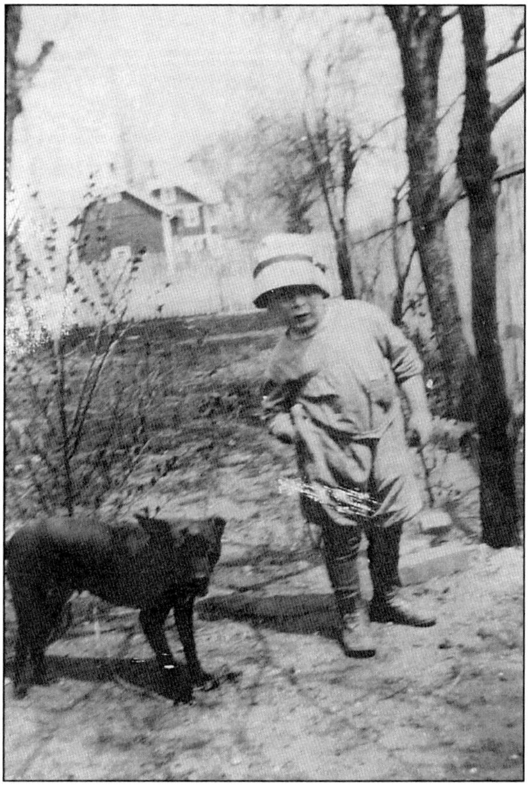

Little Walton Moore and his dog Gypsy Queen play near their home on White Road, *c.* 1913. At the 75th anniversary parade on June 7, 1998, Walton was the grand marshall of the event, having lived continuously in Little Silver all his 86 years, longer than any other current resident. (W. Moore.)

The couple pictured here are Little Silver farmer Edwin Alonzo Bowman and his second wife, Elizabeth, at the time of their marriage on January 3, 1904. His first wife, Mary, died in 1901. Bowman's farm and house at 600 Prospect Avenue are featured in chapter one of *Little Silver, Vol. I.*

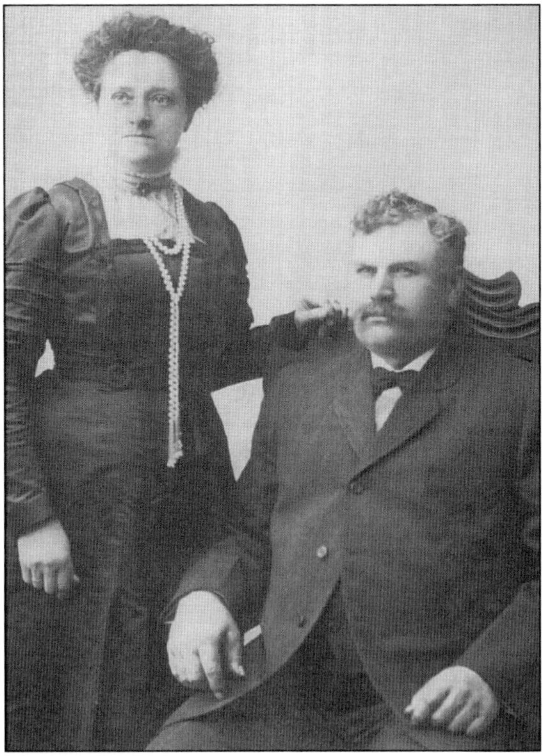

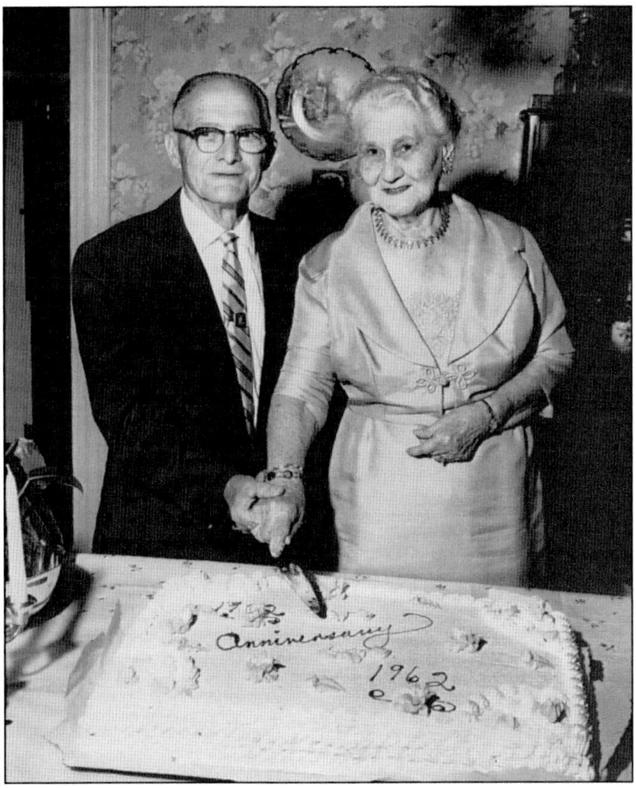

Mr. and Mrs. James F. Lane are cutting their 60th wedding anniversary cake inside their home at 600 Prospect Avenue in 1962. Mr. Lane, whose family goes way back in the local area, owned Lane's Market, a butcher shop in Red Bank. Mrs. Lane (nee Jessie Bowman) was the daughter of Edwin Alonzo and Mary Bowman (see caption above), and the mother of Frances (Lane) Burdge, whose daughter, Mary (Burdge) Jerolamon, is the lender of this photo and the photo at the top of the page of her great grandfather.

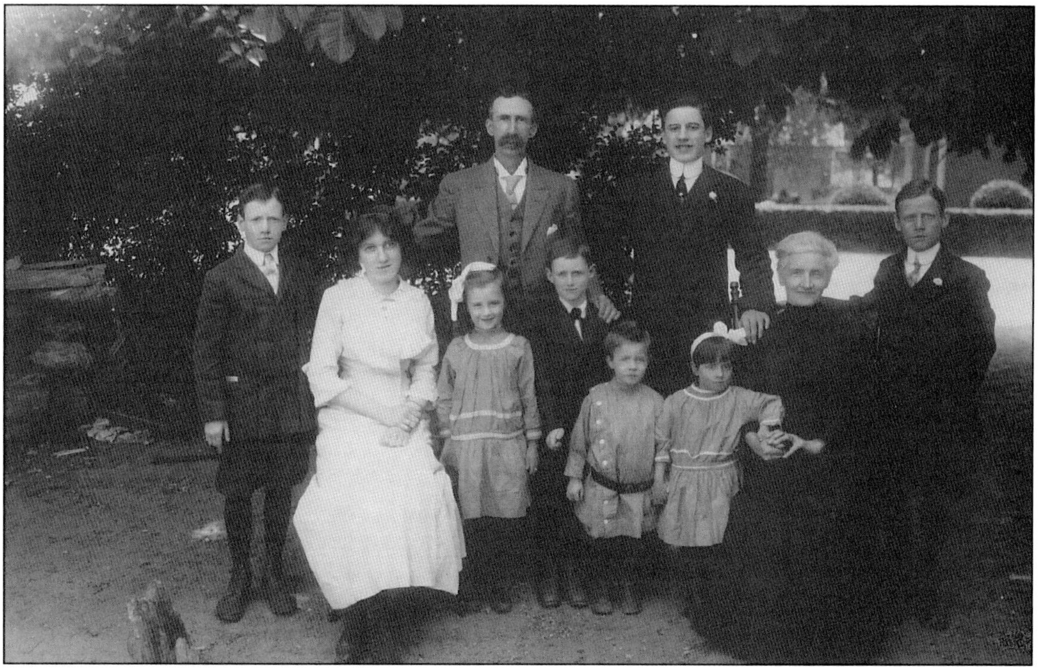

The Cook family assembled in the yard of their home at 80 Church Street (the former Lovett house) for this lovely family portrait in 1912. From left to right are as follows: (front row) Frank; Margaret; Laura; Ray, who provided this photo; Stanley; Alice; mother Hanna; and Bert; (back row) father John H. Cook, the foreman of Lovett's nurseries from 1906 to 1916, who was a leading authority on perennials; and Edwin. (Copy photo by Tom Dunn.)

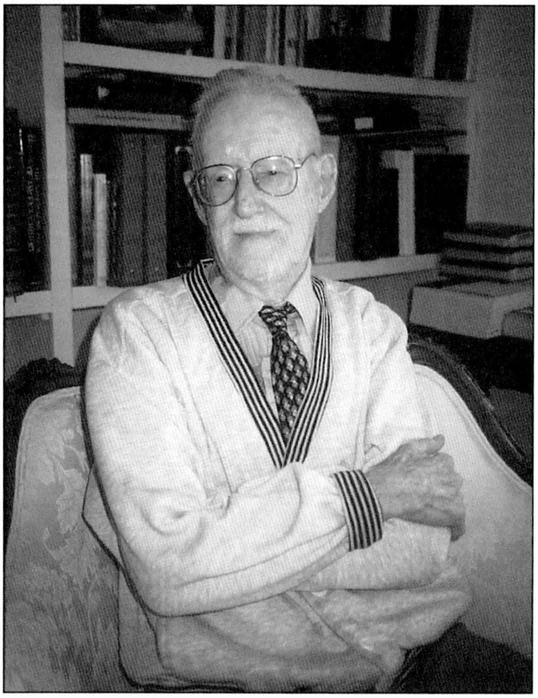

In a 1998 photo, James "Ray" Cook Sr. clearly has not changed much from the way he looked as a young boy in the center of the family portrait above from 1912! Ray, who has a wonderful memory and a great sense of humor, enjoyed his childhood days in Little Silver. He recalls many lively tales of his childhood here in the early years of the century. (Photo by author.)

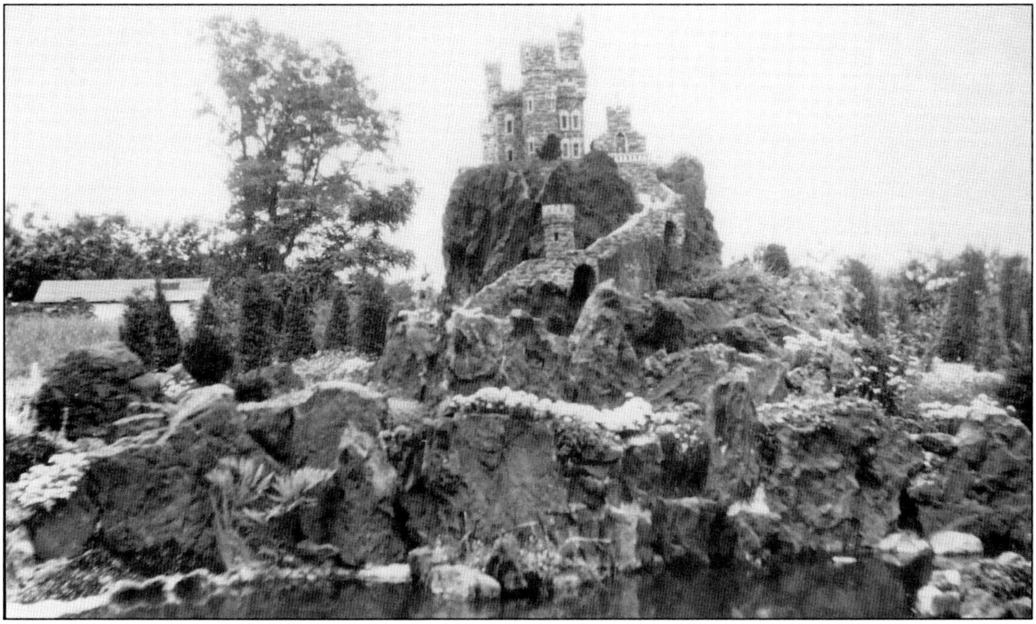

Once upon a time . . . there were castles in Little Silver? During the 1920s, intricate miniature stone castles built by Lewis Eastmond transformed the backyard of his home (the former Lovett and then Cook's house at 80 Church Street) into a fairytale setting. People came from all over to view Eastmond's creations. Wealthy owners of local estates offered to buy his work, but Eastmond declined as his artistry was purely for beautification of his property and the enjoyment of his family. The photo is courtesy of his daughter, Marjorie Eastmond Johnson.

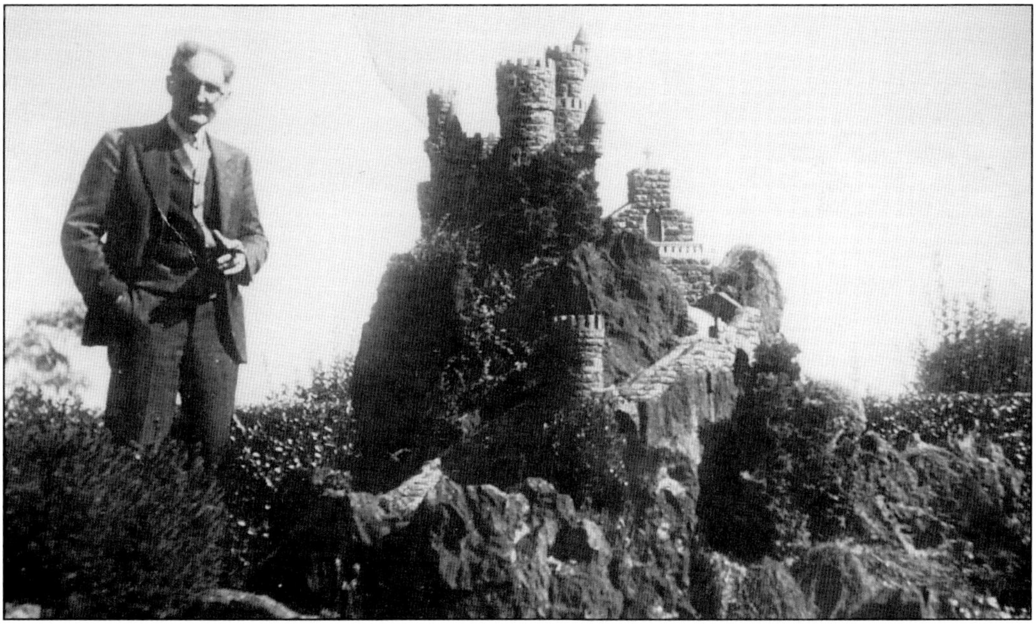

In this 1927 photo, Lewis Eastmond, who worked as a railroad engineer, stands proudly next to one of the castles he built as a hobby. Eastmond constructed a lily pond in front of the miniature palace and built elaborate castle-shaped stone posts on either side of the front walkway. The house can be seen on p. 20 of *Little Silver Vol. I.* (M. Johnson.)

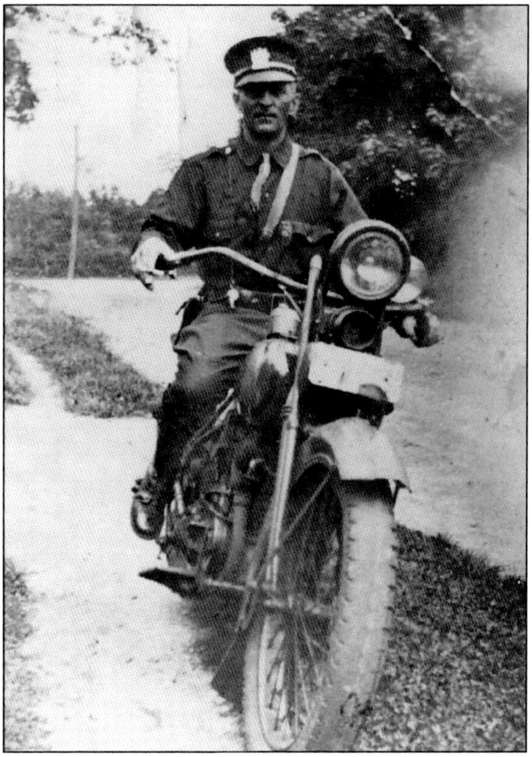

Fred Ziegler rides his first official motorcycle in 1927 when he was appointed a part-time motor police officer. A photo of Ziegler on his newer motorcycle in 1930, the year he became chief, appears in *Little Silver Vol. I*, on p. 95. Ziegler, who lived on Markham Place, especially enjoyed animals and kept dogs, cats, horses, chickens, and even a goat on the property that is now the site of the Markham Place shopping plaza. (Little Silver Historical Society.)

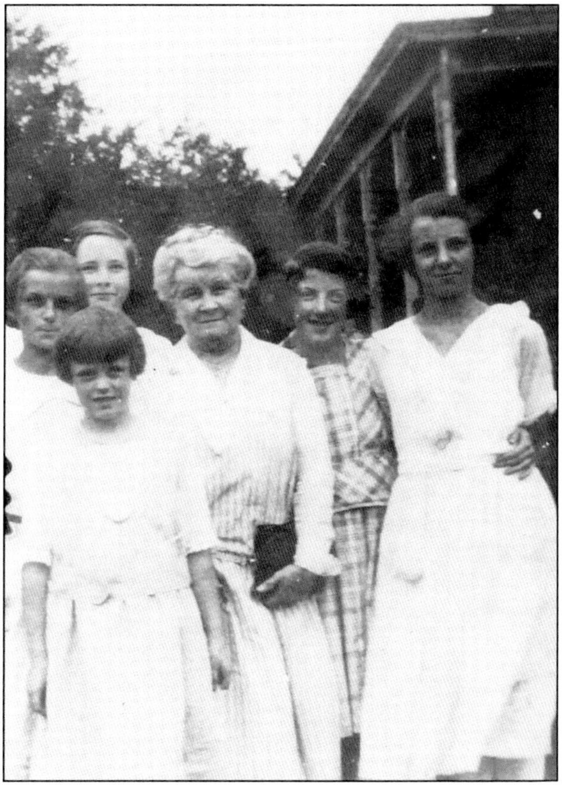

Mrs. Harvey (with white hair in center), the wife of Little Silver's first mayor, J. Elwood Harvey, stands with The Joyous Workers, a church youth group, in front of the Moore's home at 322 White Road in 1922. Lucy Ellen Wycoff Harvey was founder in 1919 of the Little Silver Sewing Society, which became the Woman's Club of Little Silver. (W. Moore.)

Edward C. Fiedler, a prominent, generous businessman who did much to improve the community of Little Silver, was a governor of the New York Stock Exchange in the 1930s. He and his wife, Jane, lived at a Lochmere, a gracious place on the Shrewsbury River. Lochmere, both the original and one built later, is shown on pp. 44–45. Mr. Fiedler served in Little Silver as a councilman, police commissioner, and the third mayor of the borough in 1936–37, completing the term of Mayor Black, who died in office.

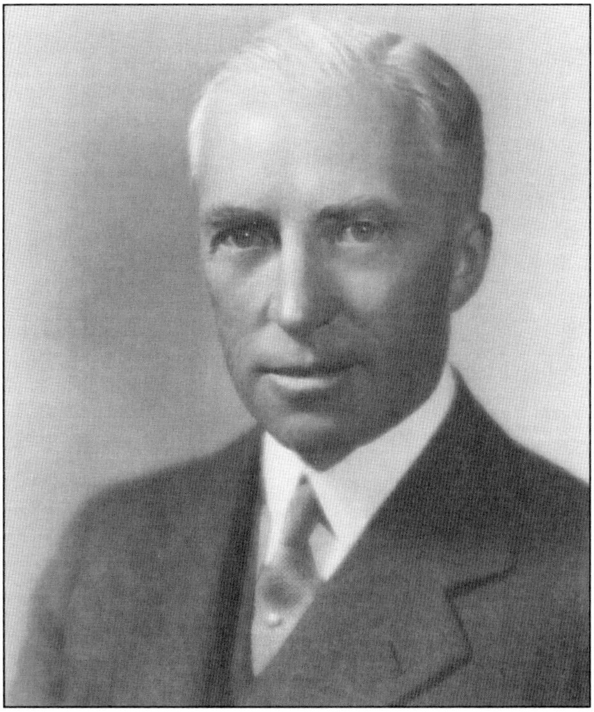

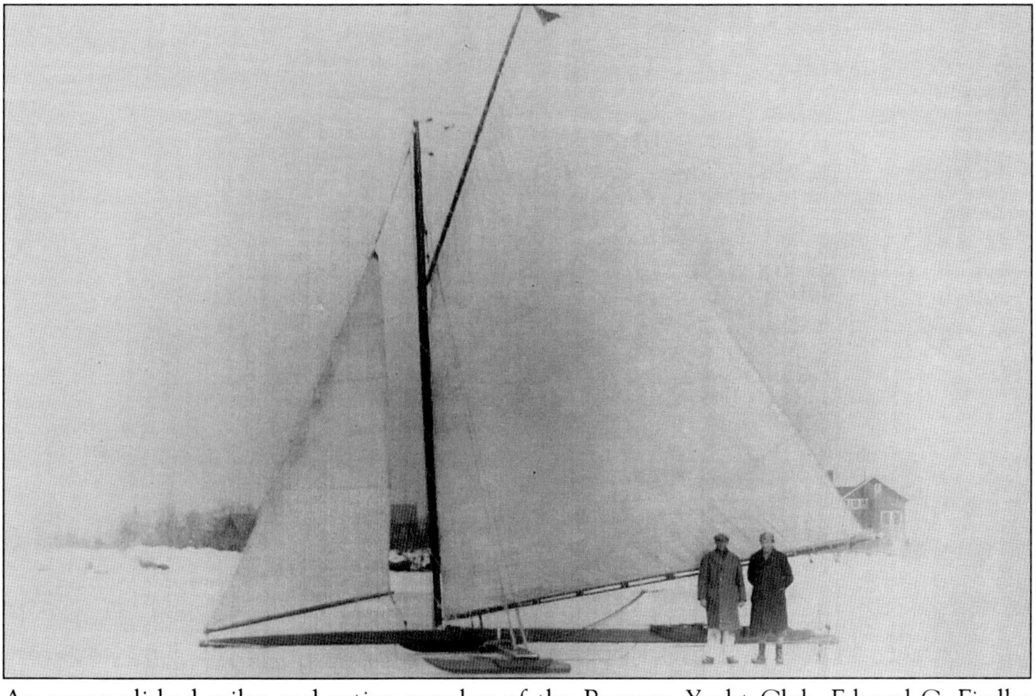

An accomplished sailor and active member of the Rumson Yacht Club, Edward C. Fiedler enjoyed racing his boat the *Aphrodite* in the summer, and his iceboat called the *Drub* when the Shrewsbury River froze in winter. "Drub" was "Burd"spelled backwards, and was named for Mr. Fiedler's friend, Charlie Burd, who built the iceboat. Mr. Fiedler is pictured here in the late 1920s or early '30s with Reuben White, caretaker of the boat club, who was from Red Bank.

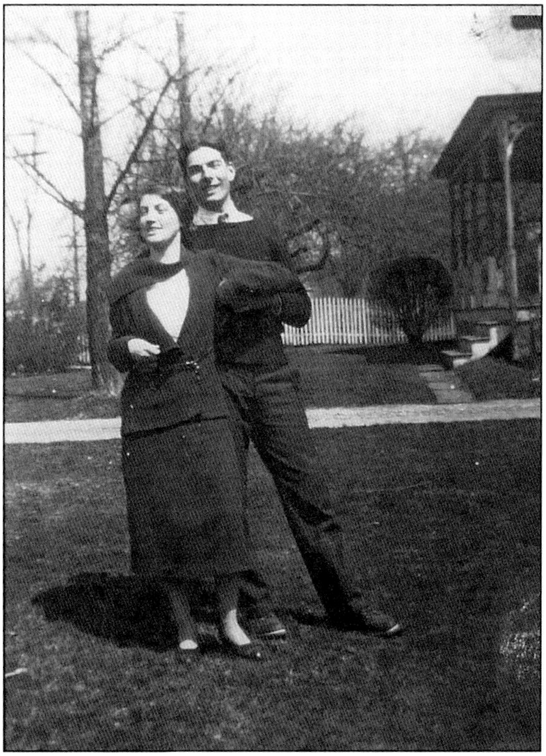

Walton Moore and his sister, Mildred Moore, are playing while someone takes a photograph in front of their home at 322 White Road in the late 1920s or early 1930s. Although it may look like Walton was literally twisting his sister's arm, they are laughing and it was all in good fun! (W. Moore.)

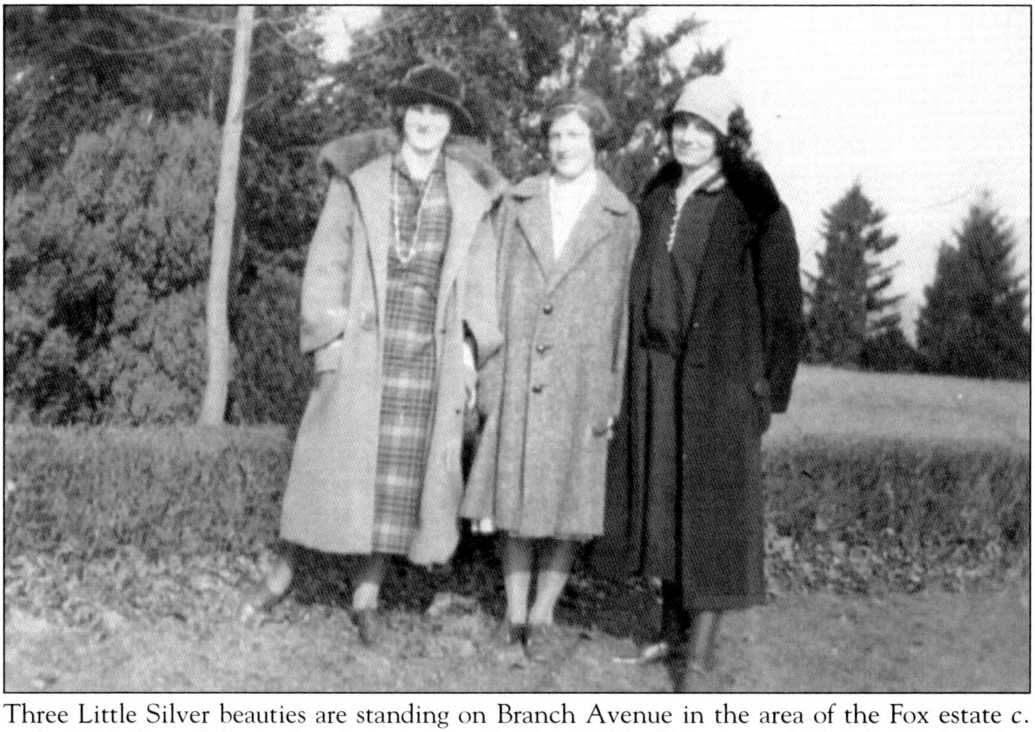

Three Little Silver beauties are standing on Branch Avenue in the area of the Fox estate c. early 1930s. From left to right, they are Anna Bublin, Mildred Moore, and Theodora Schneider. (W. Moore.)

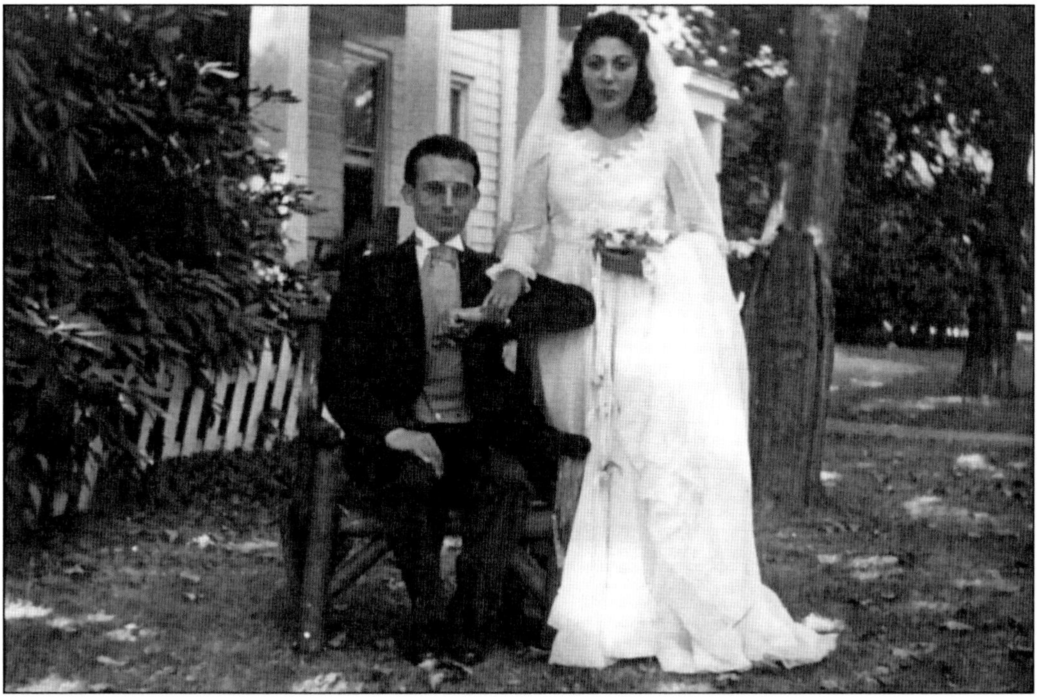

On August 27, 1944, Anthony F. and Anne M. Trufolo posed for a portrait outside the Rosevelt Tea Room on the corner of Markham Place and Branch Avenue (later the Farm House, see p. 59) where their wedding reception took place after a ceremony at St. Anthony's Church in Red Bank. Mr. Trufolo, who was a science and math teacher at Red Bank Regional High School, says that the pose was a bit of a spoof on pictures of an earlier era with the groom seated and the bride standing. (A.F. Trufolo.)

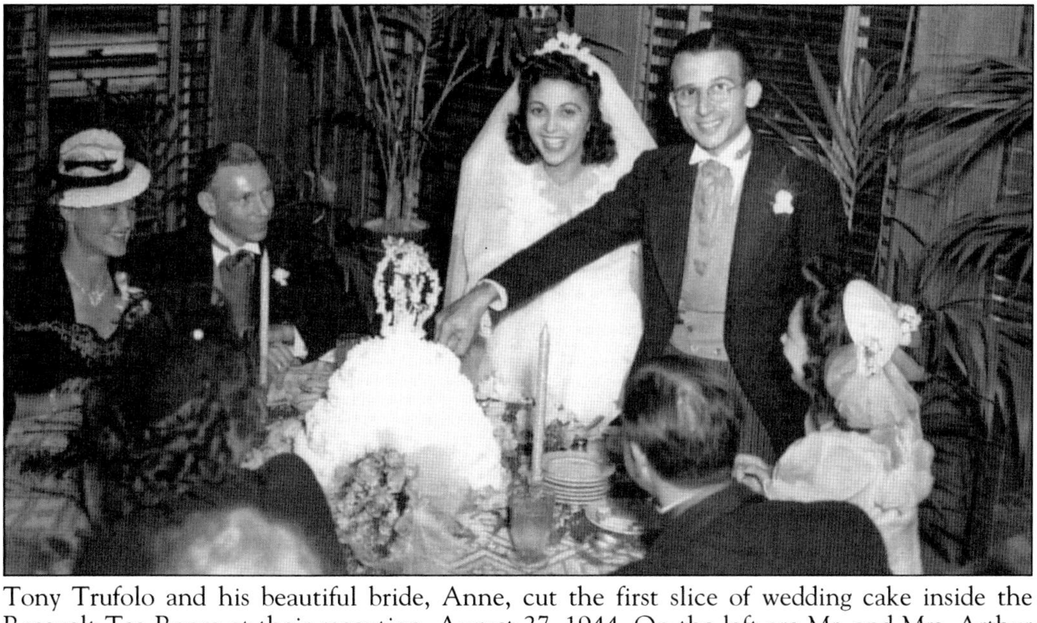

Tony Trufolo and his beautiful bride, Anne, cut the first slice of wedding cake inside the Rosevelt Tea Room at their reception, August 27, 1944. On the left are Mr. and Mrs. Arthur Freynick of Washington, D.C. (A.F. Trufolo.)

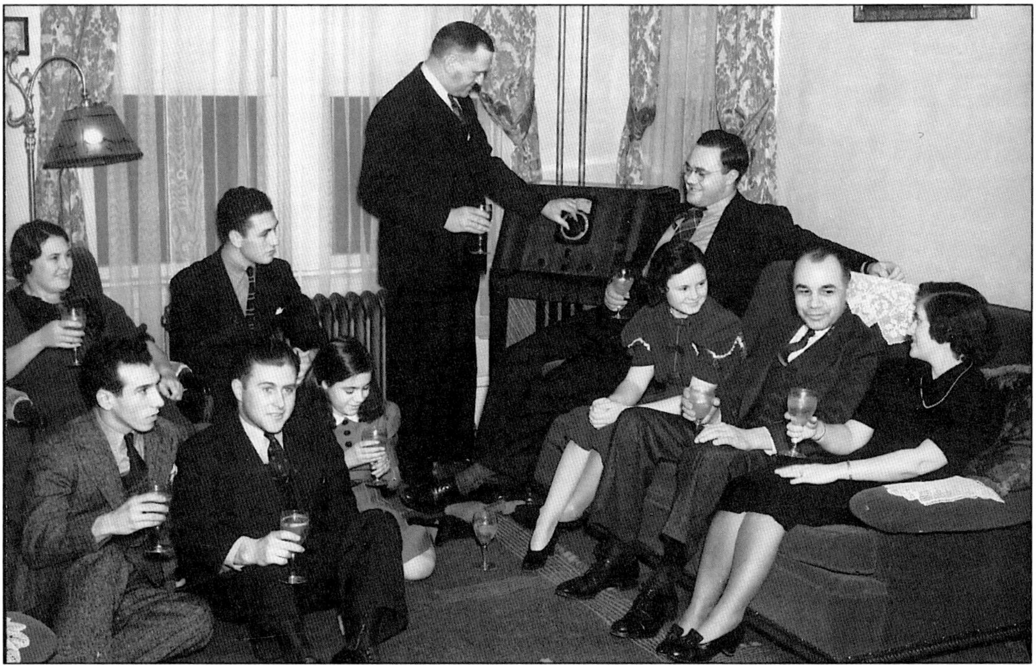

This photo of Little Silver residents appeared in a magazine ad for Bradley's Radio Service (Newman Springs Road, Red Bank) in 1938. The caption with the photograph reads as follows: "Top row: Mrs. W.F. Cogan, Edward Cogan, Mr. W.F. Cogan (turning Philco radio), W.F. Cogan, Jr., Bottom Row: Michael Cardner, Peter Lang, Sylvia Ohl, Marion Cogan, Russell Ohl, Mrs. Russell Ohl. The beginning of a New Year's party at Mr. Cogan's residence in Little Silver, finds a Philco radio in the role of assistant to the host." (M. Cogan.)

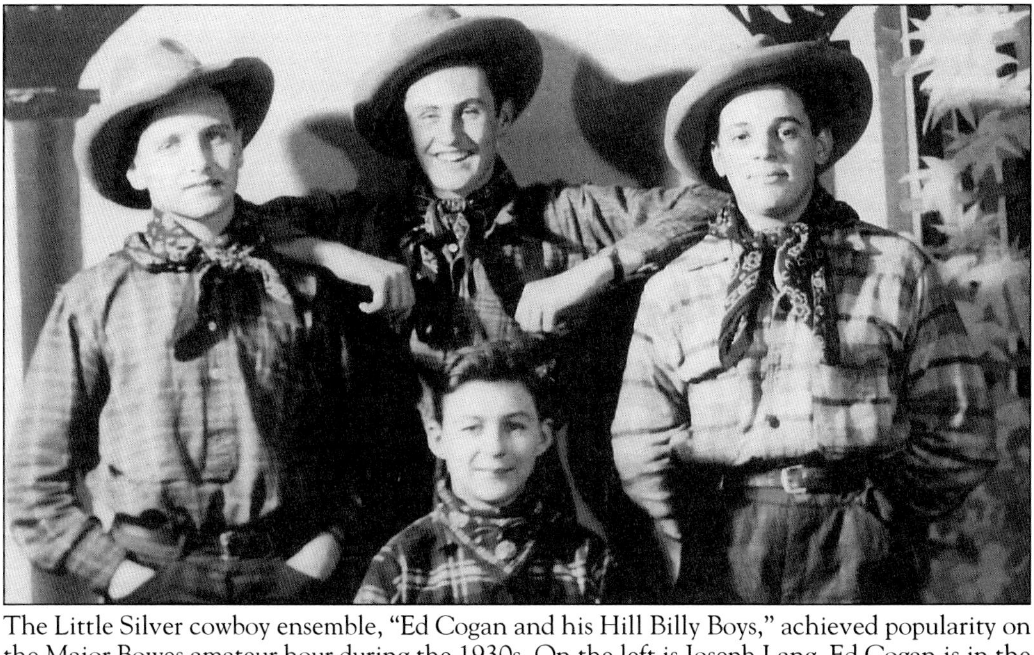

The Little Silver cowboy ensemble, "Ed Cogan and his Hill Billy Boys," achieved popularity on the Major Bowes amateur hour during the 1930s. On the left is Joseph Lang, Ed Cogan is in the middle, and Alfonso Tomaino is on the right. In front is Henry Burke. (M. Cogan.)

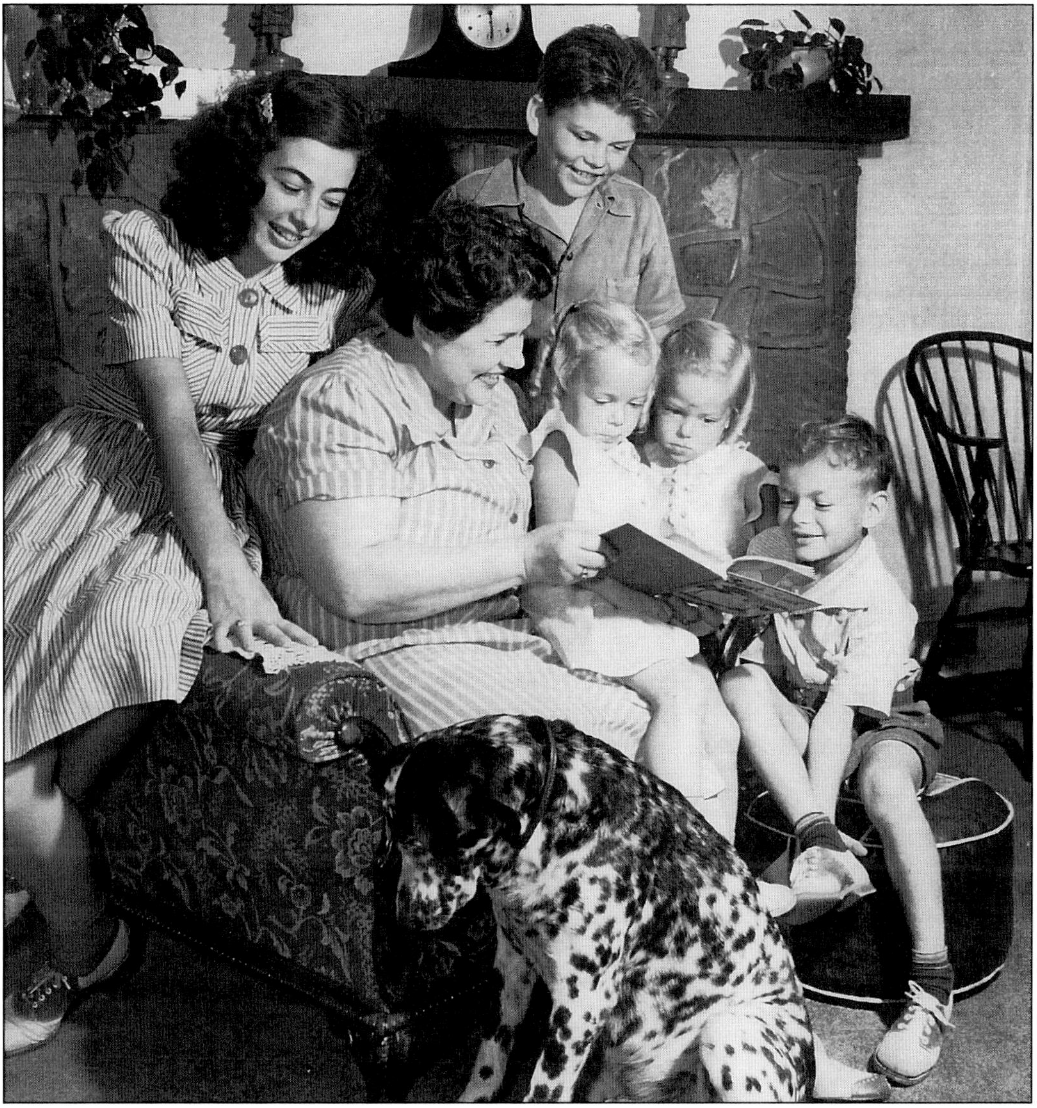

This 1943 portrait of family life shows Mrs. Edwin Burdge and her children in front of the fireplace at their 19 Orchard Place home. The photo appeared in a newspaper advertisement for "Super Suds," a product that produced "floods o'suds for dishes and duds." The caption for the photo included a quote from Mrs. Burdge: "You see I have a mighty big wash. Here's my brood. First comes Beverly, then Edwin, Mary Ann, Betty Jane, and Grover. Lots of clothes to wash . . . Lots to buy too. That's why I like new Super Suds. It's so mild . . . yet gets so much dirt out without rubbing, that clothes wear much better." The family Dalmation, unidentified in the ad, was "Buppy." Mary Ann (now Mary Jerolamon) and Betty Jane (now MacLeod) are twins (Beverly's name is now Lane). According to the ad, mother says that the twins, "just egg each other on getting' their clothes dirty. I wash about fourteen dresses a week for these two alone." The print ad also included important reminders not to waste soap due to the fact that materials used in soap making were needed for the war effort. It is also interesting to remember that in those pre-television days, there were movies and radio, but visual advertisements in print were particularly important to manufacturers. Advertisers liked to feature real life all-American families as subjects, and it was fun for the families! (M. Jerolamon.)

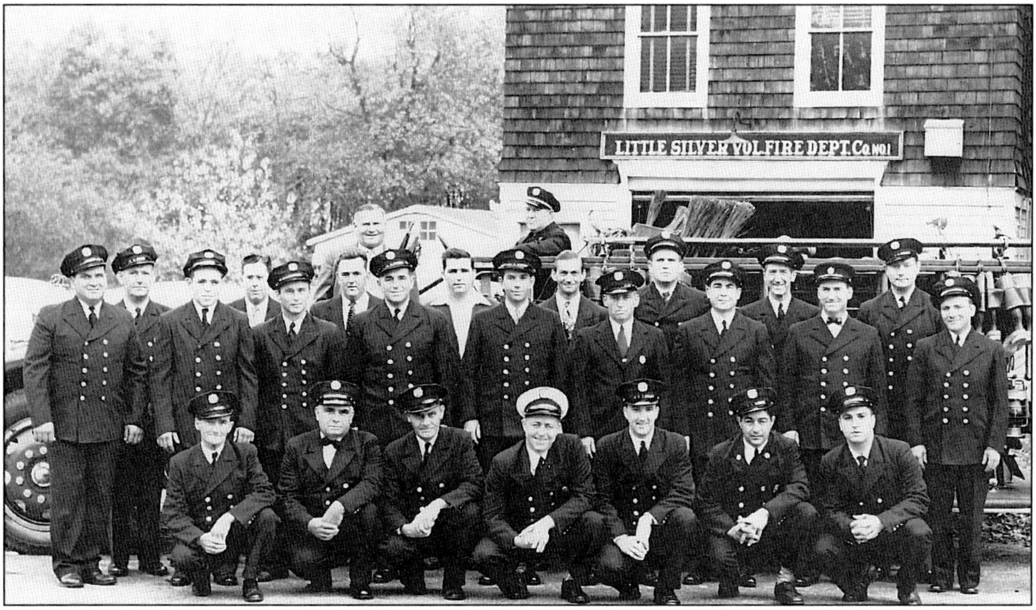

For a 1951 group portrait, the members of the Little Silver Volunteer Fire Company No. 1 stand proudly in front of the firehouse, which was still on Church Street at that time. (Courtesy of the Little Silver Fire Department.)

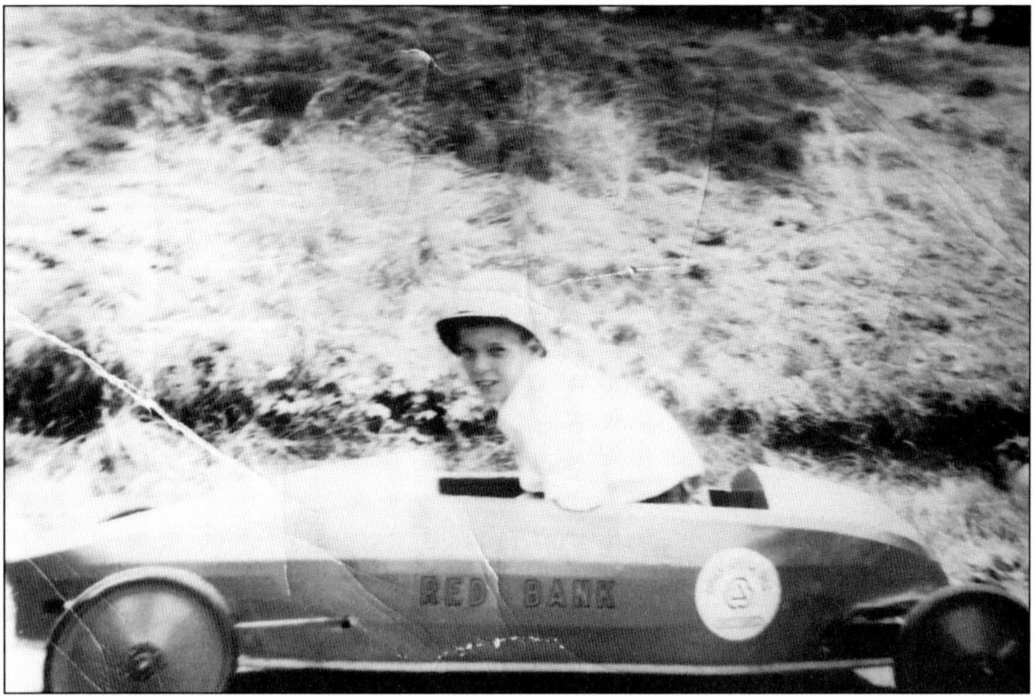

Tom Satter is ready to roll in the 1951 soap box derby, a popular event that was sponsored by local businesses. The entries would ride down Prospect Avenue in Little Silver, starting at Tower Hill, Red Bank. Storekeeper George Quackenbush built this car and it was sponsored by Globe Petroleum of Red Bank. Hopefully, young Tom didn't speed too fast as his grandfather was Police Chief Ziegler! (T. Satter.)

All dressed up in their Easter Sunday finery, *c.* 1955, best friends Nancy Liddell (right) of 8 Laurelwood Drive and Mary Christian of 24 Laurelwood Drive pause to admire a crocus. They are in front of 25 Laurelwood Drive, the home of Mr. and Mrs. Harry Killian that is now the home of the Munson family. (M. Christian.)

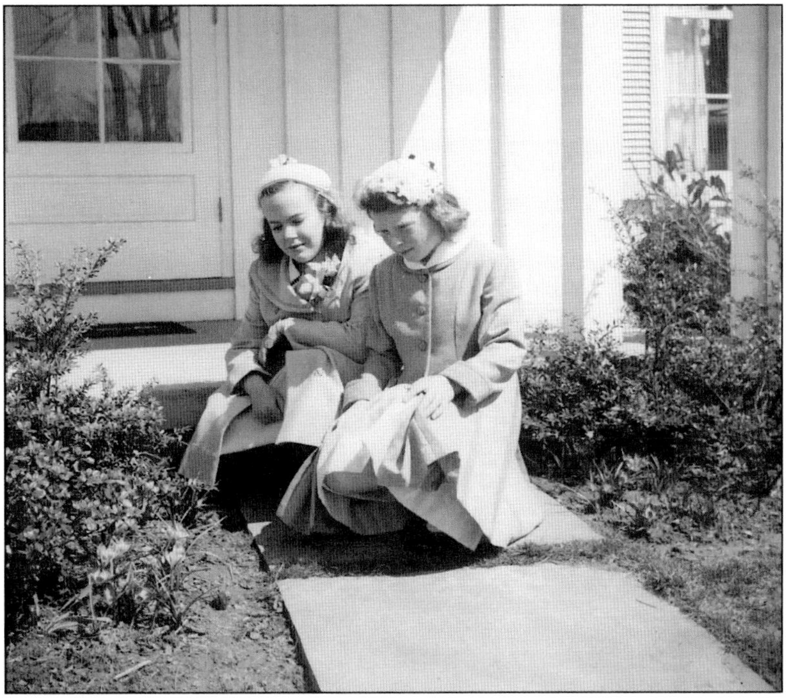

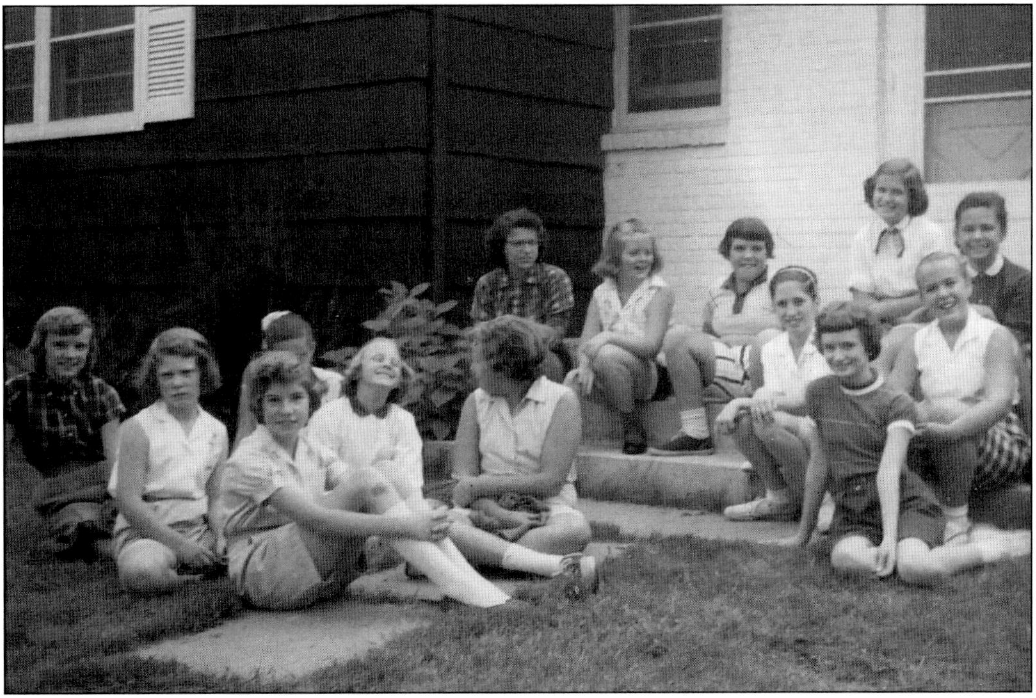

A happy bunch of Little Silver girls wearing Bermuda shorts pose in front of Mary Christian's house on Laurelwood Drive in 1956. The occasion was Mary's birthday party. From left to right are Carole Egliese, Nancy Liddell, Jackie Van Brunt, Carolyn Rush (obscured), Ginger Vander Voort, Elizabeth Howard, Charlotte Green, Betty Wright, Charlotte Doran, Lynn Nilson, Nancy Foeger, Mary Christian, and Nancy Waterman. (M. Christian.)

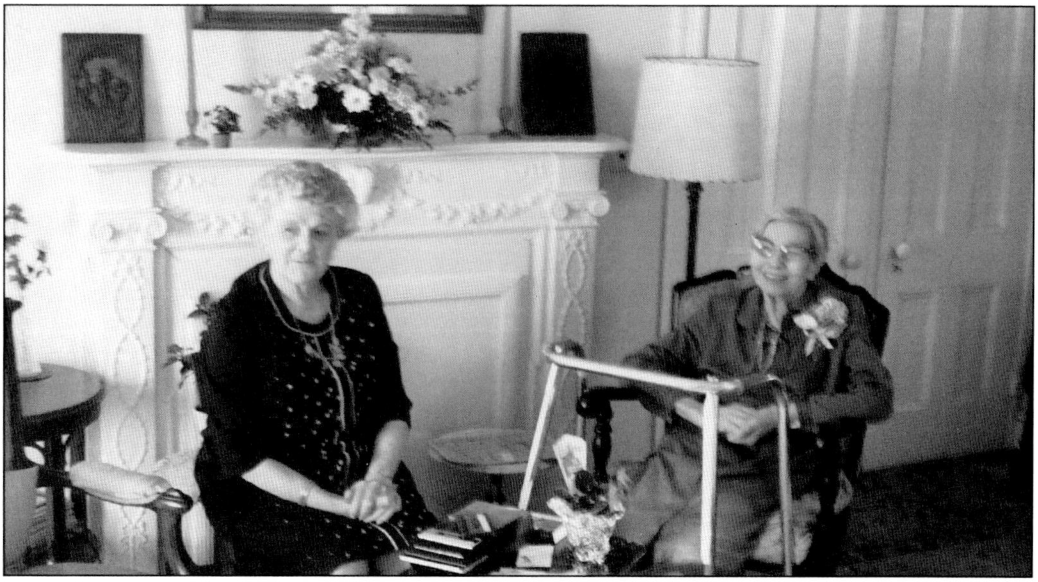

Leola Shampanore and Marie Wilby pose at the Wilby house on Rumson Road on the occasion of Miss Wilby's 94th birthday in 1982. Miss Wilby taught in the Rumson School system. Mrs. Shampanore, whose family operated the local printing business (see p. 61, *Little Silver, Vol. I*) celebrated her 100th birthday in 1995 and was honored with a proclamation from the Borough. Both ladies are now deceased. This photo was loaned by Mrs. Shampanore's daughter, Doris Shampanore Marcelli Ayers.

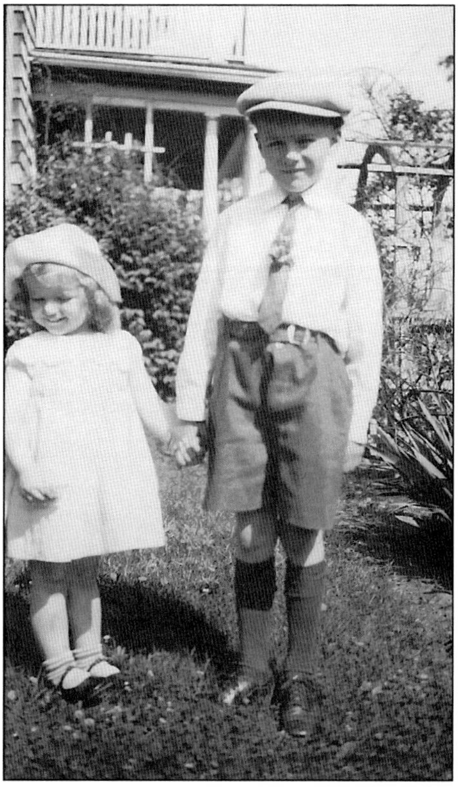

Cute as can be, this brother and sister duo are little Doris Shampanore (Doris Shampanore Marcelli Ayers) and her brother, William Harrison Shampanore Jr., known as "Bud." The photo was taken in 1935 outside the house they lived in at 50 Willow Drive. (D. Ayers.)

This adorable little girl is Janet Giersch of Little Silver in the early 1950s. The proof is from the Rue Photography Studio, a business that was located to the rear of the house at 35 Silverton Avenue. (J. Giersch.)

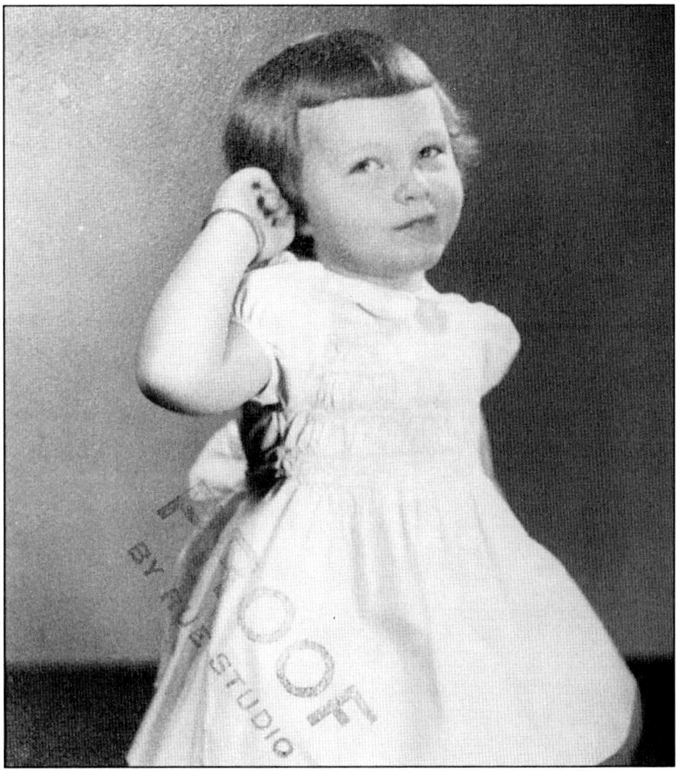

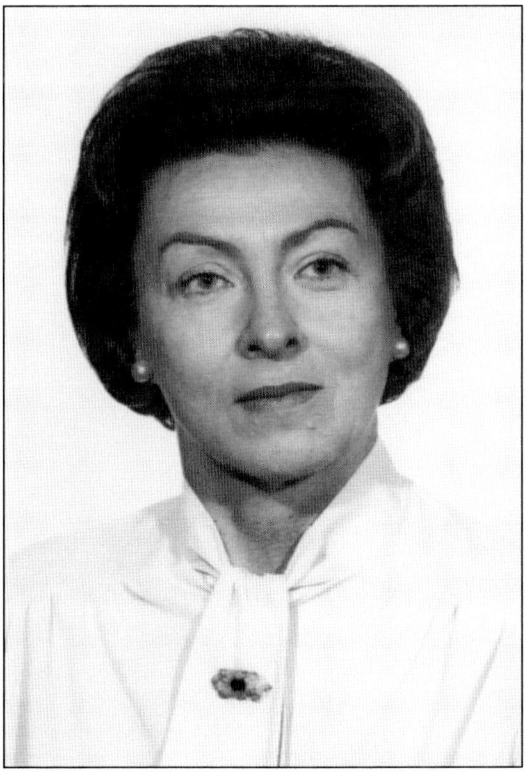

In 1976, Virginia Harrison Giersch was elected tax collector with bipartisan support and became the first woman to hold office in Little Silver. Previously, she worked on the campaign staff of 1961 New Jersey gubernatorial hopeful James Mitchell (a secretary of labor in the Eisenhower years who had a home in Little Silver). Her daughter Janet says: "Perhaps her greatest accomplishment was choosing to be a career woman in the 1960s while successfully balancing her roles of wife and mother." (J. Giersch.)

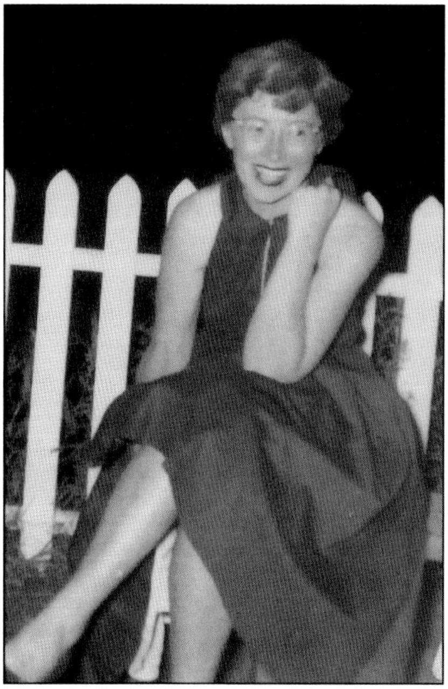

In the early 1950s, Marciadene Santelle sits by a picket fence at her home on Riverside Avenue. If only this photo were in printed in color, you could see her gorgeous red hair! This photo is one of the favorites of her husband, Dominick.

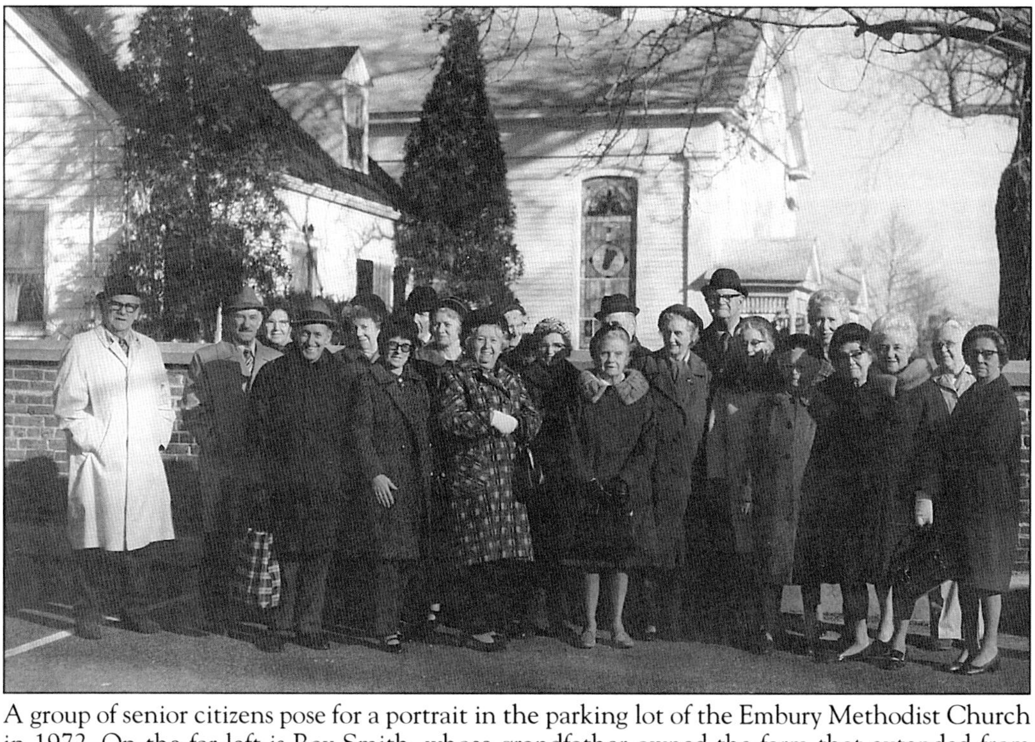

A group of senior citizens pose for a portrait in the parking lot of the Embury Methodist Church in 1972. On the far left is Ray Smith, whose grandfather owned the farm that extended from Prospect to Branch Avenue and from Tower Hill to Rumson Road. (D. Santelle.)

Mr. Stanley McIntosh, a well-known landscape architect and an expert bagpiper, is seen here at a Red Bank parade in the early 1970s. Mr. McIntosh lived on Silverton Avenue for many years and his music could be heard for blocks, much to the delight of his neighbors, who appreciated this talented and kind man. (Photo by Leon Schnitzspahn.)

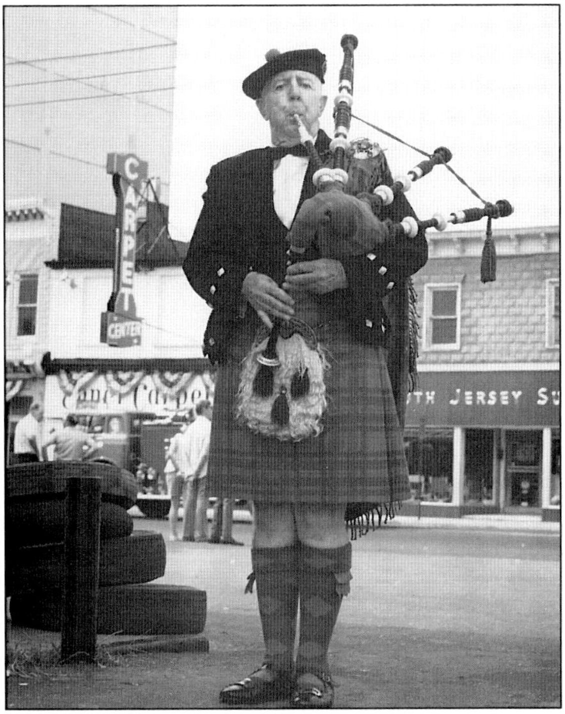

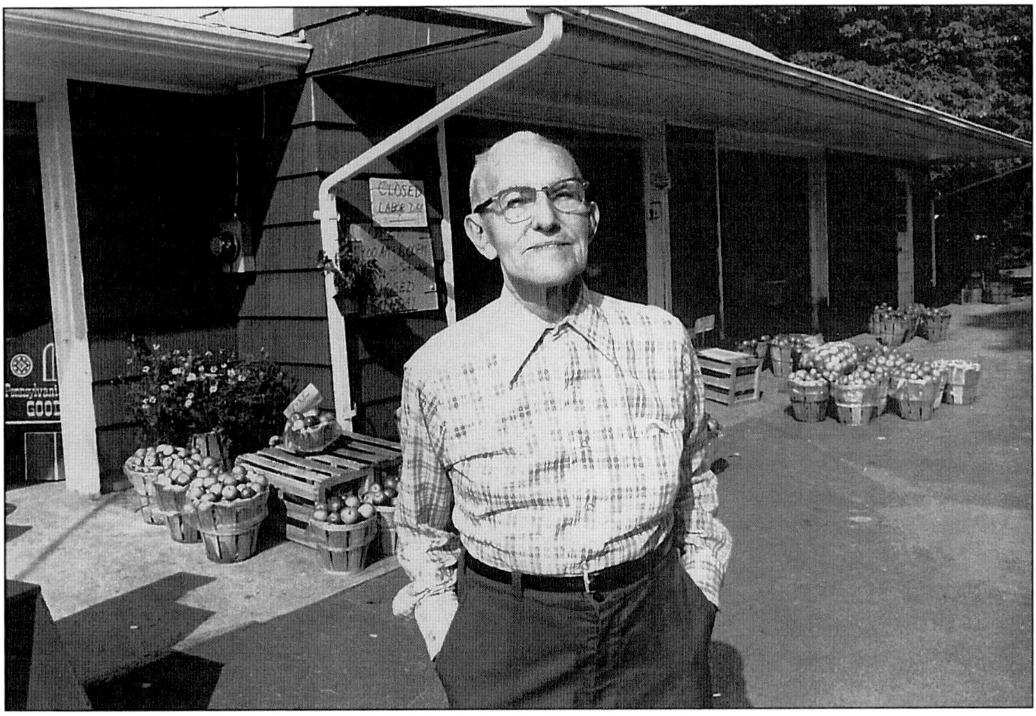

On September 10, 1974, on the occasion of his 90th birthday, Mr. Sickles posed for this photo in front of the Sickles's farm market. Most of the land that was the farm is now a park and houses. However, the popular store—greatly expanded— is still operated by the Sickles family, and offers a wide variety of fruits, vegetables, flowers, plants, and gourmet items.

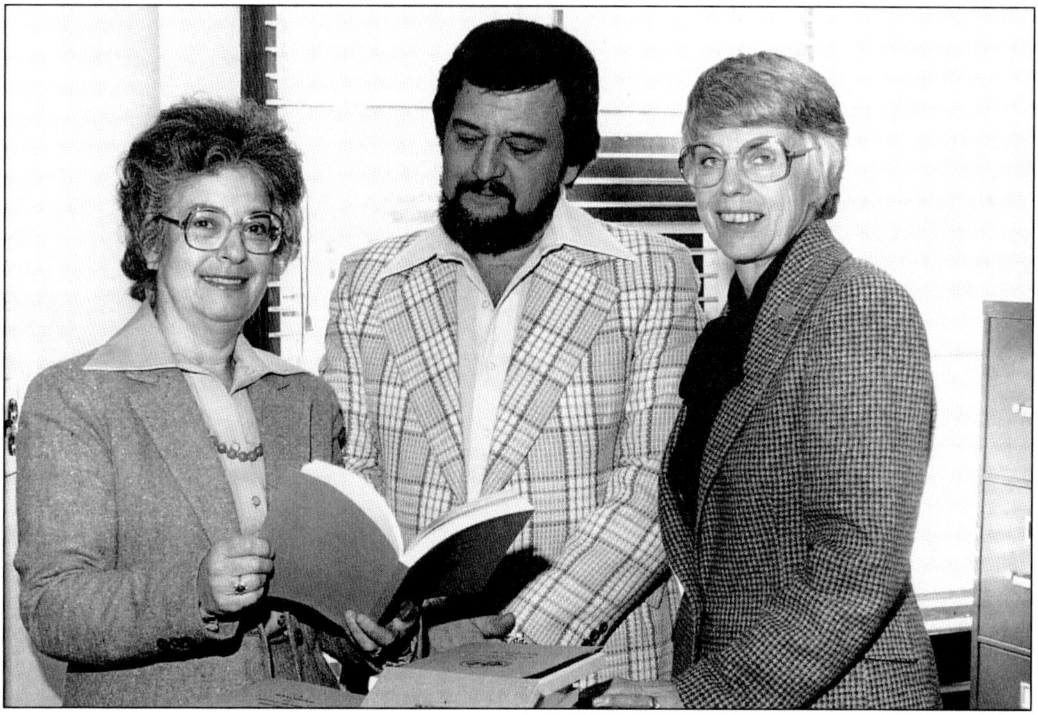

June O. Kennedy (left), Lou Ferrara of Loumel Press, and Barbara Finch take a look at the revised edition of *A Sketchbook of Little Silver History* by Mrs. Kennedy when it was released in 1980. The well-researched book is still available and provides a comprehensive look at the town's history. It was first published in 1973 in conjunction with the 50th anniversary of the borough. (J.O. Kennedy.)

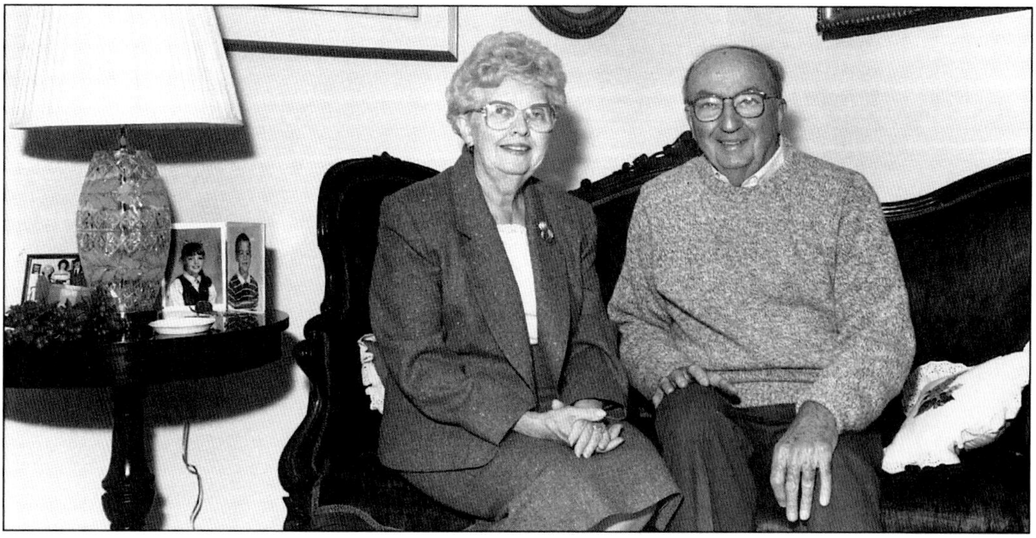

Mr. and Mrs. Henry Pope (pictured here in a *Two River Times* photo from March 13, 1991) have done so much for Little Silver over the years that it is impossible to fit all their accomplishments into one little caption! Henry and Elaine (Inman) have been area residents since 1936 and both attended Red Bank High School. Mr. Pope served six years on the board of education and 12 years as a borough councilman.

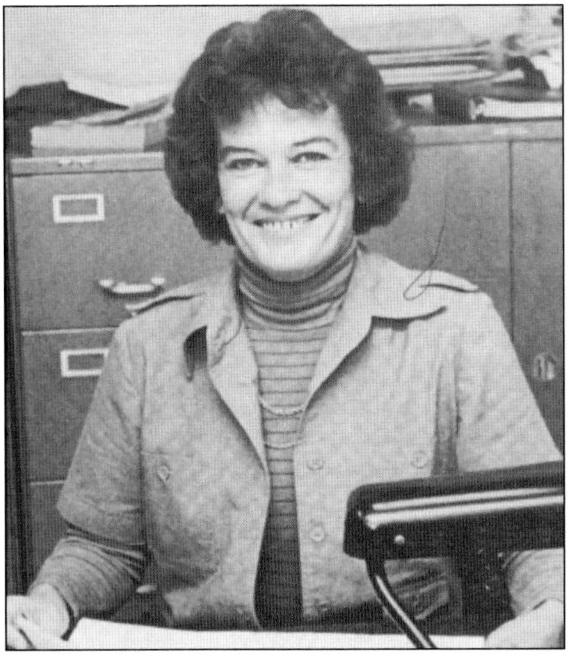

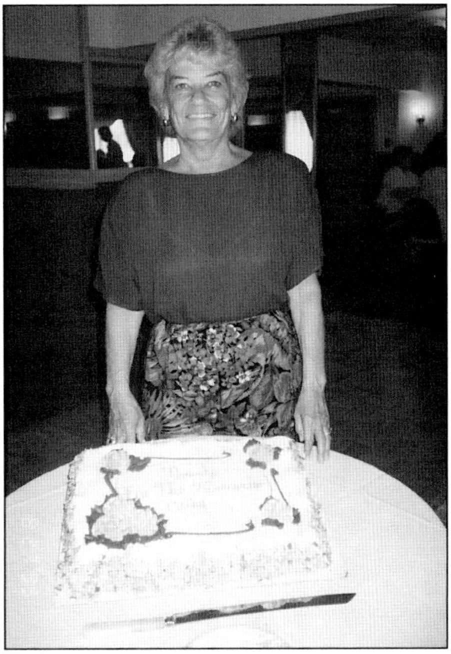

Left: Catharine C. Wright, a resident of Little Silver since 1957, was employed by the Borough in various capacities since 1959 and served as tax collector. Besides her many accomplishments and dedication to public service, Cathy's sense of humor and style are greatly appreciated by all. *Right:* Cathy Wright prepares to cut the cake for her retirement party in 1995.

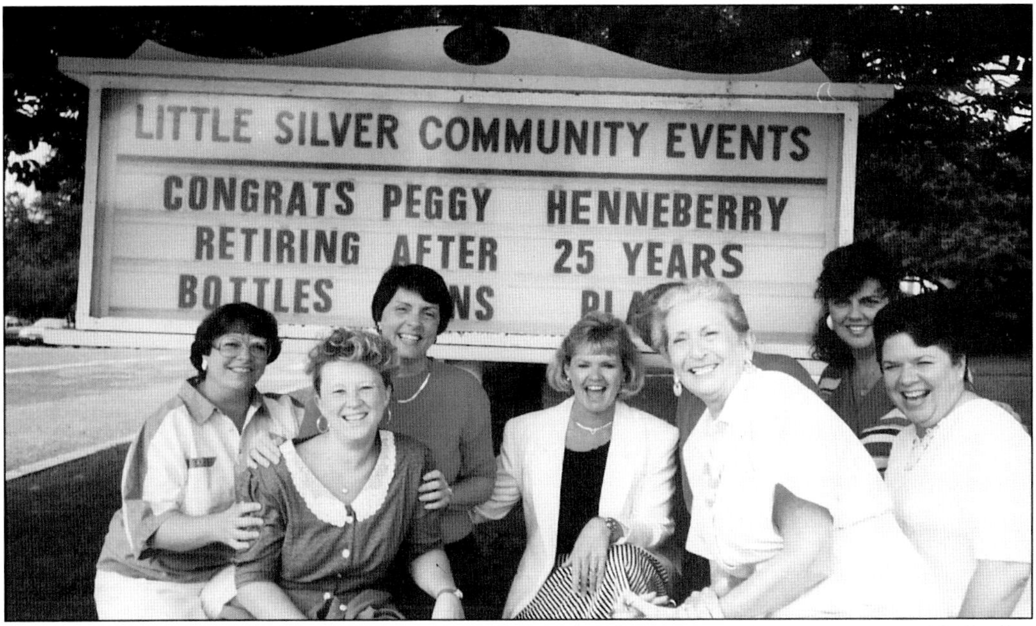

On the occasion of Peggy Henneberry, asst. borough administrator's retirement in 1993, this photo was taken with her co-workers outside Borough Hall. Peggy jokes about how she seems to be ready to be recycled according to the sign! Identifiable from left to right are Helen Gormley, Diane Ramsey, Amy Hirsch, Vicki Hennelly, Peggy Henneberry, Lynn Gale, and Barbara Procino. (M. Henneberry.)

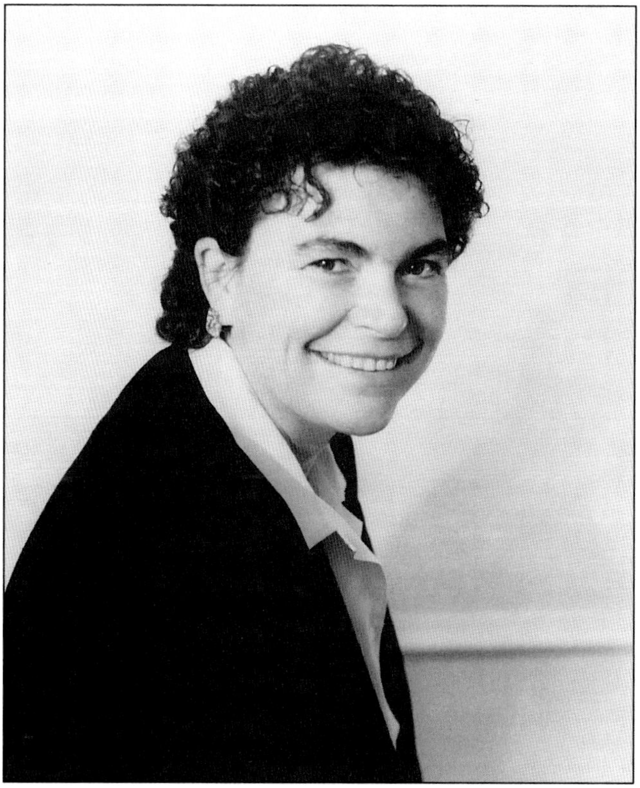

Susan M. Love, M.D., renowned surgeon and author of informative bestsellers *Dr. Susan Love's Breast Book* and *Dr. Susan Love's Hormone Book*, grew up in Little Silver. Dr. Love now lives in California but lectures extensively around the country. She appeared at Monmouth University as the first speaker on May 6, 1997, in a series sponsored by the Women's Council for the Cancer Center at Monmouth that raises funds for the Jacqueline M. Wilentz Comprehensive Breast Center.

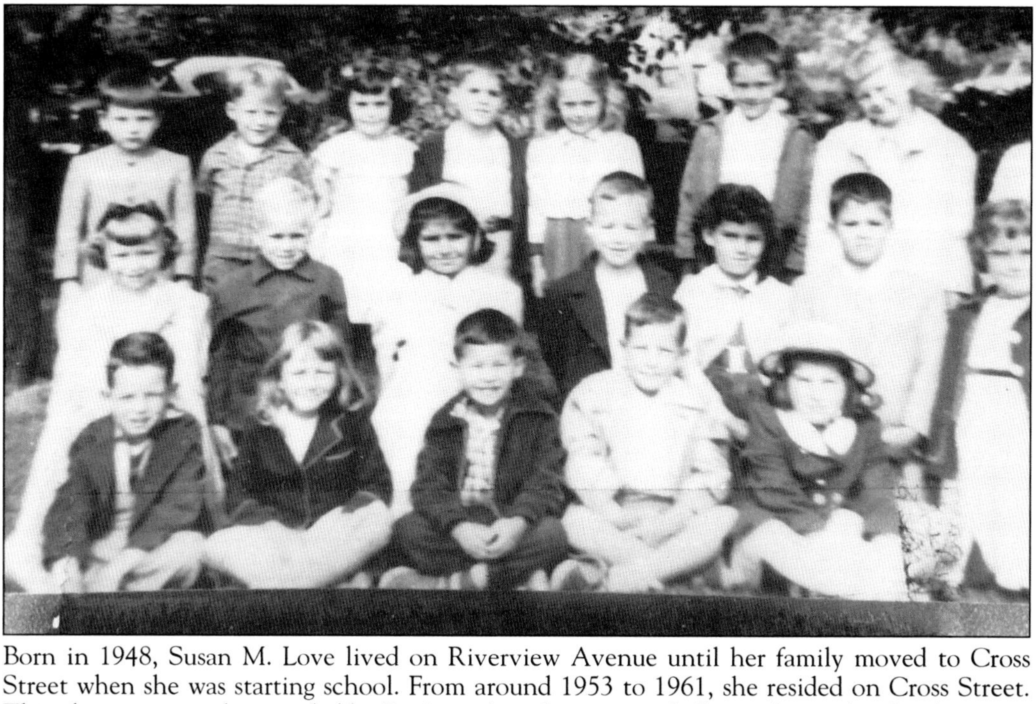

Born in 1948, Susan M. Love lived on Riverview Avenue until her family moved to Cross Street when she was starting school. From around 1953 to 1961, she resided on Cross Street. This photo, graciously provided by Dr. Love from her personal album, depicts her kindergarten or first-grade class at Markham Place School. She is third from the left in the top row.

Six

School, Sports, and Recreation

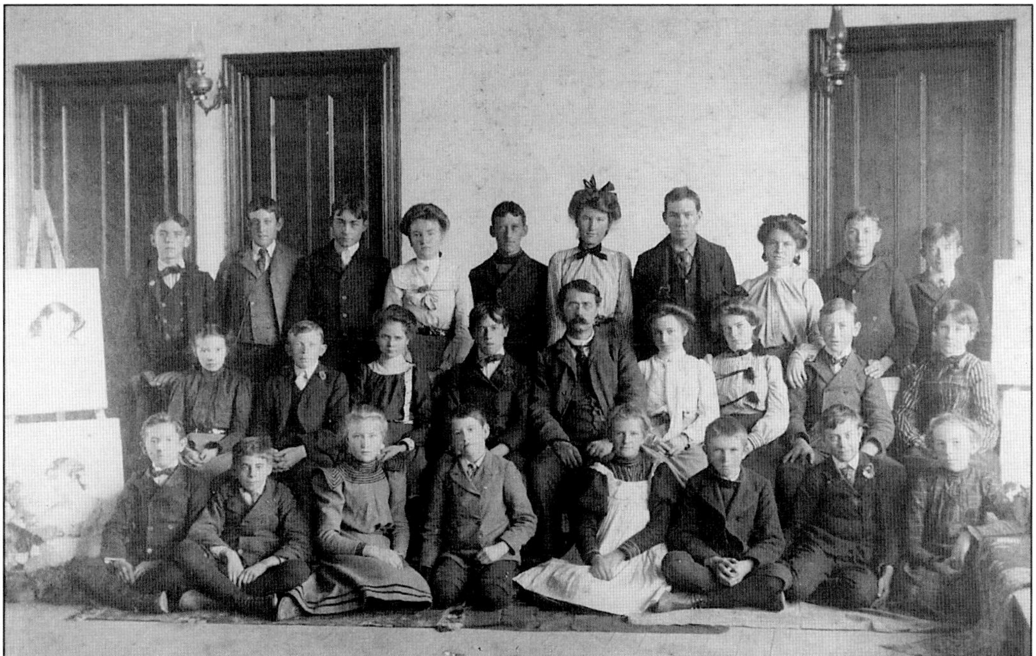

The students in this Little Silver grammar school photo, *c.* 1901, are flanked on either side by drawings on easels which might show that this was an art class or art appreciation class. The teacher sitting in the center is Professor Robinson. The school was located on Prospect Avenue in the building that would become the Borough Hall when Markham Place School opened in 1934. (Little Silver Historical Society.)

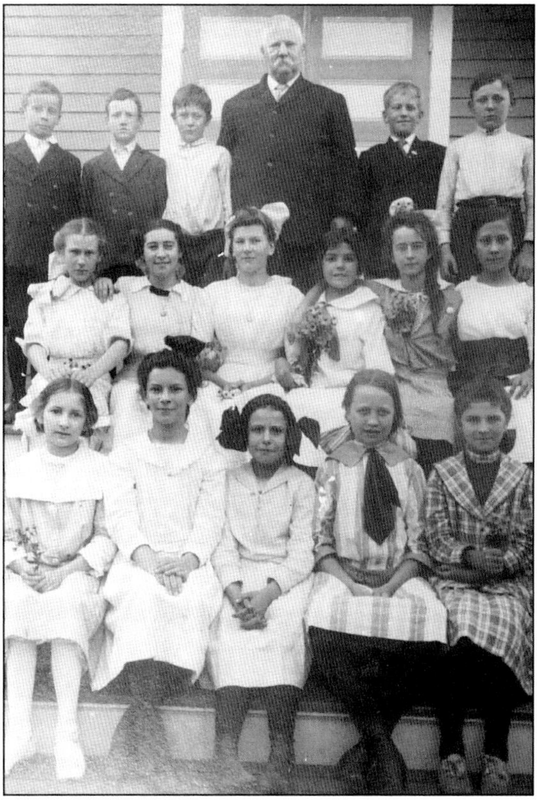

A Little Silver grammar school photo from 1912 shows the girls wearing the stylish hair bows of the era. Anna Elgrim is seated in the front row, far right, wearing a pretty plaid dress. The teacher is Mr. Shaw. (G. Kingston.)

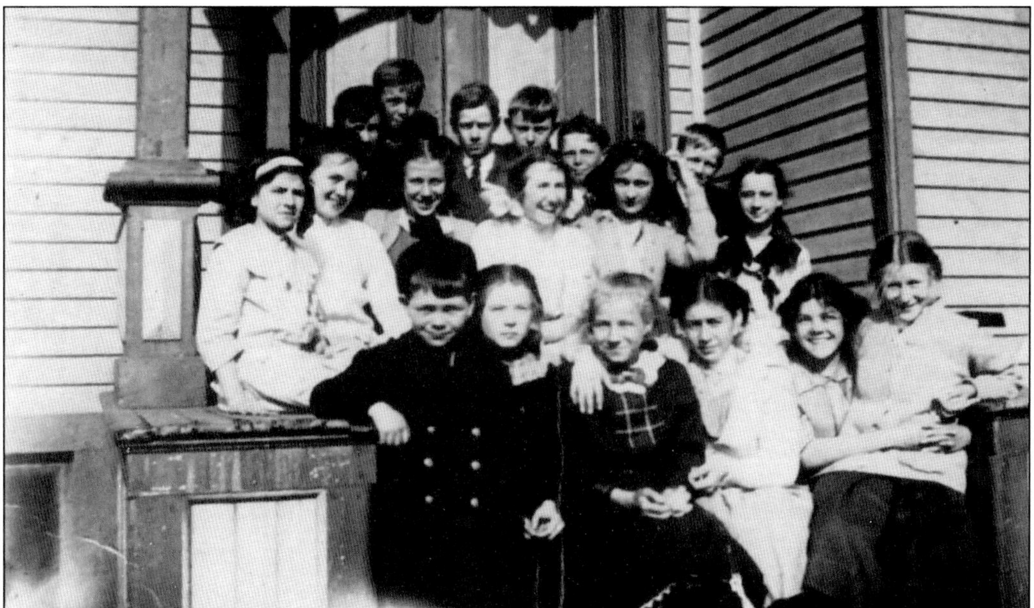

The eighth-grade class of 1913 appears to be a happy group as they strike carefree poses for this class picture. (G. Kingston.)

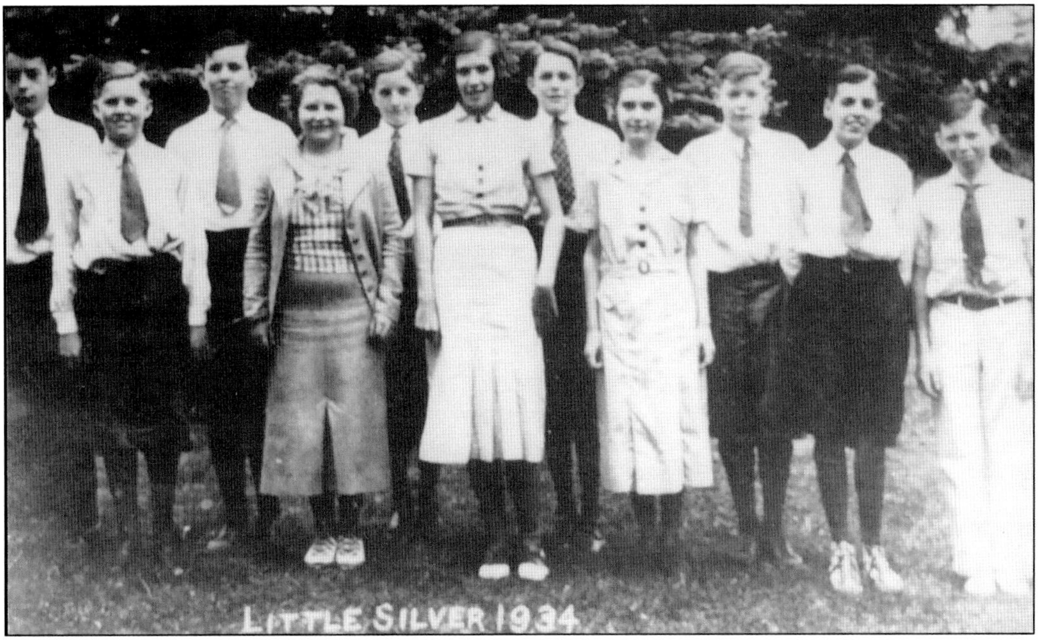

The last eighth-grade class to graduate from the old Prospect Avenue School before Markham Place School opened was the Class of 1934. From left to right are Lloyd McNally, Thomas Foster, Clark Kemp, Martha Ann Ruddy, Lester Truax, Marjorie MacConnell, George Shoemaker, Lillian Golden, Lawrence Seibert, Howard Alexander, and William Haviland. (H. Pope.)

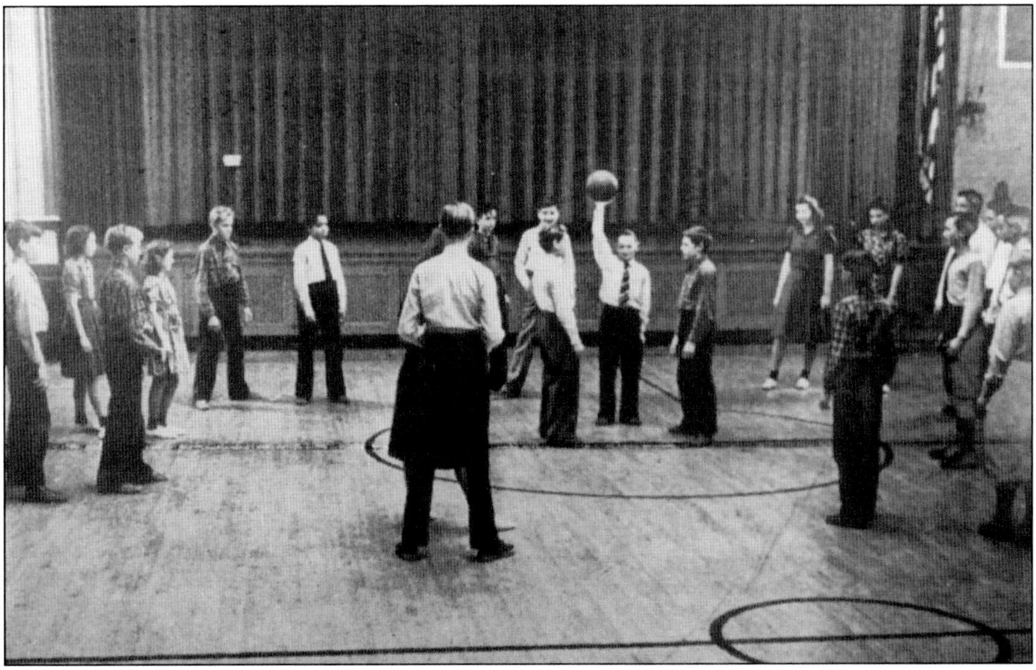

This photo of a gym class at Markham Place School appeared in a *Monmouth Pictorial* in the late 1930s. The eighth-grade students are playing "Captain Ball." One half hour a day was allotted for "health education." (R.A. Schoeffling.)

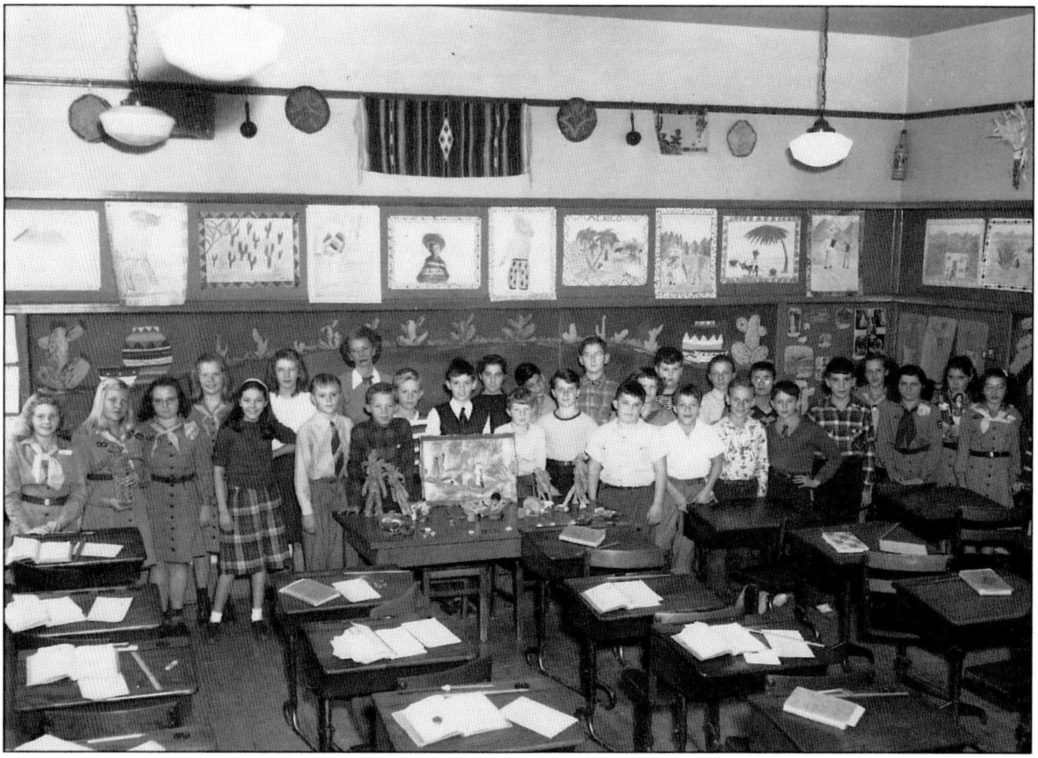

A classroom photo taken at Markham Place School in November 1947 clearly shows the student's projects about Mexico. There are several Brownie scouts wearing their uniforms in this image. (Dorn's.)

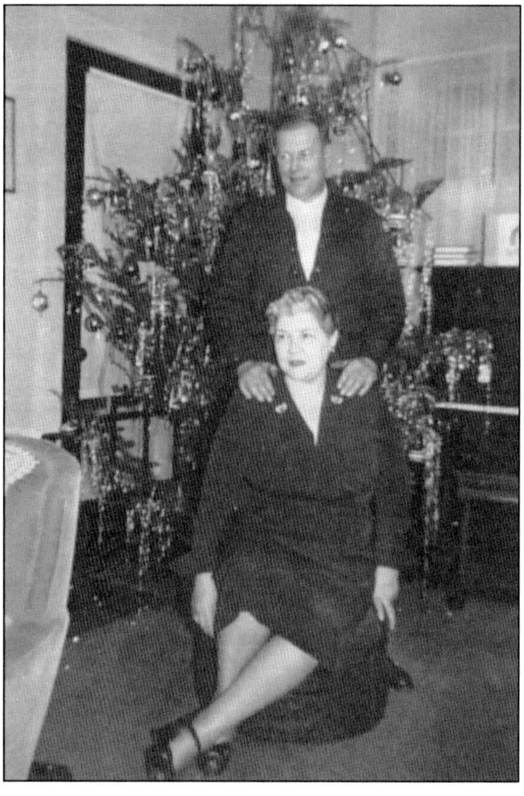

Frances and Ed Burdge pose for a holiday portrait at their home, 19 Orchard Place, in 1952. Mrs. Burdge, the daughter of Mr. and Mrs. James Lane (see p. 79), was a teacher and mother who served as secretary and president of the Little Silver P.T.A., president of the Monmouth County PTA, and vice-president of the New Jersey Congress of PTA's. Mr. Burdge owned and operated Burdge's Garage on Branch Avenue. (M. Jerolomon.)

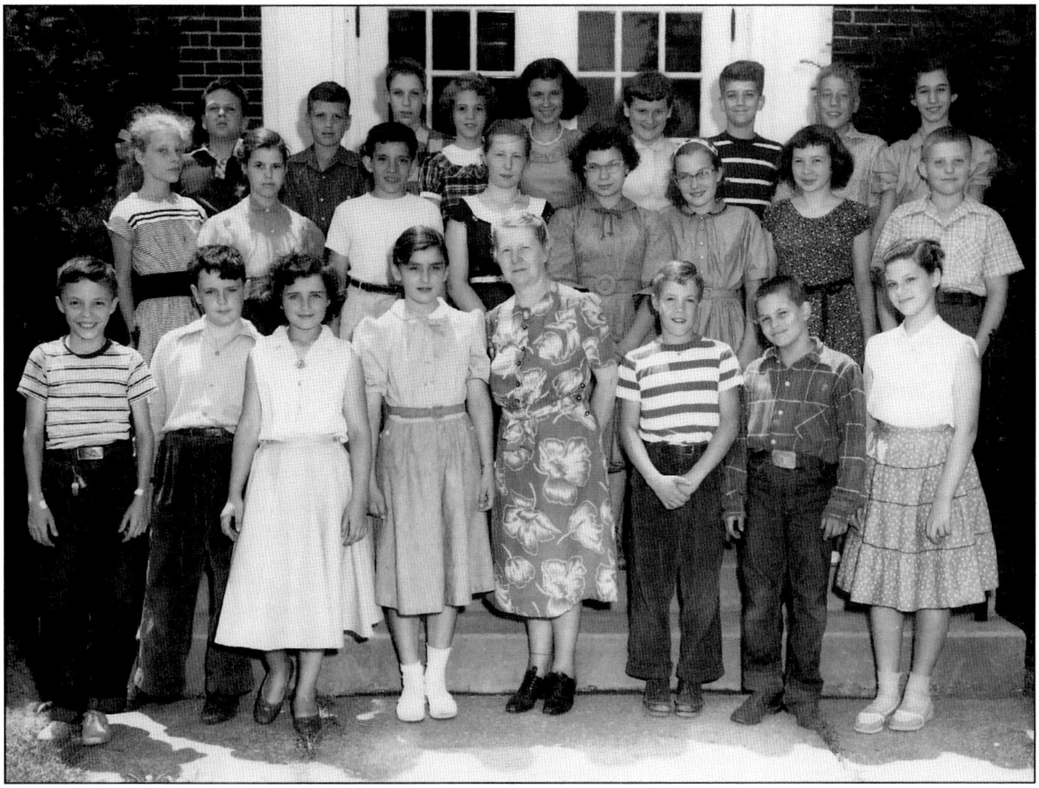

Miss Agnes Hackett, who started teaching in the Little Silver School in 1913, stands proudly with her sixth-grade class in June 1953. The well-liked Miss Hackett, who had great concern for the welfare of children, taught every grade in the school and served at one time as principal. She advocated the idea of a regional high school long before the present one became a reality, and she opposed compulsory retirement for teachers. (Dorn's.)

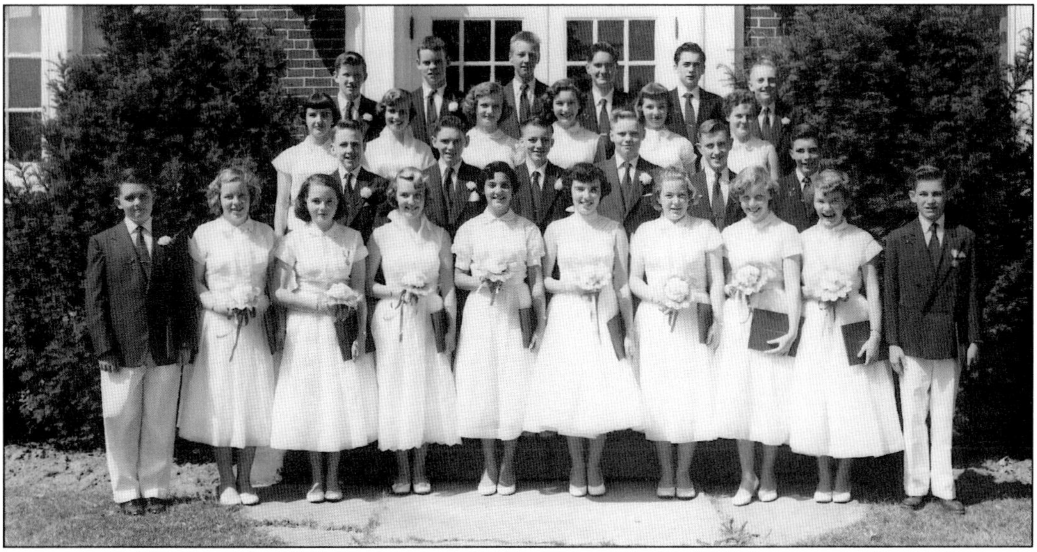

The Markham Place graduating Class of 1953 stands proudly holding their eighth-grade diplomas in hand. Notice how the girls all hold nosegays and the boys wear boutonnieres. (Dorn's.)

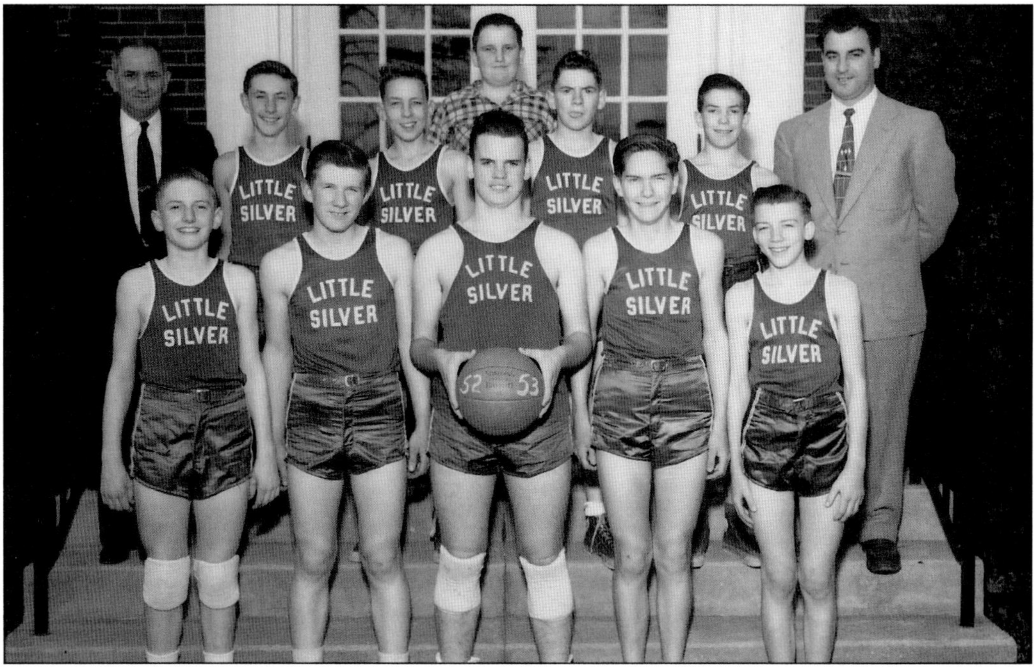

The 1952–53 school basketball team poses proudly on the steps of the Markham Place School with Bradley Dupree holding the ball. On the left is Mr. Thompson, who was principal and later superintendent. (Dorn's.)

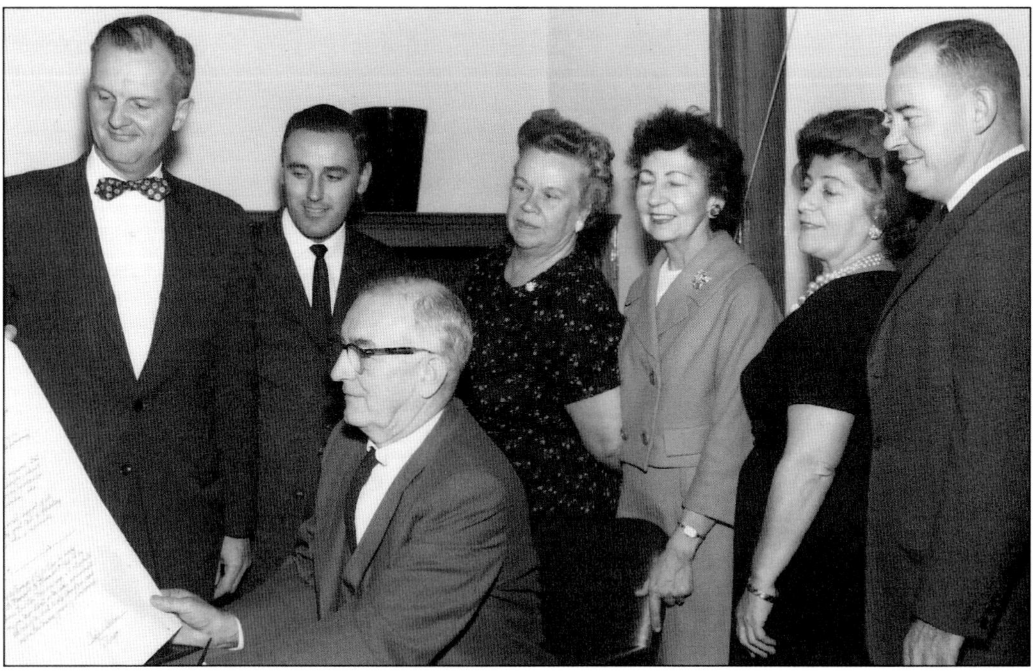

In 1962, Little Silver Mayor Stephens (seated) and the school staff admire an educational proclamation at the Markham Place School. Standing, from left to right, are Mr. Vanderhoff (superintendent), Mr. Doug Horan (principal), unidentified, Mrs. Kosky (teacher), Mrs. Joyce(teacher), and unidentified. (Dorn's.)

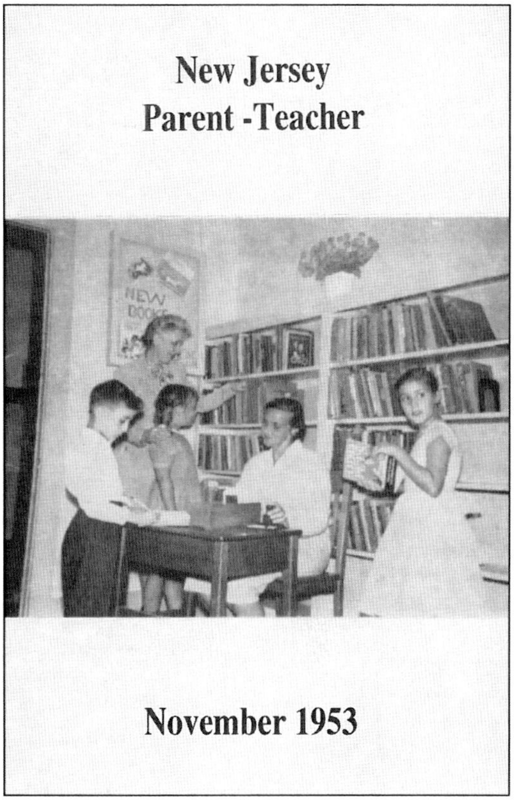

New Jersey
Parent -Teacher

November 1953

The November 1953 issue of *New Jersey Parent-Teacher* featured a Little Silver photo on the cover and an article about how the PTA organized a centralized library in the school system. On the right is John Maimone, Mary Christian is looking at the books with an unidentified woman, and Kate McLean is on the right. Sitting at the desk is Barbara Wynkoop. (M. Christian.)

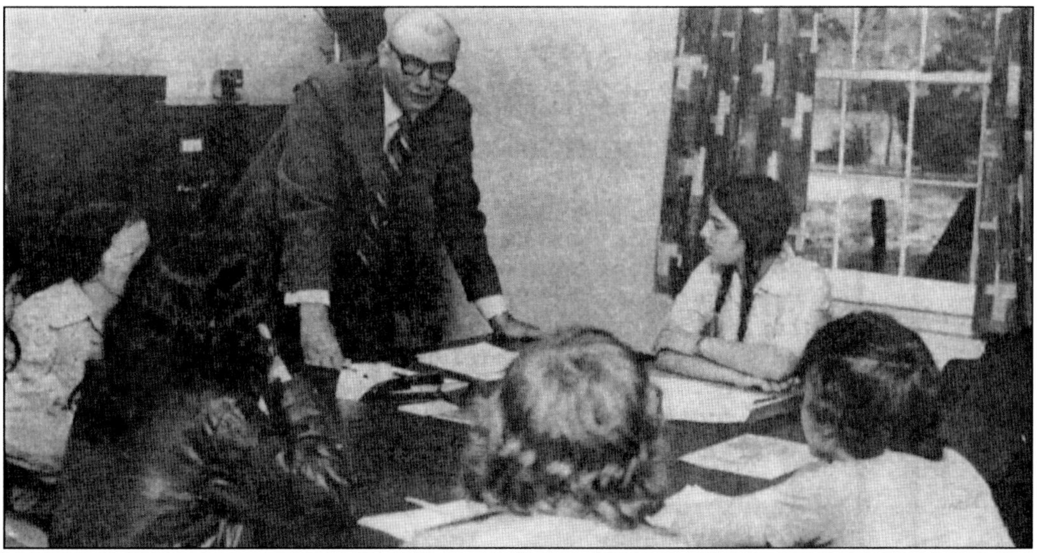

On Student Government Day in 1973, Mayor Charles F. Rell is pictured addressing an attentive eighth-grade class at Borough Hall. (From *The Little Silver Newsletter*, May 1973; June O. Kennedy was the editor at that time and provided this photo.)

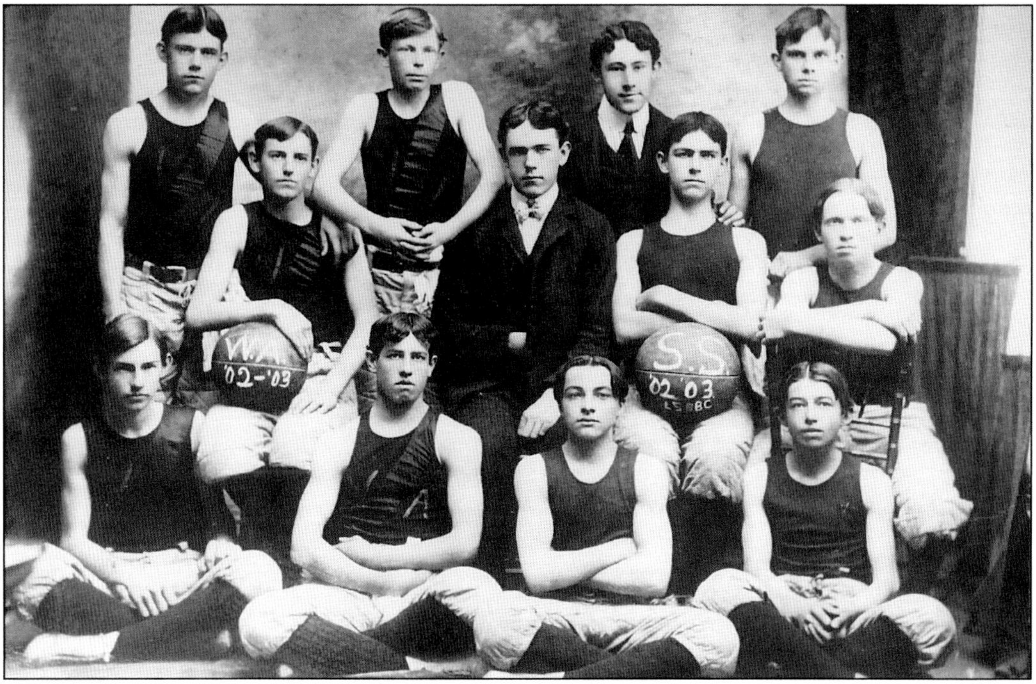

The 1902–03 "Wide Awakes" basketball team look somber for their portrait. The Shooting Stars (note the S.S. on the basketball), from left to right, are as follows: (front row) Hal Parker, Clark Kemp, Wesley Lane, and ? Lane; (middle row) Ken Parker, Fitzmaurice, George White, and unidentified; (back row) Clark Fitzsimmons, Fred Moore, Tommy Fitzmaurice, and Scott Conover. (Borough of Little Silver.)

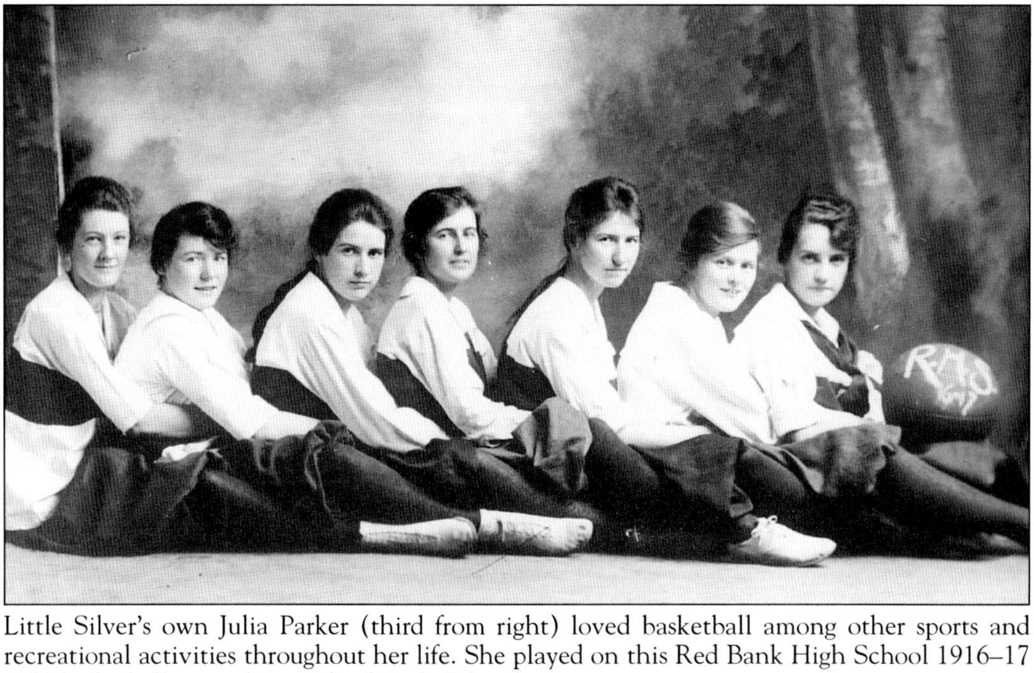

Little Silver's own Julia Parker (third from right) loved basketball among other sports and recreational activities throughout her life. She played on this Red Bank High School 1916–17 girls' basketball team. (Borough of Little Silver.)

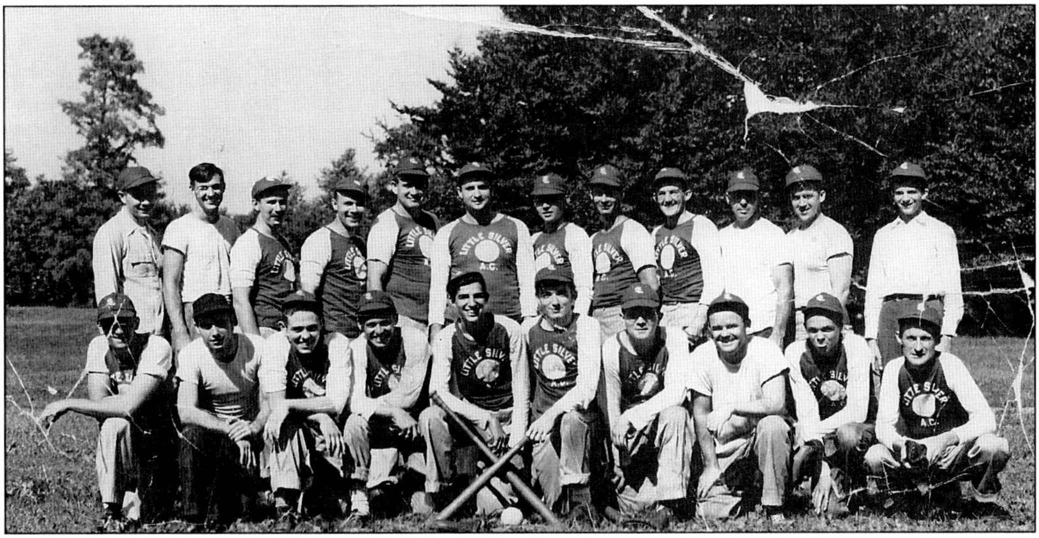

In 1948, members of the Little Silver Athletic Club softball team got together for this group portrait. From left to right they are as follows: (front row) J. Bocceloto, V. Soverio, Bob Stout, A. Conklin, J. Bacigalupi, B. Burns, F. Bruno, P. Patterson, Karl Bergman, and "Skinny" Robson; (back row) John Robson, Joe Kellenyi, Don Wright, H. Greenwood, A. Pound, J. Soverio, R. Tetley, H. Young, K. White, L. Van Brunt, R.C. O'Connor, and L. Bacigalupi. (R. Tetley.)

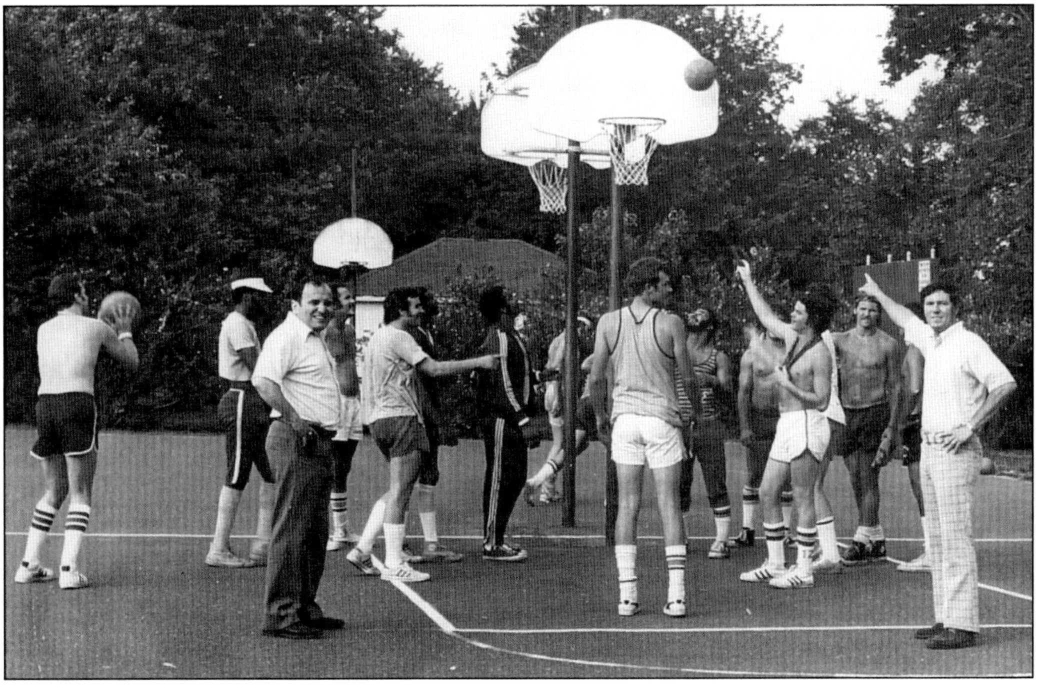

In 1975, Dan Dorn Jr. (right), who was president of the Community Appeal, points to the new basketball hoops as Anthony Bruno (who has served in Little Silver as a councilman, mayor twice, and borough attorney) looks on. The Community Appeal of 1974 paid for the paved basketball courts on Rumson Road. Some of the players in this photo are Sackowitz (shooting), Jim Tetley, Steve Hill, the Allgood brothers, and Paul Rich. (D. Santelle.)

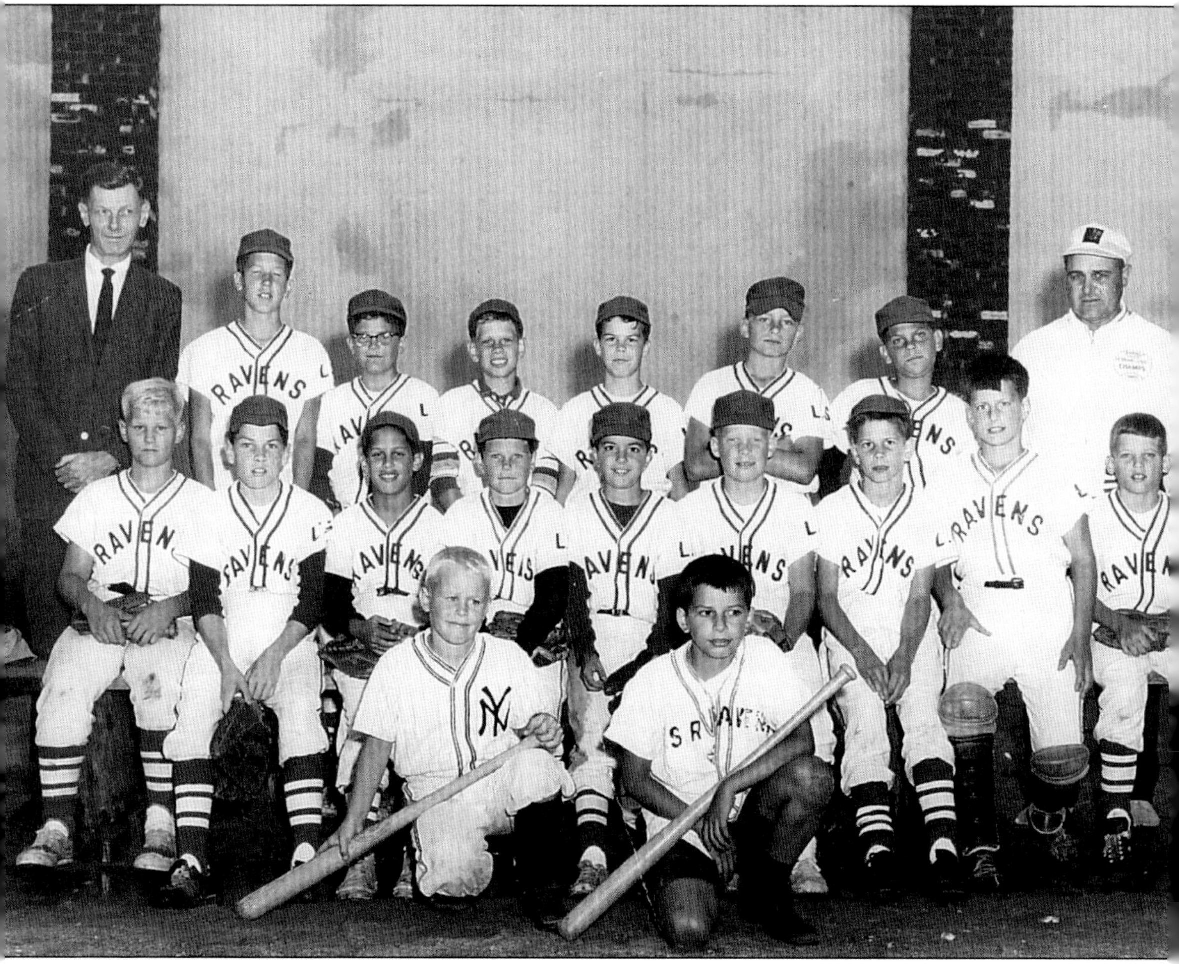

The Little Silver Ravens were the undisputed 1964 Seaboard champs and made local baseball history. They were managed by Dom Santelle (far right in the back row) and assisted by Warren Van der Voort (in the suit and tie on the right). Members of the impressive team, from left to right, are as follows: (front) bat boys Stewart Deans and Ron Tomaino; (first row, seated) Bob Hewitt, pitcher-left fielder; Keith Vander Voort, right fielder; Terry Mond, third base-pitcher; Bobby Frick, left field; Rich Ciambrone, utility outfielder; John Van Kirk, third-base-pitcher; Bill Fleming, centerfielder (who executed a triple-play!); Earl Twigg, catcher; and Dave Kelly, second base; (back row, standing) Jamie Deans, ace pitcher who went 10-0 that year; Jim Connolly, pitcher-catcher; Steve Maginn, second base-catcher; Tim Betz, left fielder; Jim Golson, third base pitcher; and Ken Bodeep, shortstop-third base. Twenty-five years later, this outstanding team's portrait was published as a "Vintage Snapshot" and the '64 Ravens were honored in sports editor Rich Nicoletti's *Daily Register* column on August 9, 1989. Nicoletti wrote in praise of manager Dom Santelle: ". . . he led many Little Silver kids in a healthy direction to higher levels in sports. He has always done that, whether it has been on his tennis court at his home on Riverview Avenue, or on some baseball diamond. In 1964, the Little Silver Ravens, directed by Santelle and his assistant Warren Van der Voort, were the scourge of the Seaboard 9-12 Baseball League. The team finished the season at 21-3. Santelle didn't just inherit a bunch of outstanding players—he developed them." Dom Santelle is to be commended, then and now, as he has devoted so very much of his time and his talent to promoting and developing recreational activities and facilities in Little Silver."

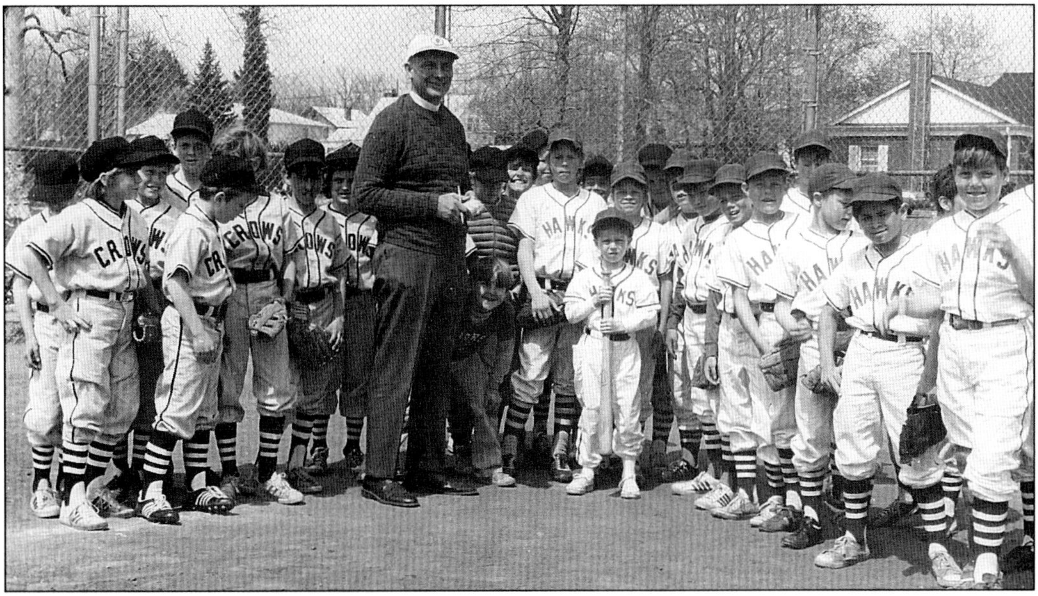

In 1973, Mayor Rell coached baseball. He is seen here at the Markham Place ball field with some members of the Hawks and the Crows.

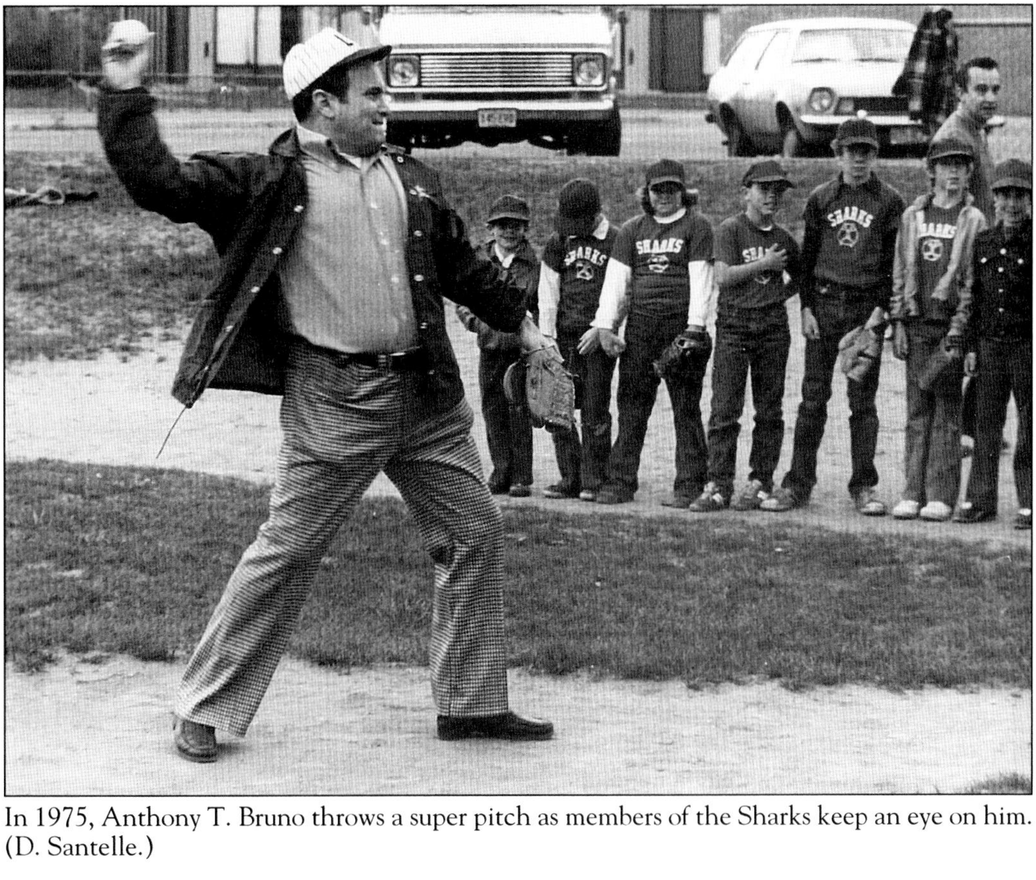

In 1975, Anthony T. Bruno throws a super pitch as members of the Sharks keep an eye on him. (D. Santelle.)

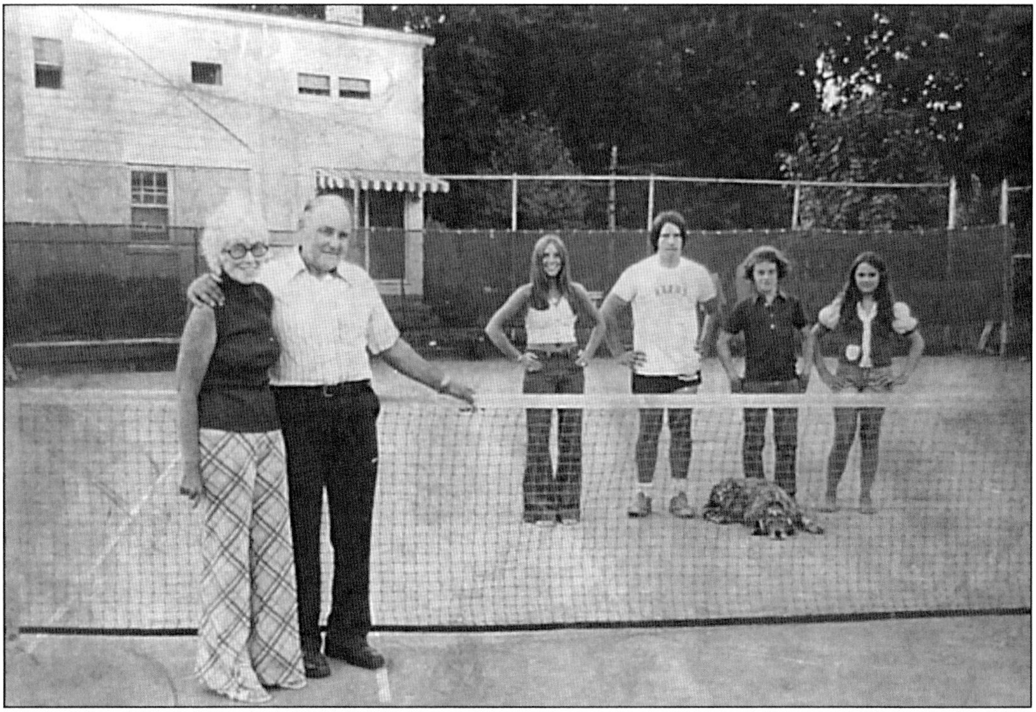

Dom and Marciadene Santelle, with their children (from left to right are Judy, Mark, Paul, and Patti) and their dog "Misty," line up for a newspaper photo on the family's tennis court in 1973. The occasion was the Santelle's 25th anniversary. (Santelle's copy of an *Asbury Park Press* photo by Herman Gerechoff.)

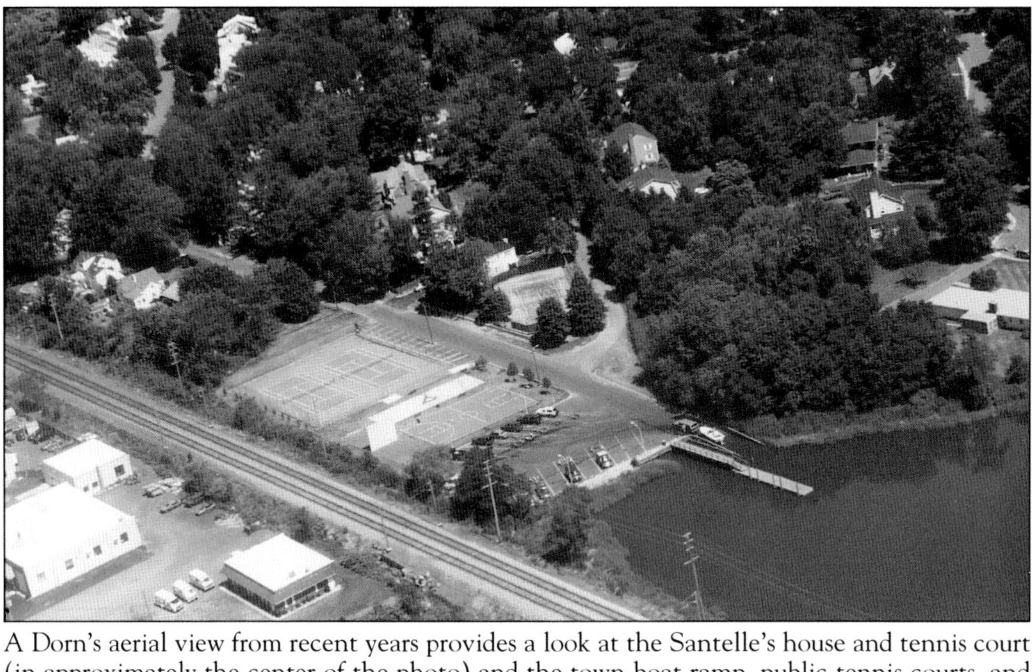

A Dorn's aerial view from recent years provides a look at the Santelle's house and tennis court (in approximately the center of the photo) and the town boat ramp, public tennis courts, and park that was named for Dominick Santelle and dedicated in 1997. (D. Santelle.)

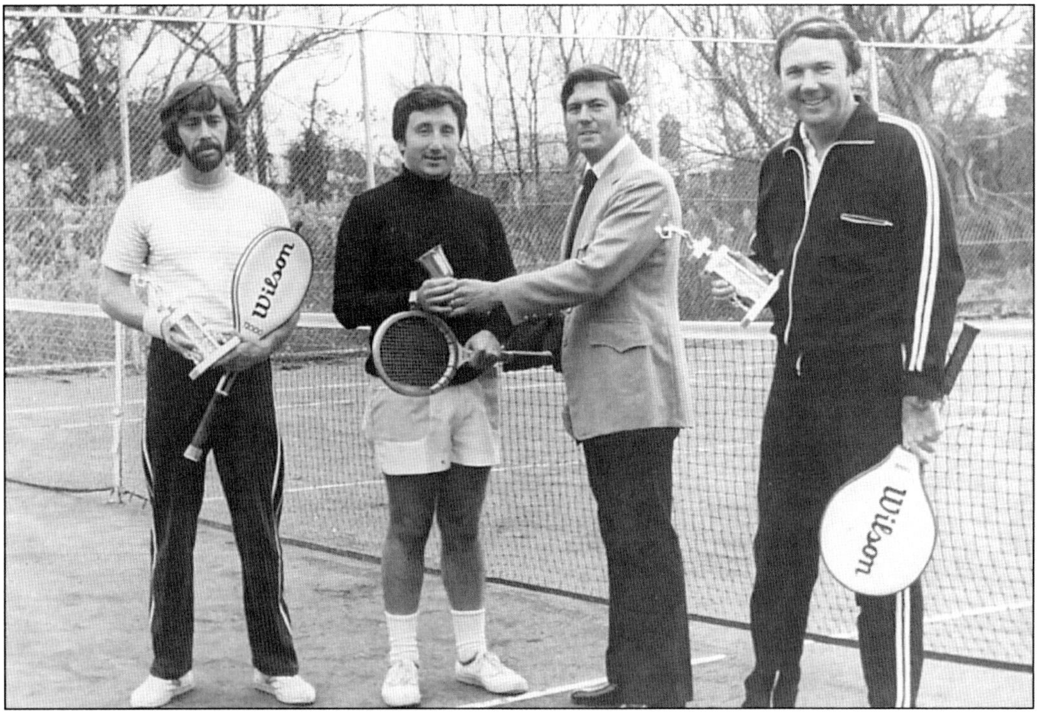

The Little Silver 1975 Men's Doubles champs are seen here being congratulated by Dan Dorn Jr., who ran the Little Silver Community Appeal. From left to right with tennis rackets are Dwight Kehoe (runner-up), Dr. S. Rothman (first place), and Joe Seaman (runner-up). (D. Santelle.)

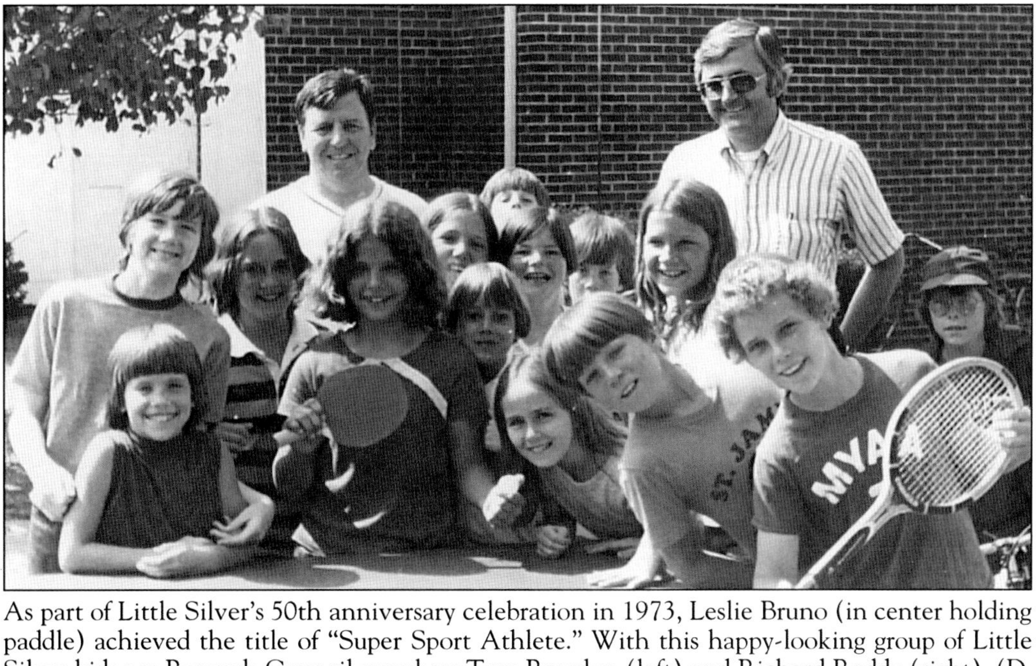

As part of Little Silver's 50th anniversary celebration in 1973, Leslie Bruno (in center holding paddle) achieved the title of "Super Sport Athlete." With this happy-looking group of Little Silver kids are Borough Council members Tom Reardon (left) and Richard Roddy (right). (D. Santelle.)

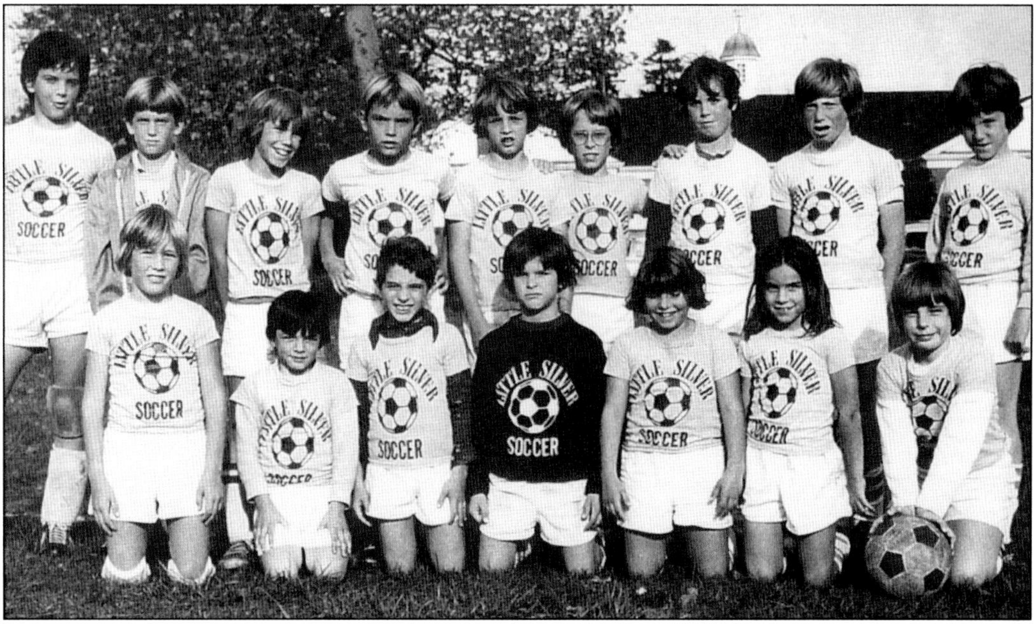

The soccer program in Little Silver developed rapidly as a popular sport for kids in the early 1970s and remains active today. In this 1976 photo are the following, from left to right: (kneeling) unidentified, Chris Norton, Bernie Nicoletti, Mark Marotta, Lia Bruno, Kathie Williams, and unidentified; (standing) Jon Schmidt, Tommy Dixon, Scott Cunningham, Billy Bowie, Jeff Lyn, ? Peterson, Michael Creedon, Scott Thomas, and unidentified. (L. Bowie.)

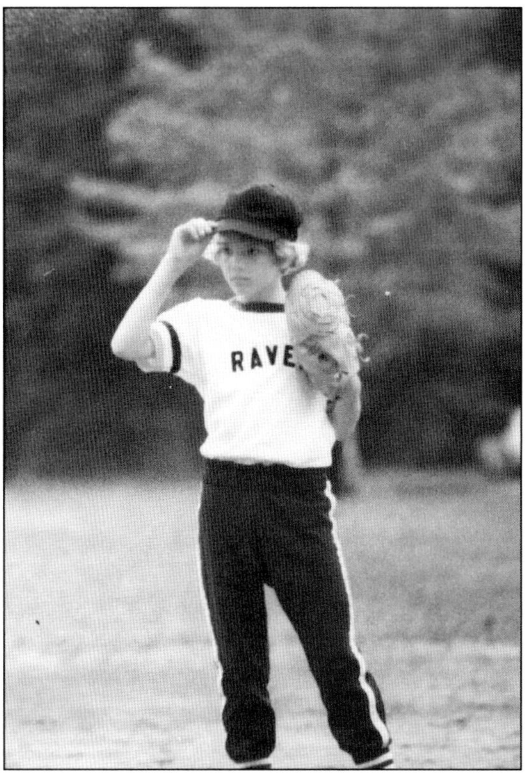

Billy Bowie pitches for the Ravens at an October 1977 game. This photo belonging to the Bowie family is in tribute to William ("Billy") Bowie III (October 16, 1965–February 3, 1998).

Seven

Parades, Fairs, and Special Events

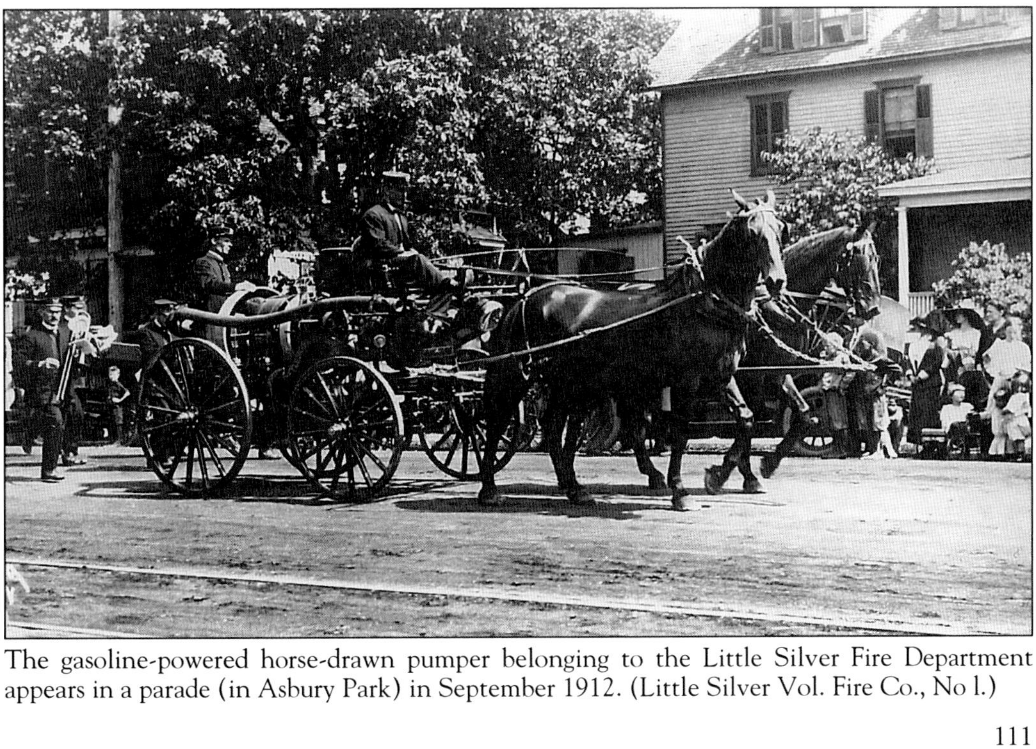

The gasoline-powered horse-drawn pumper belonging to the Little Silver Fire Department appears in a parade (in Asbury Park) in September 1912. (Little Silver Vol. Fire Co., No l.)

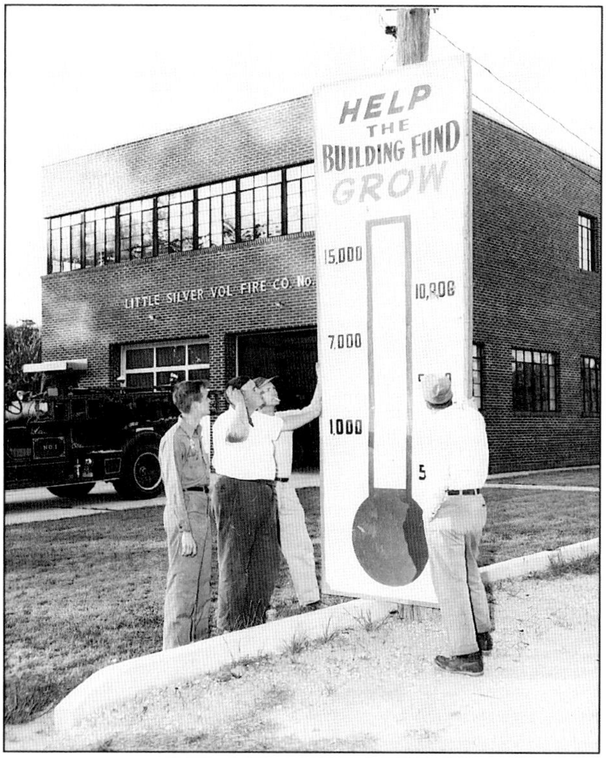

In 1953, from left to right, Joe Bacigalupi, Al Pound, Harry Carter, and a man who is not identified are checking the building fund "thermometer" to keep track of funds for a good cause, the expansion of the firehouse. The post-war modern-looking firehouse seen in this photo was replaced with Colonial styling when the new Colonial-style Borough Hall was built in 1966. (Dorn's.)

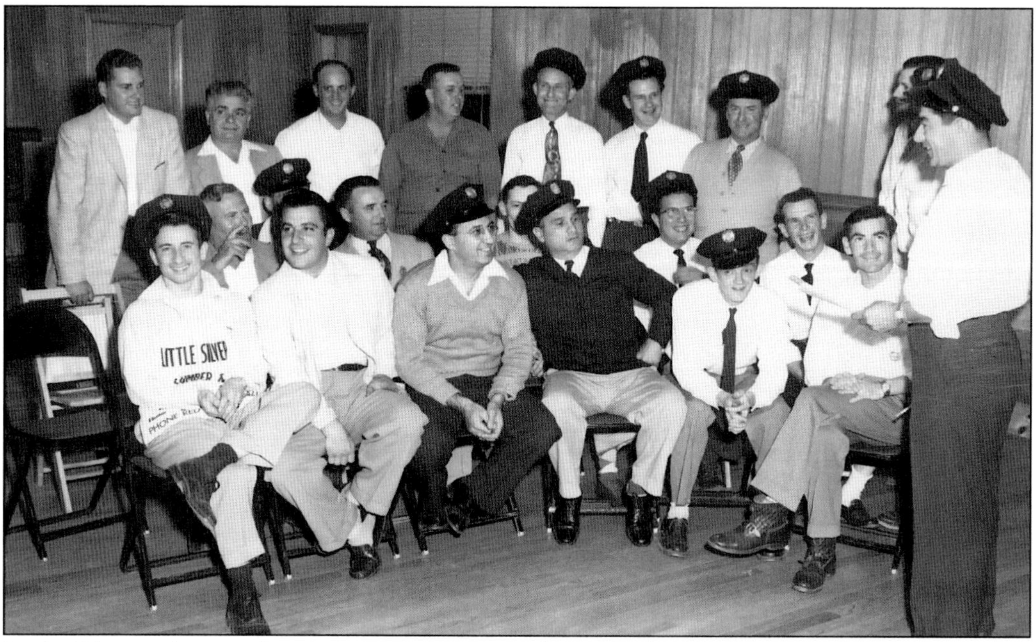

Little Silver volunteer firemen are meeting to plan a fund-raising fair in 1953. From left to right they are as follows: (front row) G. Darragh, O. Marcelli, B. Geradi, A. Bruno, R. West, R. Carter, and Chairman D. Mazza (standing in front); (middle row) those who are not obscured are Dick Parker, R. Fields, and F. Bruno; (back row) B. Davison, E. Grilli, ? Clarke, H. Dressler, R. Robson, D. Wright, and D. Parker. (Dorn's.)

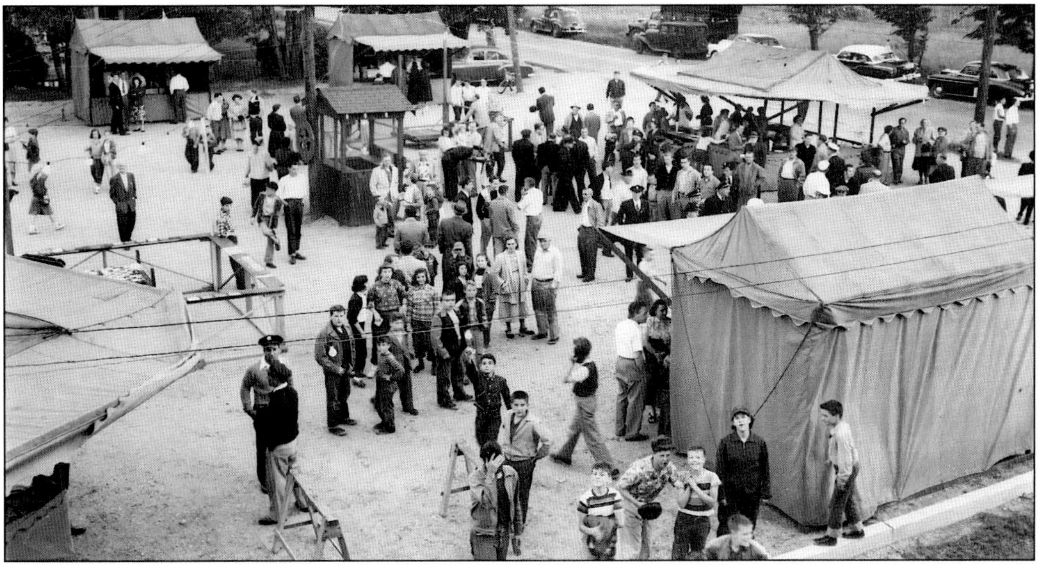

The Little Silver Fireman's Fair of June 1953 looks like an ordinary old-fashioned carnival in this view of the grounds on Prospect Avenue, but the fair made headlines when it was raided for disregarding a state law prohibiting gaming wheels, dice, and other gambling at such events. (Dorn's.)

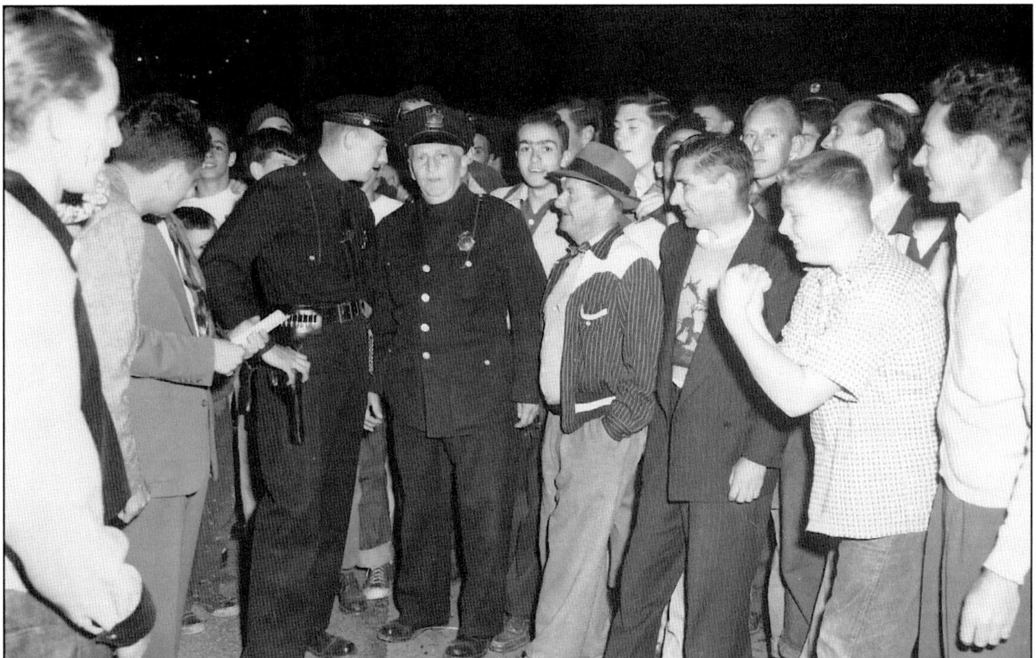

Little Silver Police Chief Fred Ziegler deals with the outraged crowd at the Fireman's Fair of 1953. The fund-raising event was shut down by Monmouth County Prosector J. Victor Carton and the state police. It was quite a memorable event for a small town, and was even written up in *Life* magazine. As it turned out, the Grand Jury did not indict the Fire Co. and the positive side to the event is that it paved the way to allow games of chance at fund-raisers for charitable groups. (Dorn's.)

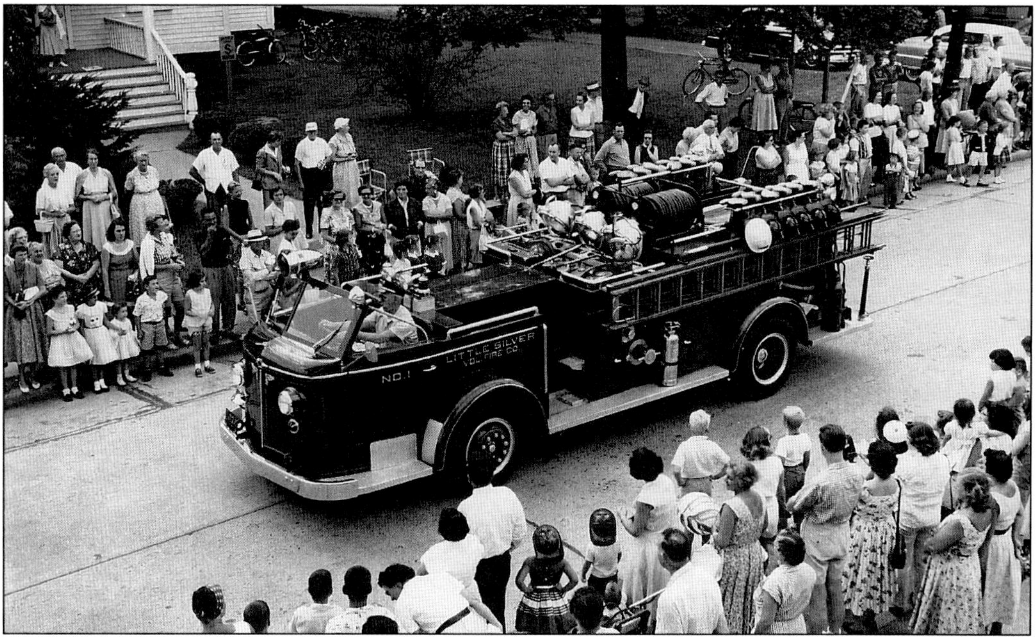

In the summer of 1956, a parade that marched south on Prospect Avenue commemorated the 50th anniversary of the Little Silver Fire Department. The steps of the old Borough Hall can be seen in the upper left corner. It's fun to look at the clothing people are wearing and the cars in the background that are all so very recognizable as the '50s.

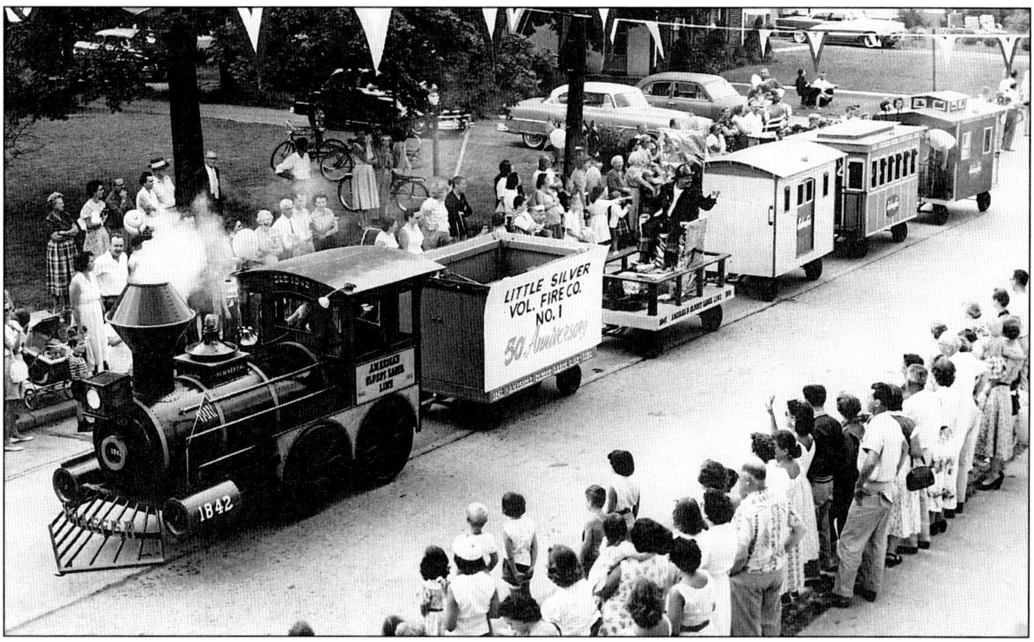

One of the highlights of the parade in honor of the fire department's 50th anniversary that delighted the crowd was this Schaefer beer train obtained by James Annarella, owner of Shore Point Distributing Co. and a member of the fire department. Richard Parker is seated in the center car. (Little Silver Fire Company No. 1 provided the photos on this page and the following page of the 1956 event.)

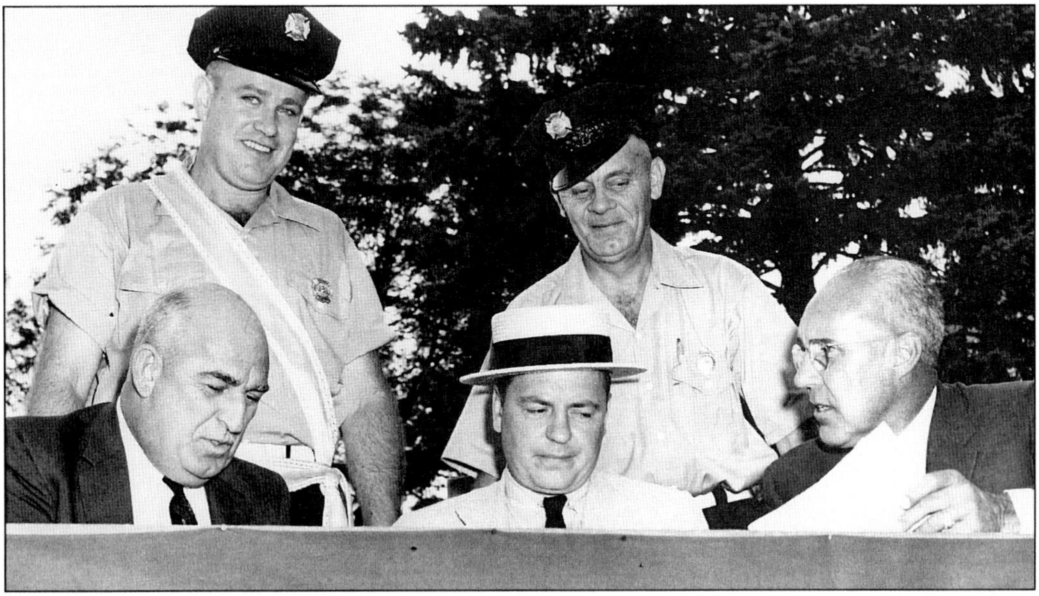

At the 1956 Little Silver Fire Company's 50th anniversary parade, Al Pound, president of the fire company and grand marshall of the event, is standing on the left and to his right is Warren Herbert. Seated, from left to right, are J. Stanley Herbert (president of the Monmouth County Fireman's Bowling Association), New Jersey State Senator Richard Stout, and Elmer Hess, who sold fire equipment.

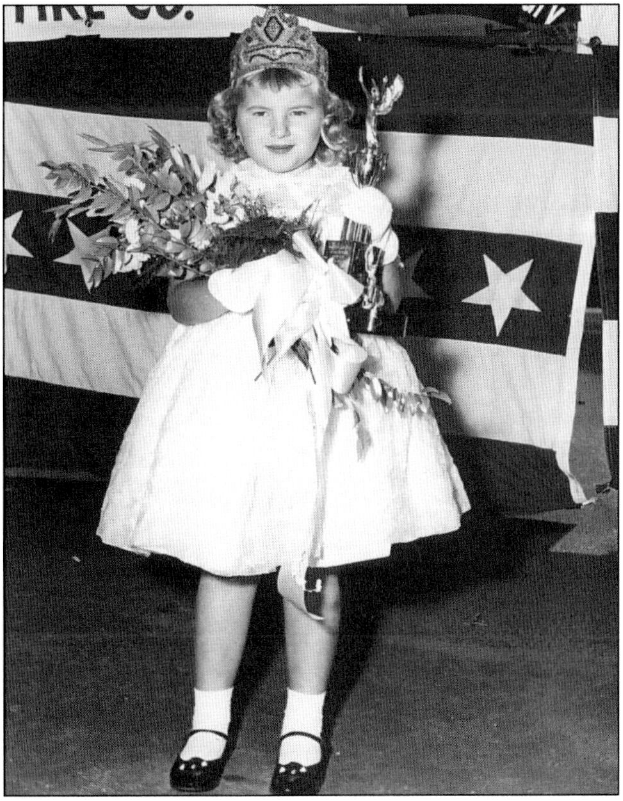

Five-year-old Patricia Pinedo, daughter of Mr. and Mrs. Carlos Pinedo, who lived at 20 Winding Way, reigned as queen of the Little Silver Fire Department's 50th anniversary parade on August 25, 1956. She was elected by the 700 schoolchildren of the borough. Her father was working here only temporarily and the family returned to their homeland, Venezuela, soon after the event.

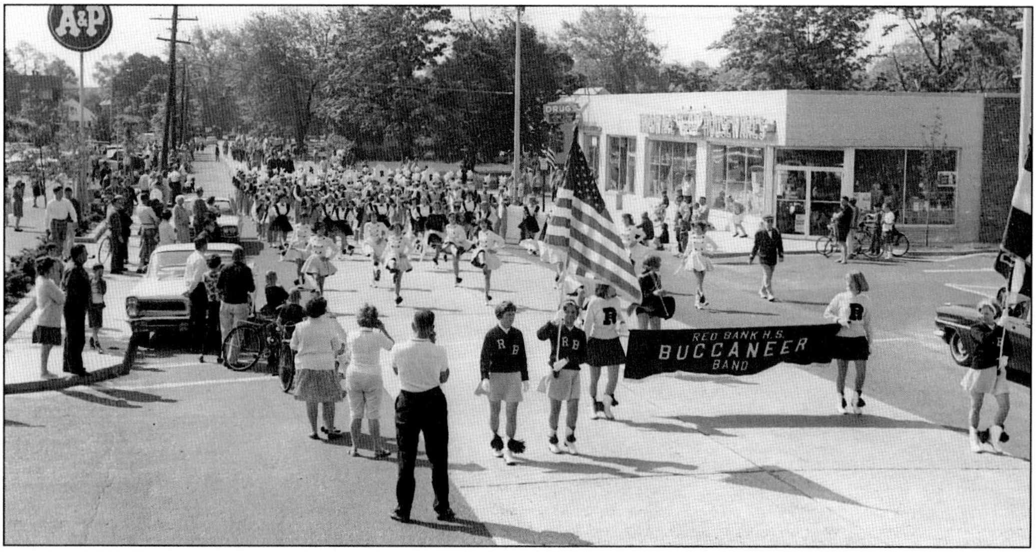

In 1965, the Red Bank High School Buccaneer Band struts down Prospect Avenue. Holding the American flag on the left is Beryl Marx and with a flag on the far right is Patti Fritsche. The twirler just behind the banner is Patti Gale. This photo gives a good view of the street and the lot on the corner of Markham Place where the Shrewsbury Bank is now located. (Dorn's.)

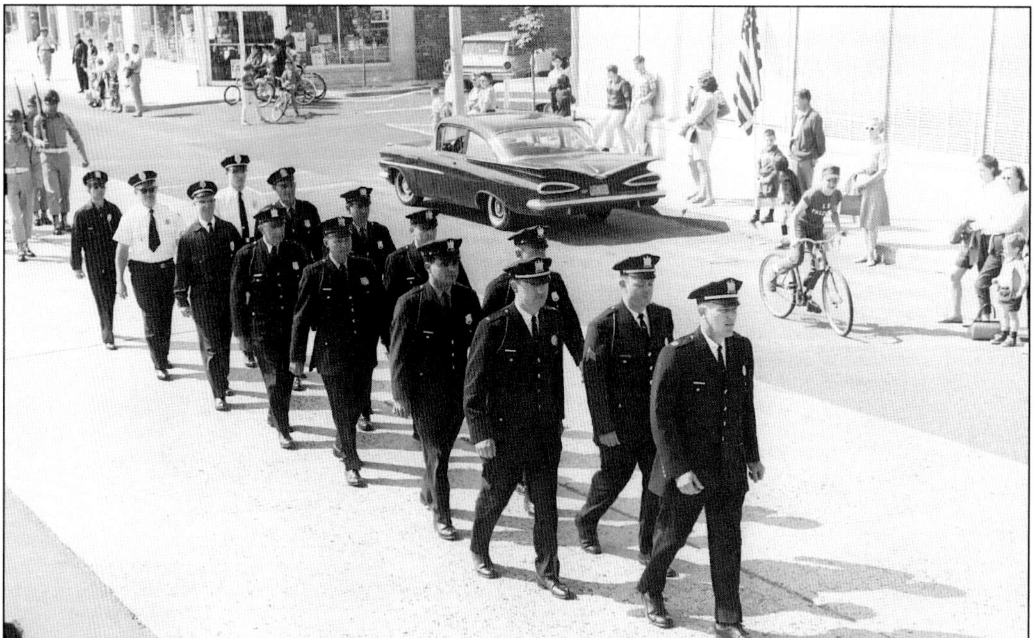

Little Silver's finest marches down Prospect Avenue in the same 1965 parade as above. In front is Capt. Walter Stearns, followed by, from left to right in pairs, Lt. D. Kennedy and Sgt. J. Fagan, Ptl. T. Bruno and Ptl. D. Clapp, Special Officer R. Tetley and Ptl. H. Giblin, Col. A. Coleman and Pt. A. Wright, Special Officer C. Rowe and Special Officer Warren Herbert, and two unidentified auxiliary officers. In the rear is Special Officer N. Ranineri. Lt. Kennedy's mother is watching on right (wearing sunglasses) and that parked car, fins and all, belongs to her. (Dorn's.)

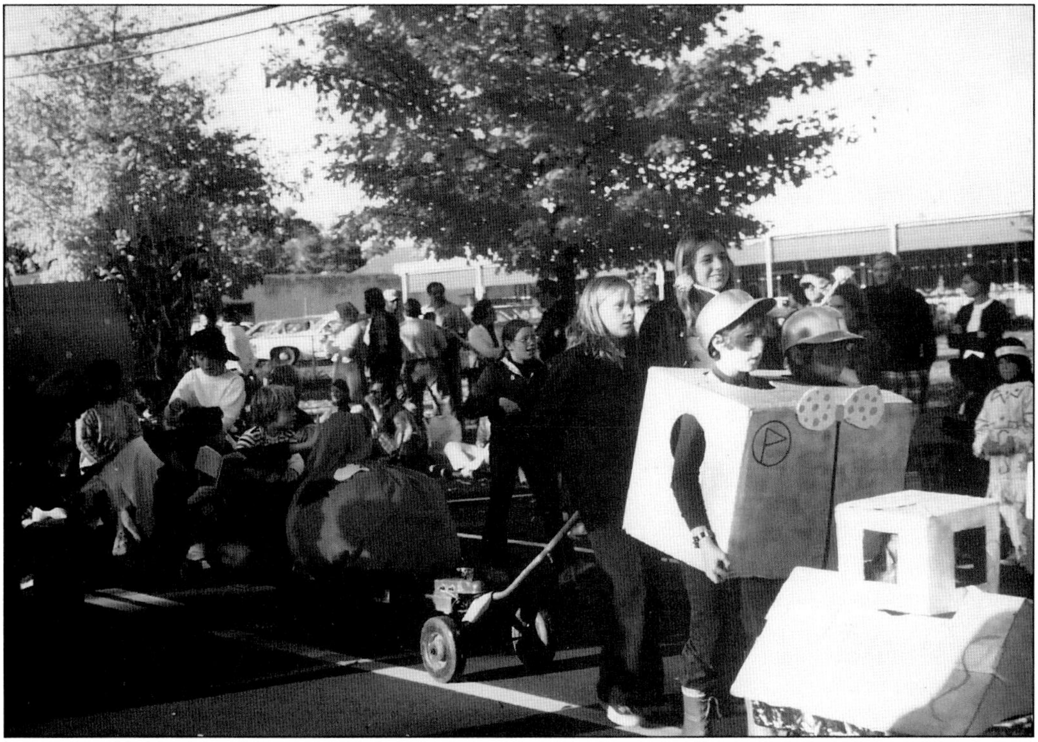

The annual Halloween costume parades for borough children sponsored by the Little Silver Fire Department have been a popular event since they began in the 1960s. This photo is of the parade in 1974 and features a group on the right portraying "Charlie Brown and the Great Pumpkin."

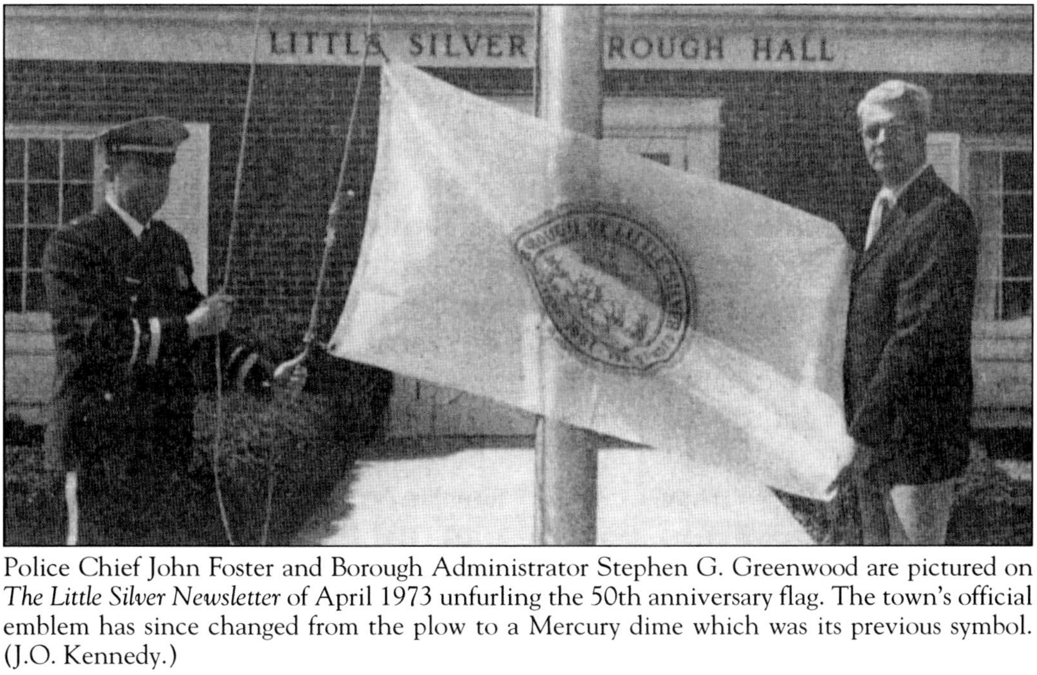

Police Chief John Foster and Borough Administrator Stephen G. Greenwood are pictured on *The Little Silver Newsletter* of April 1973 unfurling the 50th anniversary flag. The town's official emblem has since changed from the plow to a Mercury dime which was its previous symbol. (J.O. Kennedy.)

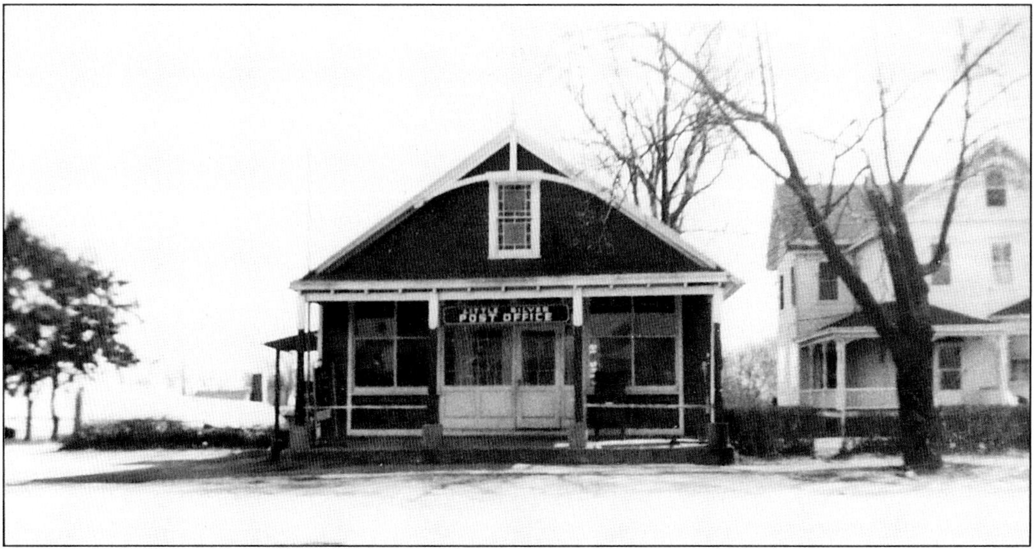

Here is how the old Little Silver Post Office on Church Street looked in the early years of the century. The house on the right was a parsonage for the Embury Methodist Church and Lovett's Nurseries were on the left. In 1956, the present post office building opened nearby. In 1973, the Double G Land Corporation offered the building to the Borough. That year Mayor Rell formed the Little Silver Historical Society and efforts began to relocate the old post office as a museum.

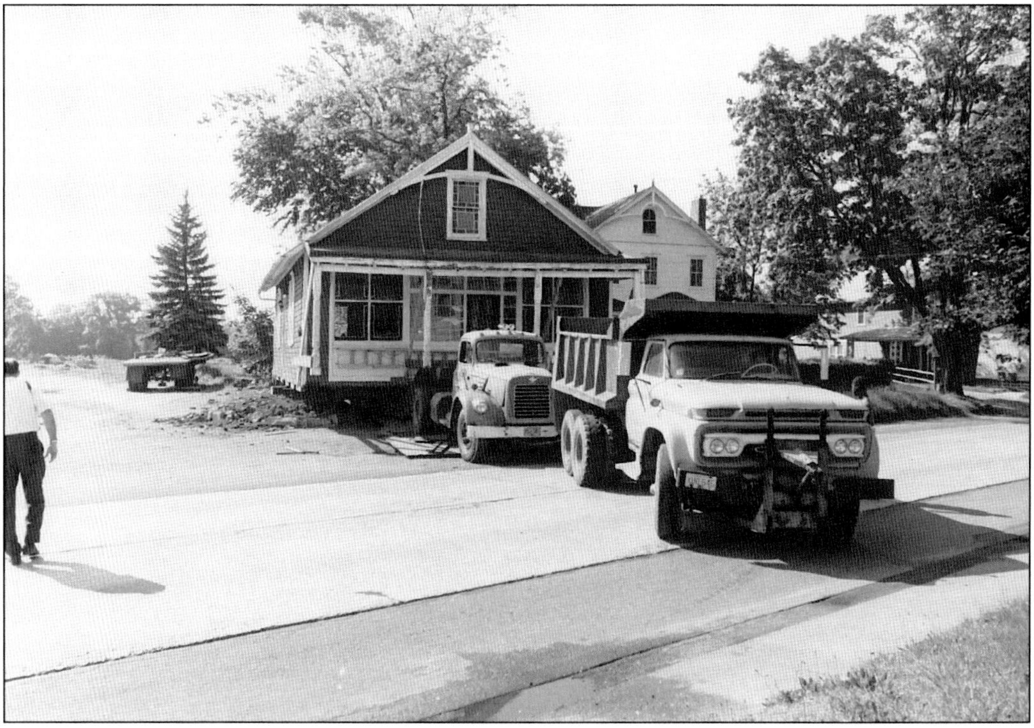

After successful fund-raising drives, the Little Silver Historical Society's museum became a reality. On May 31, 1973, Duffy Fisher of Middletown moved the building to its present location near the public library. Here the trucks begin to relocate the former post office from its Church Street location.

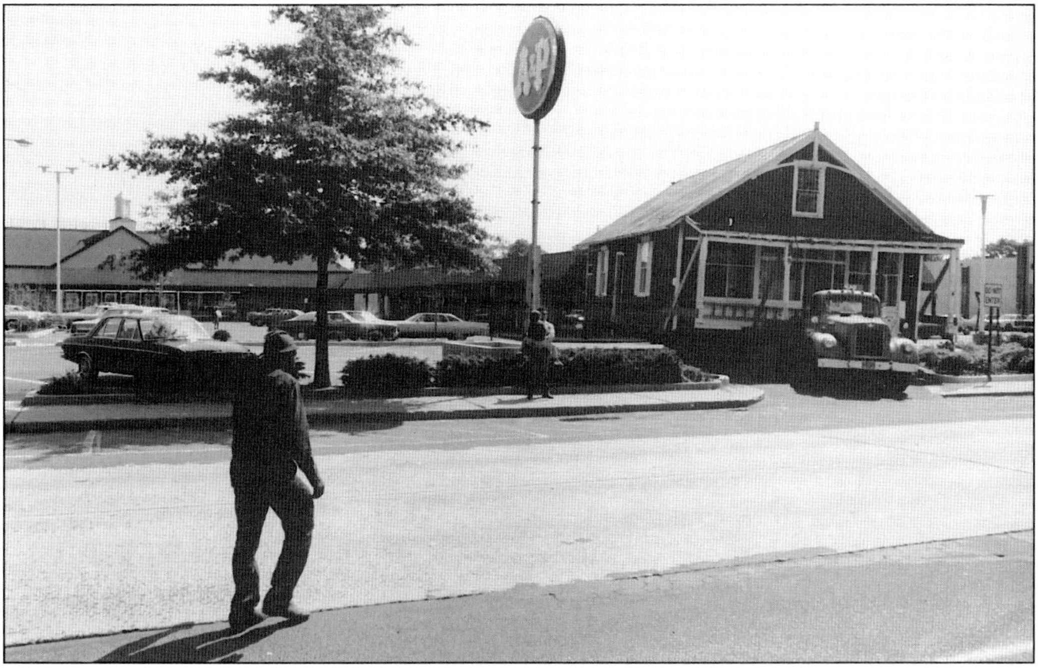

Imagine seeing this spectacle as you try to turn into the A&P parking lot! On May 31, 1973, many people watched in awe as the old post office was moved through the Prospect Avenue shopping center and across the street to its new location as a museum.

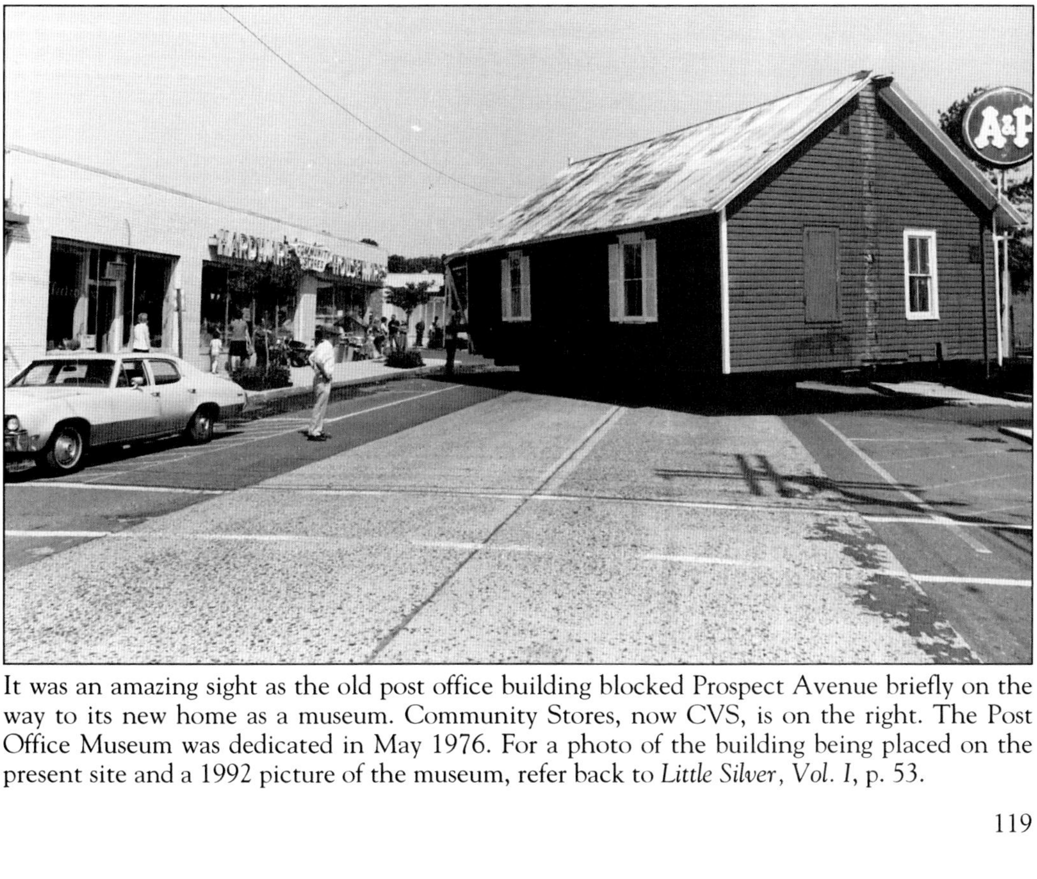

It was an amazing sight as the old post office building blocked Prospect Avenue briefly on the way to its new home as a museum. Community Stores, now CVS, is on the right. The Post Office Museum was dedicated in May 1976. For a photo of the building being placed on the present site and a 1992 picture of the museum, refer back to *Little Silver, Vol. I*, p. 53.

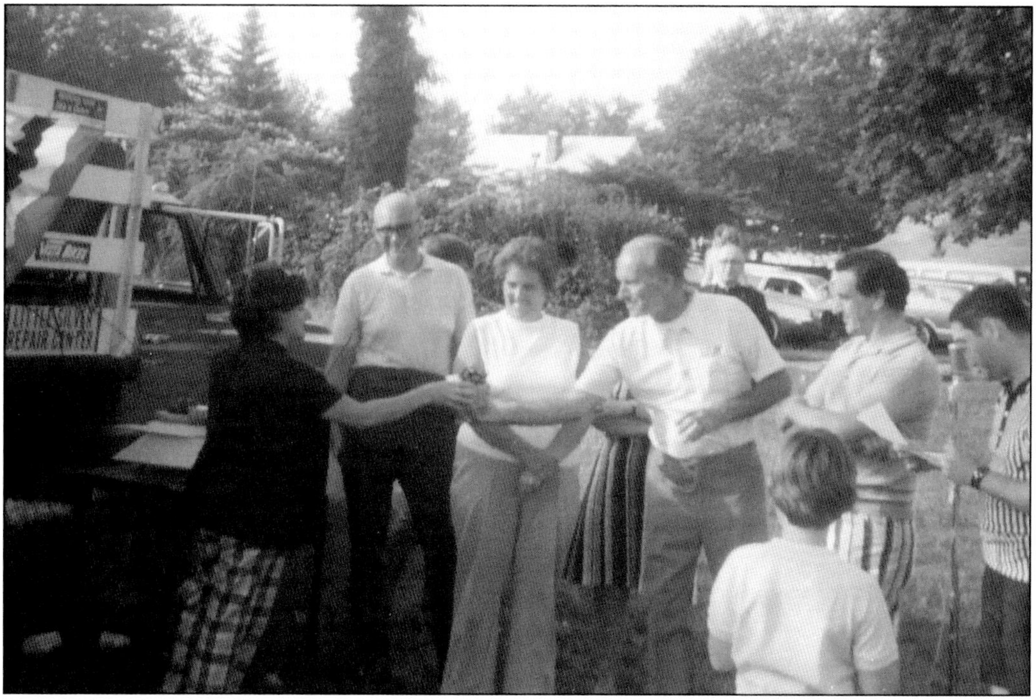

For Little Silver's 50th anniversary fair in 1973, those residents who were 50 years old were recognized. Here Carl Giersch is receiving his award. (J. Giersch.)

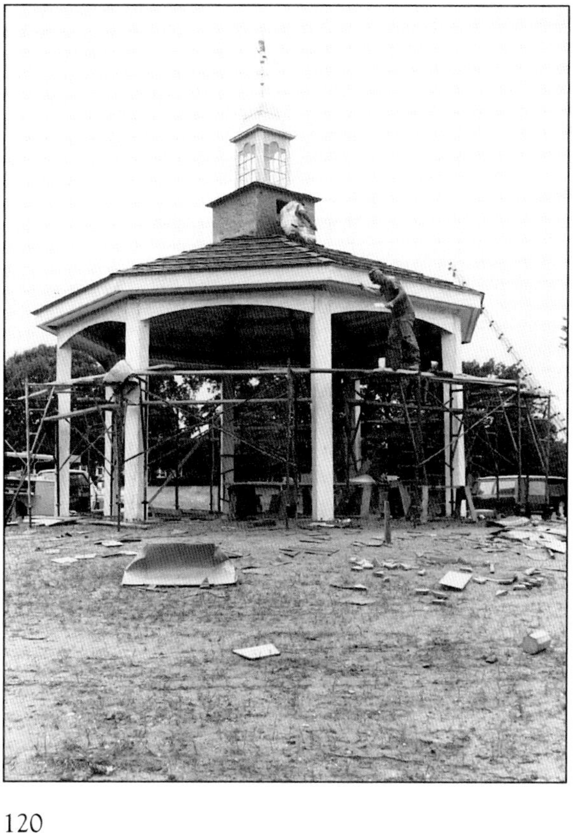

Construction is being completed in 1976 on Little Silver's gazebo that was planned soon after the borough's 50th anniversary as a bicentennial project. The gazebo on Markham Place is the site of many a good old-fashioned band concert and is a lovely setting for taking photographs.

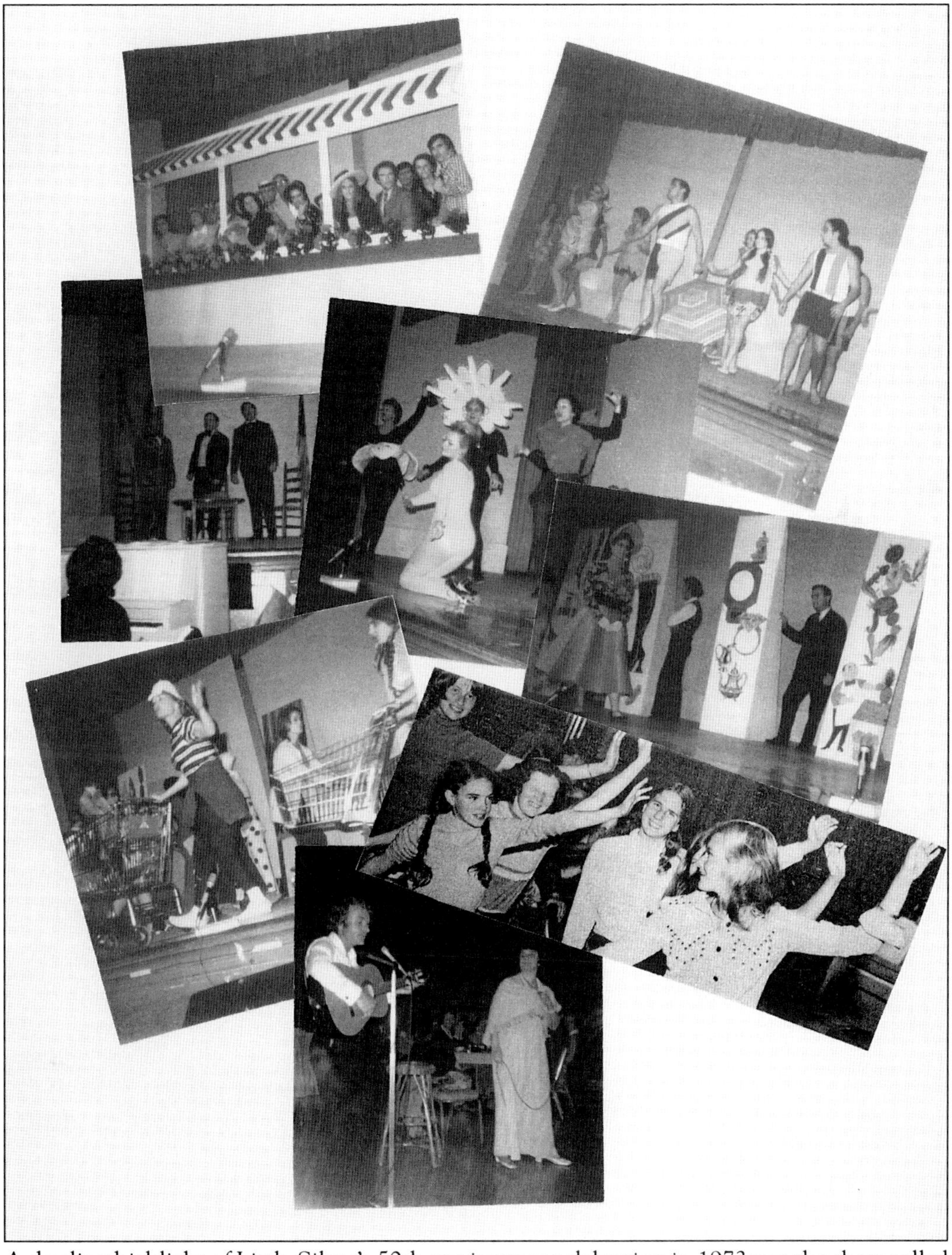

A dazzling highlight of Little Silver's 50th anniversary celebration in 1973 was the show called *Gold n' Little Silver*. The revue choreographed by Arlene Simon that featured local talent is remembered here in a montage (assembled by the author) from photos in the collection of June O. Kennedy.

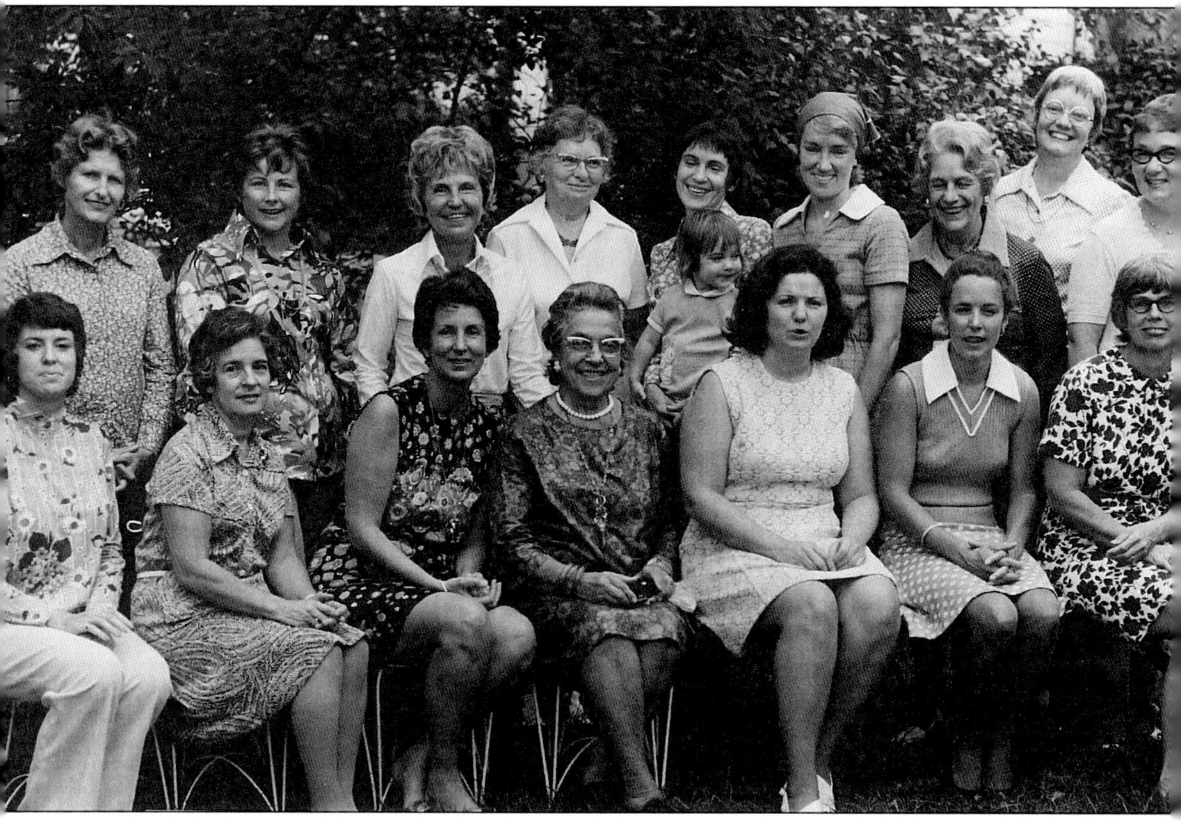

Little Silver commemorated its 50th anniversary in 1973 and then the nation's 1976 bicentennial year with a variety of activities. An enduring project from that period is the quilt consisting of 35 squares depicting the borough's history. About half of the quiltmakers "posed for posterity" in this July 1976 photo. From left to right, top to bottom, the squares (seen in photo on top of opposite page) represent: l. "Monmouth Civic Chorus," Sheila McKenna; 2. "The New York and Long Branch," Sarah B. Eitelbach; 3. "Pirate's Cove," Mary Lou Chace; 4. "Parker's Pond," Paulette Maloney; 5. "Ice House," Welsch; 6. "L.S. Point Bridge," Bobbie Spearle; 7. "80 Little Silver Point Road," Paulette Welsch; 8. "The 4 Season's Sickles's Farm," Helen King; 9. "M.L. Campbell Blacksmith," Marty Locilento; 10. "Tragedy and Comedy," Renee Maxwell; 11. "Local Windmills," Barbara Patterson; 12. "Boro Entrance Sign until 1975," Emily Swift; 13. "Little Silver Woman's Club," Anita Rosen; 14. "Sewing Circle and Mayor's Gavel," Frances Harvey; 15. "Firehouse, 1907," JoAnn Barecca; 16. "John Slocum and Indian Wrestle," Linda Rabon; 17. "Grandview 1890," Jan Parker; 18. "Boro Seal," Marilyn Millar and Barbara Seaman; 19. "Little Silver R.R. Station," Patti Jeydel; 20. "Sailing," Thelma Johnson; 21. "The Little-Silver," Jean Lee; 22. "Historical Society Seal," June Kennedy; 23. "1889 Parkerville Map," Barbara Finch; 24. "N.J. Assoc. of Nurserymen Seal," Betty Bertelson; 25. "Wildlife," Linda Gay Finley; 26. "Gold 'N Little Silver Stage Show 1973," Priscilla Marrah; 27. "4th of July Picnic, 1973," Lynn Thompson; 28. "Little Silver P.S. 74 Bell," Sue Seiter; 29. "Post Office Museum," Judith Messerli; 30. "Sickles' Pond," Susan Stanton; 31. "Crabbing," Sheila McKenna; 32. "Saint John's Chapel," Marty Locilento; 33. "Ecology-Space Age," Adeline Genadio; 34." Embury Methodist Church—1868," Alice Choquette; and 35. "Lovett's Nursery, 1878," Margaret McNally.

The Little Silver "Bicentennial Quilt" that belongs to the Little Silver Historical Society is shown here in the chamber room of the Borough Hall while on display to commemorate Little Silver's 75th anniversary in 1998. A complete list of the patches depicting the borough's history and names of the local quilters who made the 35 squares is on the previous page.

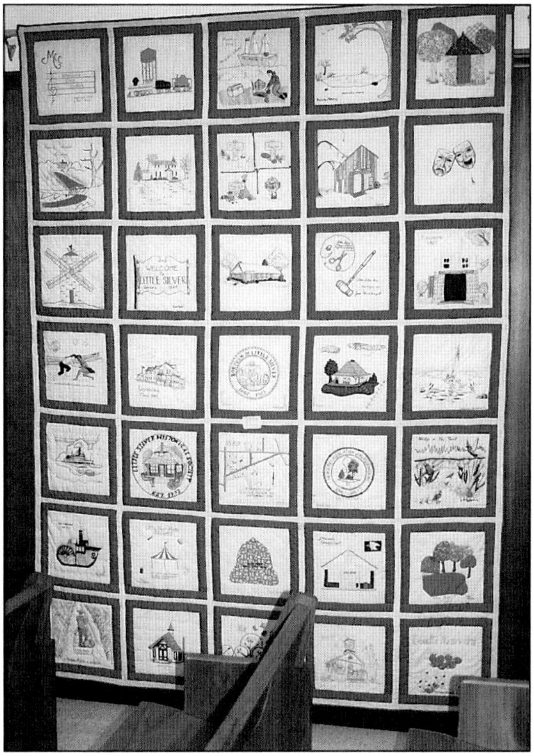

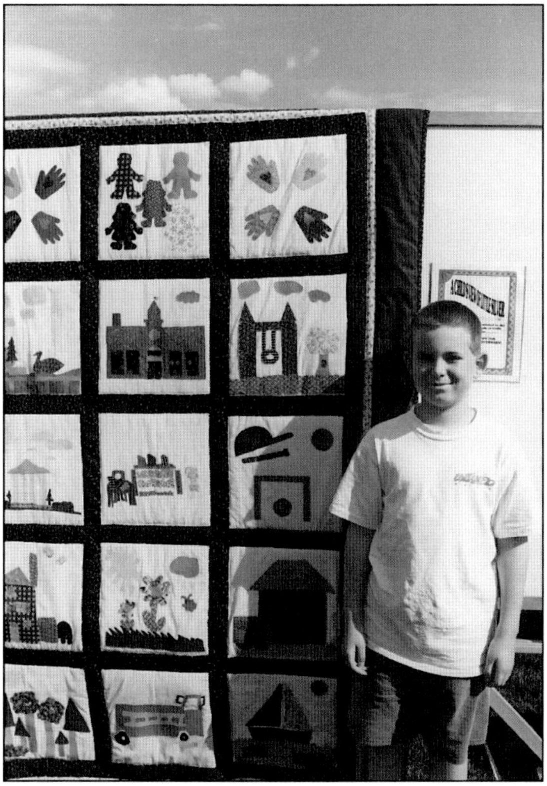

For Little Silver's 75th anniversary, borough children participated in a variety of special school projects. "A Child's View of Little Silver," a quilt designed by students in Grades K, 1, and 4 and coordinated by Susan Rolak, is pictured here as displayed at the 75th anniversary picnic, June 7, 1998. Standing by the delightful quilt is Kevin French, one of the young artists. Kevin, who designed the "playground" square, is a great-great-grandson of Little Silver's first police chief, Fred Ziegler.

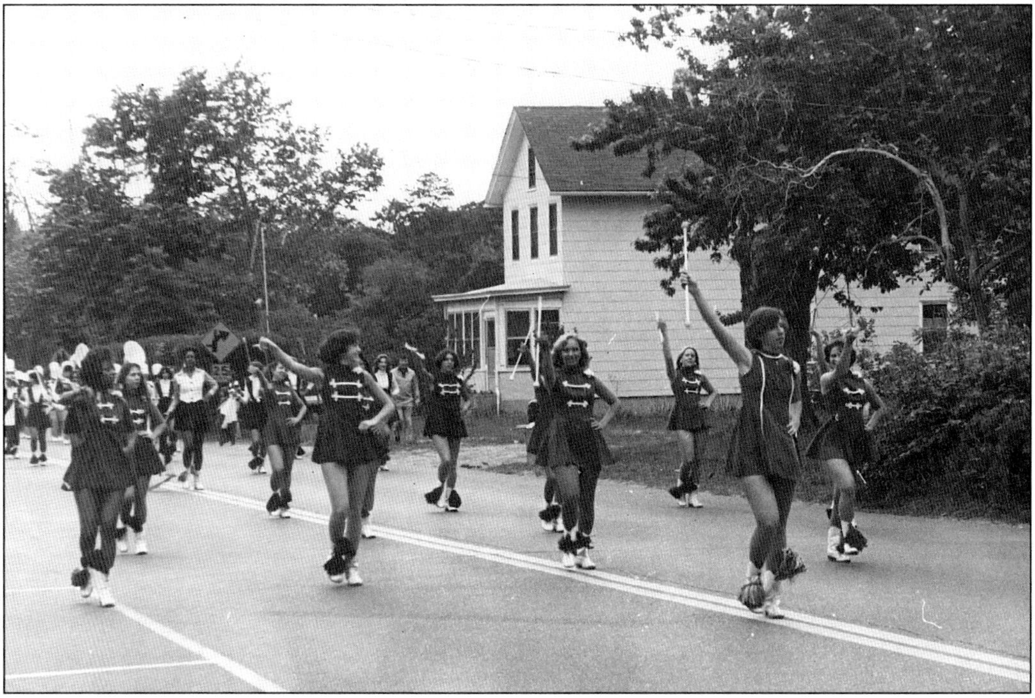

At a 1977 parade in Little Silver, Captain Betsy Pope leads the Red Bank Regional High School majorettes down Prospect Avenue. From left to right they are as follows: (front row) Karen Douglas, Linda Judge, Angela Citarella, Pope, and Cheryl Kerner; (second row) Sheila DeStefano, Loretta Clancy, Jehora Antinozzi (obscured), and Patti Holmes. Laura Godwin, captain of the flag twirlers, is seen leading her group following directly behind the majorettes. (H. Pope.)

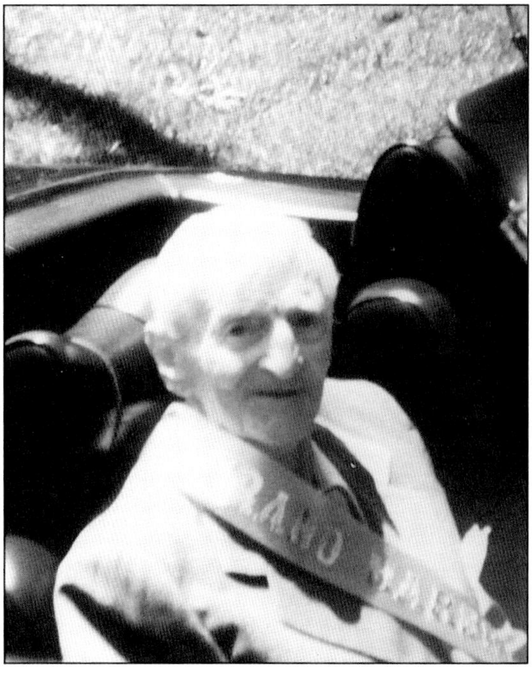

Retired Police Chief Fred Ziegler rides as grand marshall in the July 1981 parade to commemorate the 75th anniversary of the Little Fire Department. He died later that year at the age of 92. Ziegler, a well-loved man with many accomplishments to his credit, became a Little Silver legend. (T. Satter.)

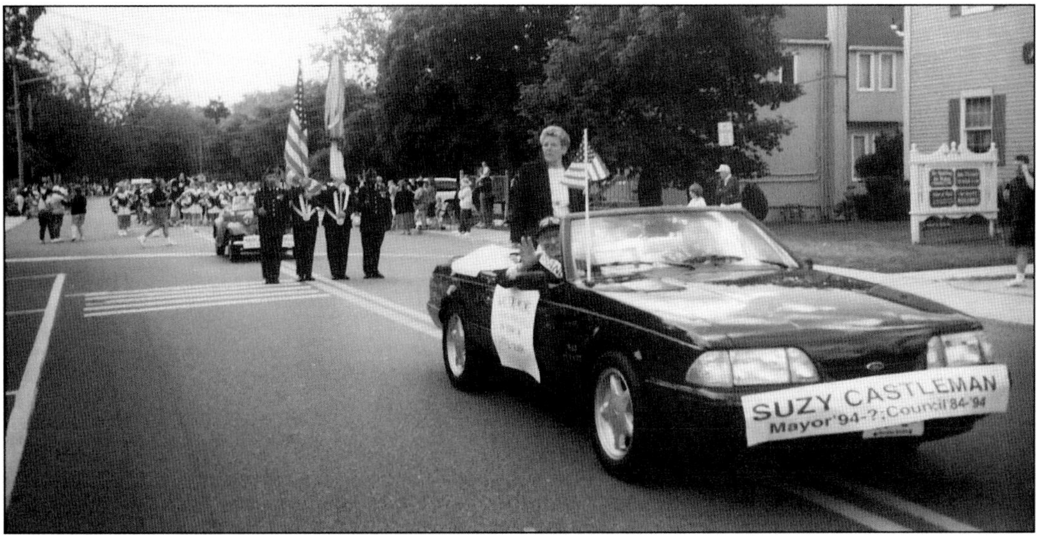

Little Silver Mayor Suzy Castleman and Grand Marshall Walton Moore (who has lived 86 years in the borough) wave to spectators along Prospect Avenue during the June 7, 1998, 75th anniversary parade in front of the firehouse on Prospect Avenue. They are followed by the U.S. Army Color Guard. Chairpersons of the 75th anniversary committee Meg and Jim McNally and Gail and George Drawbaugh coordinated the festivities with the assistance of dedicated people from the community.

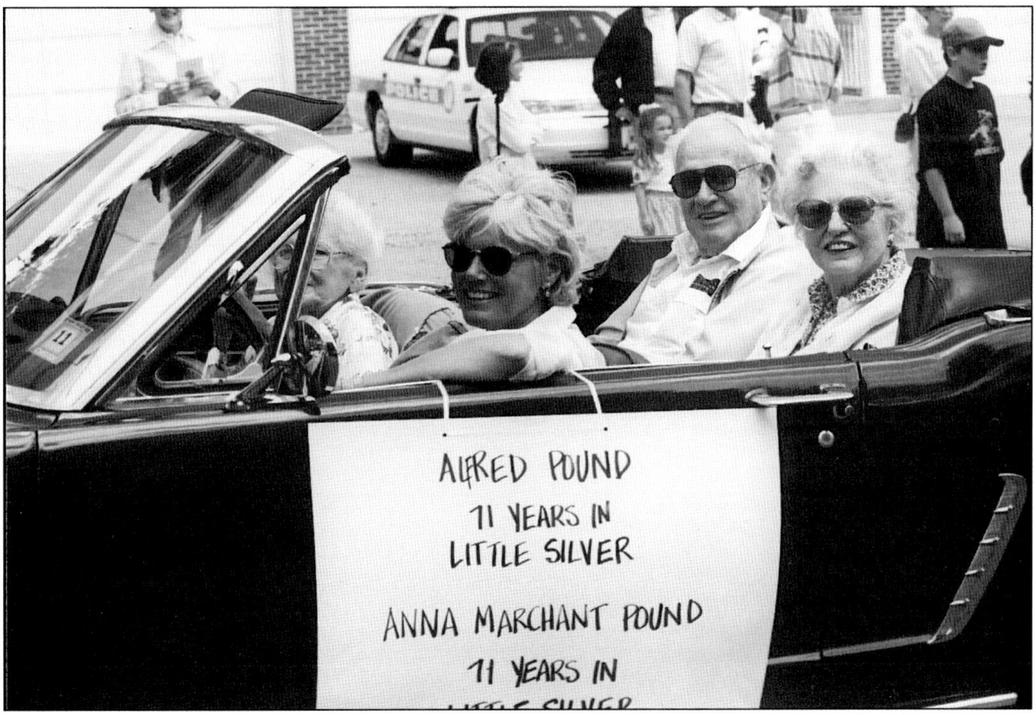

As a feature of the 75th anniversary parade, a total of 14 residents who have lived 65 years or more in the borough rode in special cars. Here Al and Anna Pound, both 71 years in Little Silver, ride by looking happy in their sunglasses on what was a glorious day for the celebration! (75th anniversary parade photos by author.)

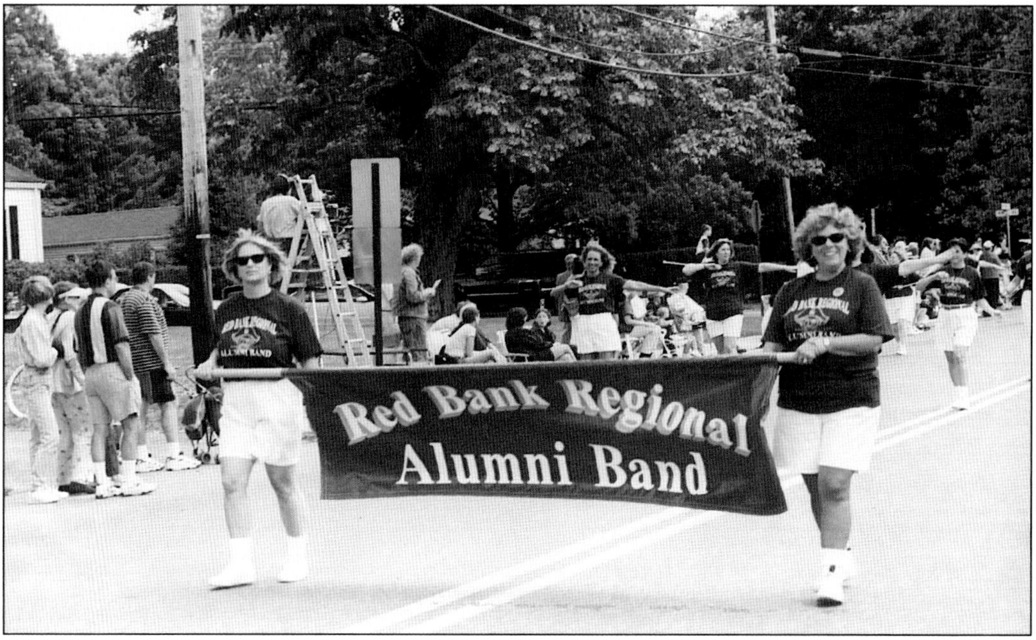

Here comes that rousing hit of the 75th anniversary parade of June 7, 1998—the Red Bank Regional Alumni Band! Carrying the banner are Lisa (Drawbaugh) Barnes (left, Class of 1980) and Sandy (Ferrogiari) Wells (right, Class of 1965). Directly behind them are the majorettes followed by the flag twirlers.

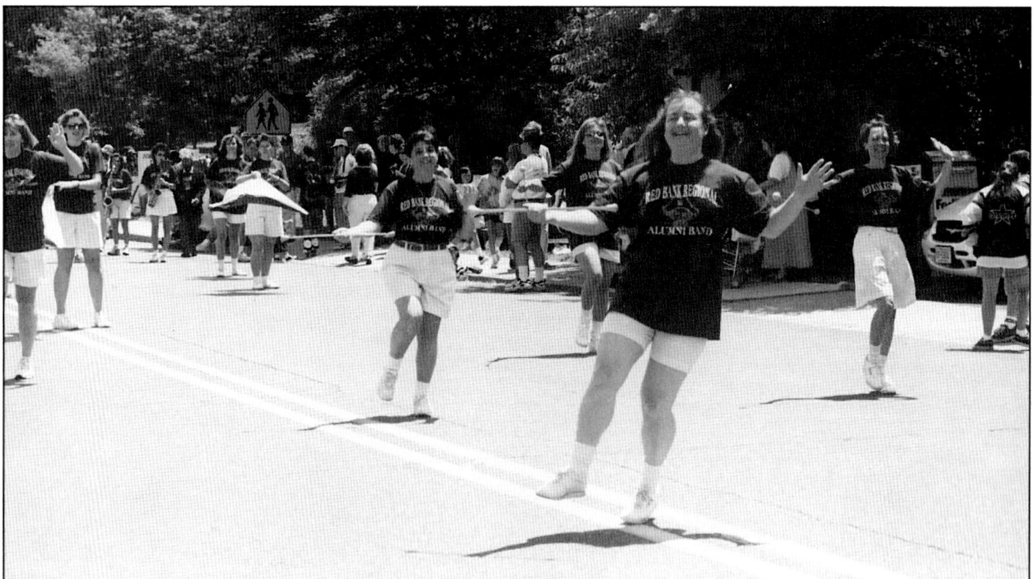

Gail (Miknich) Semliatschenko (Class of 1976), twirling coordinator of the Red Bank Regional Alumni Band, leads the majorettes at the June 7, 1998 parade. The twirlers closest to the center of this photo are, from left to right, Debbie (Setaro) McNish (Class of 1971), Karen (Tetley) DiNocera (Class of 1975), and Kathy (Miknich) Capozzi (Class of 1979). The other twirlers in the group are Angela (Citarella) Nelson (Class of 1978), Betsy (Pope) Aras (Class of 1977), and Ellen (Lehtonen) Branin (Class of 1955).

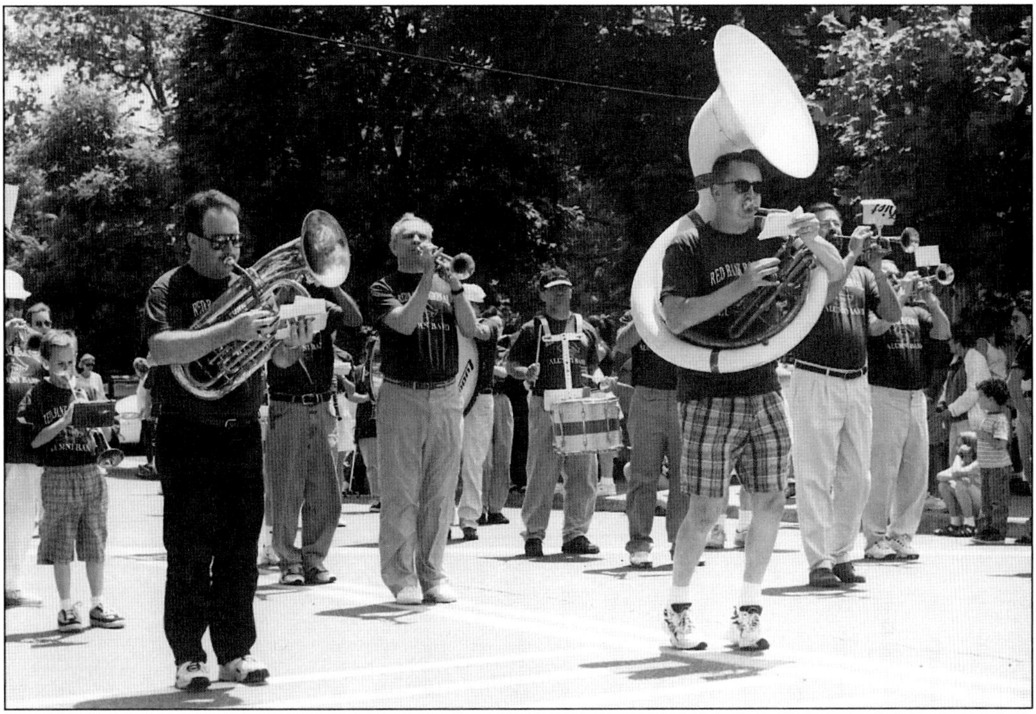

Members of the Red Bank Regional Alumni Band play their instruments with great gusto as the crowds at the 75th anniversary parade cheer them on! Some of the musicians seen in this photo are John W. Luckenbill III (boy with trumpet on right), Artie Weinkofsky on baritone, John W. Luckenbill Jr. (center with trumpet), Emile Talarico (with drum), Paul Murphy (with the tuba), and on far right are trumpeters Tom Forbes and Douglas Runge.

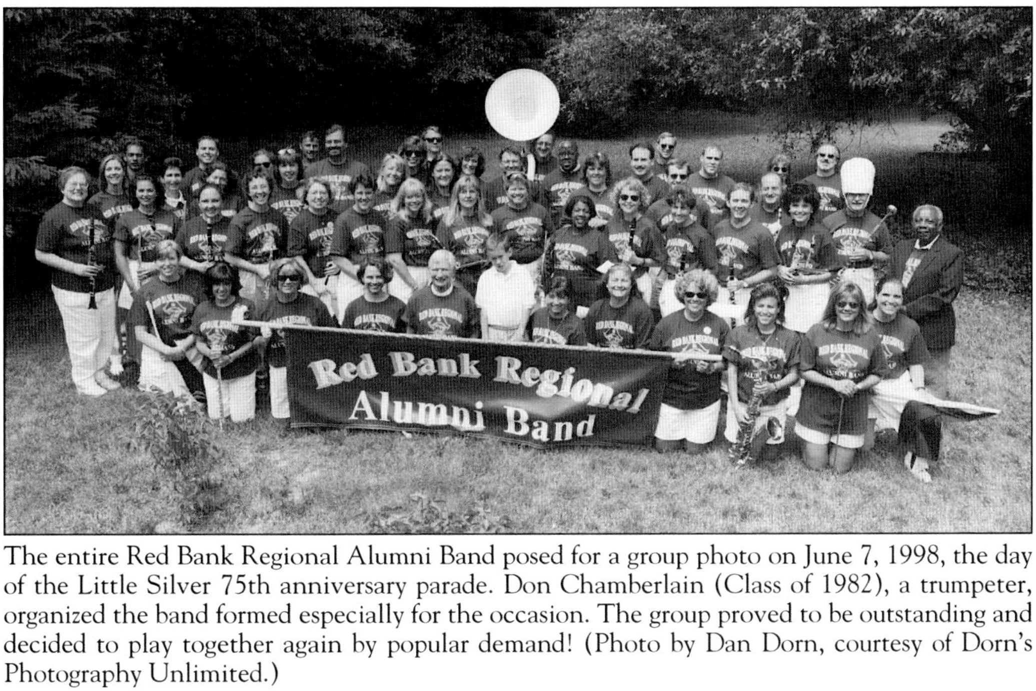

The entire Red Bank Regional Alumni Band posed for a group photo on June 7, 1998, the day of the Little Silver 75th anniversary parade. Don Chamberlain (Class of 1982), a trumpeter, organized the band formed especially for the occasion. The group proved to be outstanding and decided to play together again by popular demand! (Photo by Dan Dorn, courtesy of Dorn's Photography Unlimited.)

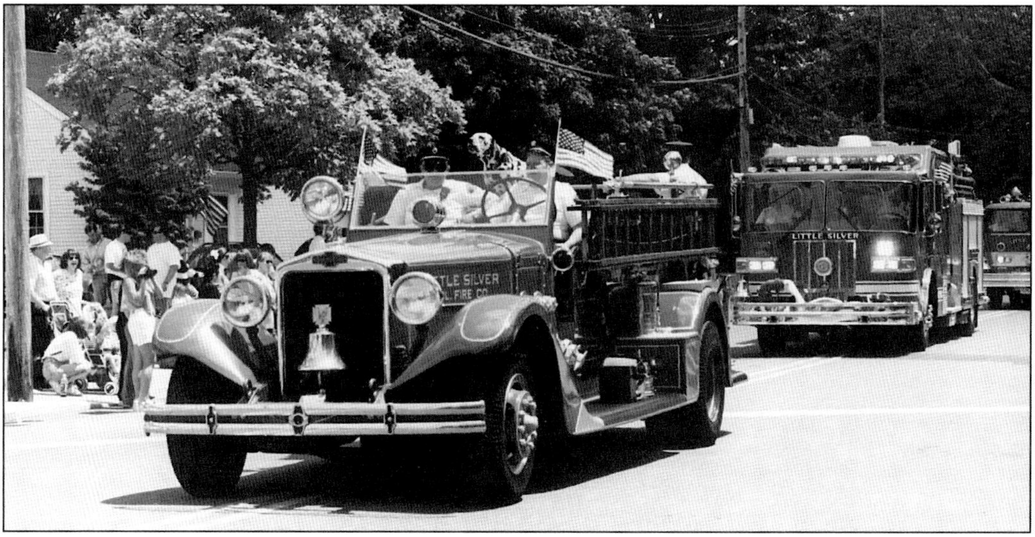

Here come the fire trucks near the end of the parade with The Little Silver Volunteer Fire Company No.1's historic 1935 American LaFrance leading this brigade at the borough's 75th anniversary parade on June 7, 1998. Ed Burdge (driving), Walt Sterns, and "Squirt" the Dalmation ride on the truck.

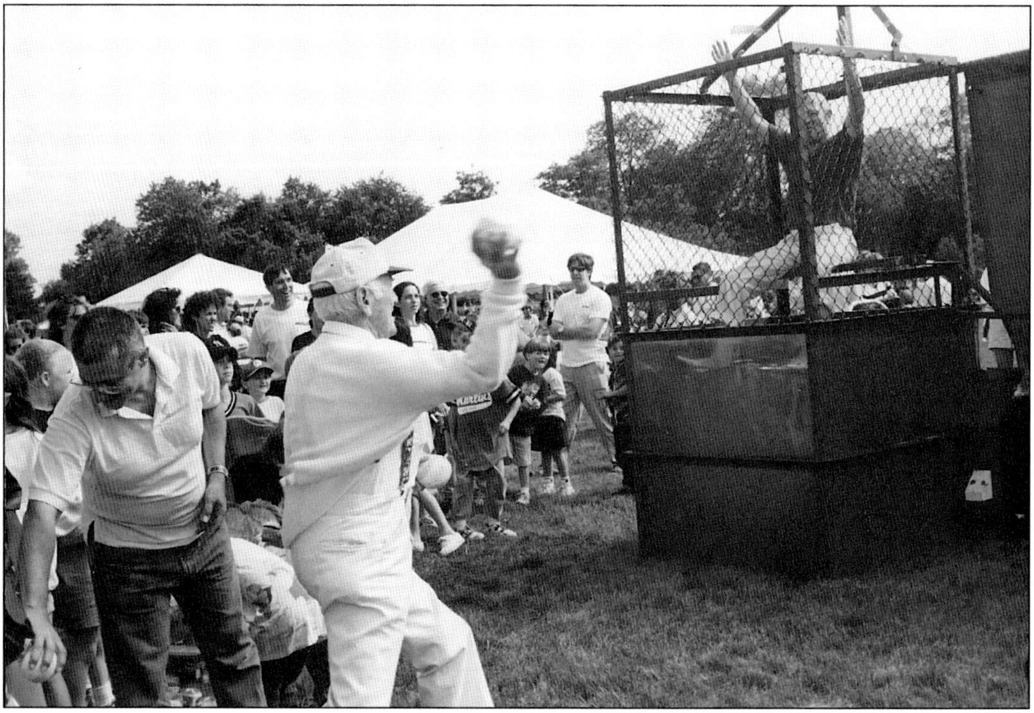

Perhaps this will become a classic photo of the dunk tank, sponsored by the Armstrong Agency, at Little Silver's 75th anniversary picnic that was held at Sickles Farm Park immediately following the parade on June 7, 1998. Dan Dorn Sr. (known as "The Chief") takes aim to dunk his son, Dan Dorn Jr. (of Dorn's Photography Unlimited, Red Bank). Yes, the Chief was successful! The author enjoyed taking this photo, and she hopes that it will provide a chuckle for this volume's finale.